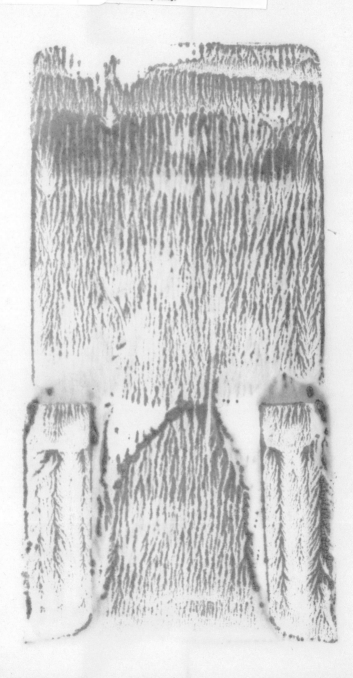

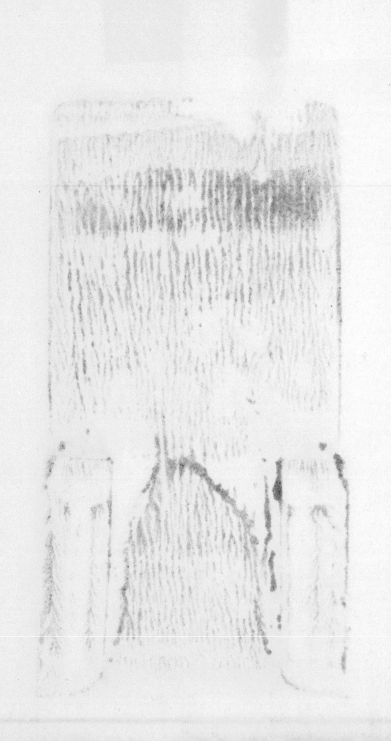

Ten Fascinating Women

ELIZABETH TUDOR
In this portrait we can see the rising of "that bright occidental star,
Queen Elizabeth of most happy memory".

Ten Fascinating Women

ELIZABETH JENKINS

COWARD-McCANN, INC.
New York

Preface

These sketches were first published in 1955 and have been out of print for several years. The women who are the subjects of them make, I still think, an extremely interesting collection. Many of them have of course been frequently written about, but the stories of Martha Ray, Elizabeth Inchbald and the Duchess of Lauderdale, will, I believe, be new to a number of readers. The stories of the other seven will, I hope, like most good stories, bear re-telling.

I must plead this excuse particularly for the sketch "Elizabeth Tudor" to anyone who has read my *Elizabeth the Great*. It was reading the sketch in this collection which caused the American publishers, Coward-McCann, to commission a full-length biography of Queen Elizabeth, which Messrs. Victor Gollancz published here in 1958.

ELIZABETH JENKINS

Contents

List of Illustrations

Martha Ray

Two gentlemen were debating as to whether a figure in the distance was Lord Sandwich. One of them settled the matter. "It is certainly Lord Sandwich," he said. "You observe, he is walking down both sides of the street at once." Lord Sandwich's shambling walk was not his only peculiarity; his bold-featured face was deadly pale and gave rise to the saying that he looked as if he had been half-hanged and cut down by mistake. His constitution was an iron one; he never felt discomfort in the heat or wore an overcoat in the depths of winter. This imperviousness was not only physical but moral. During his tenure of office as First Lord of the Admiralty he was the object of violent public hatred, at which he never turned a hair. Appointments were made of inexperienced and inefficient administrators who could be trusted to vote with Sandwich's party. The results of this régime were epitomized in 1782, when the *Royal George* sank off Spithead in still water. A great piece fell out of the ship's bottom and she went down with all hands, including the Admiral.

In spite of his uncouthness, his harshness, his lack of scruple, Lord Sandwich had, when he liked to use it, great personal charm. His country seat in Huntingdon, Hinchinbrook, was not only the magnificent establishment of an eighteenth-century nobleman, it was also the home of a cultured man. Lord Sandwich was devoted to music, and though he played nothing but the kettle-drums himself, he loved to hear playing and singing, and the concerts given at Hinchinbrook were famous. He was the friend and patron of Giardini, the celebrated singer; his private secretary, Joah Bates, was a distinguished musician. He had also, under his roof, a soprano of brilliance and exquisite sweetness: her name was Martha Ray.

She had been baptized at St. Paul's, Covent Garden, but her childhood was spent at Elstree in Hertfordshire, as the daughter of "a dissolute stay-maker", who had apprenticed her at thirteen years old to a milliner in Clerkenwell. At the end of her five years, when she was eighteen and he was forty-two, Lord Sandwich had taken her into keeping. How the connexion was made is not known. The few people who knew them both intimately said that his Lordship and Miss Ray were equally cautious in never dropping a word about the matter. Some said that it was through the medium of that "Mrs. H", "famous in the annals of gallantry", who has been drawn by Hogarth, decoying the country girl in Plate 1 of "A Harlot's Progress". Another account said that Lord Sandwich, passing a shop in Tavistock Street where Miss Ray was employed, heard her singing a song. At all events the affair which began as a vulgar intrigue developed into the one attachment of Sandwich's life. He had been unhappily married and was separated from his wife, who had the upbringing of their children, and Martha Ray became a companion whom he could not do without. His friend Joseph Cradock said that her modesty and her retiring behaviour were such that, considering the disparity of their ages, it would have been possible to be in the same house with them and suppose that she was Lord Sandwich's protégée rather than his mistress; and in some respects her relationship to her elderly protector was that of a child, for Lord Sandwich gave her a very thorough education. She was taught the accomplishments of a fashionable woman, but above all she received a musical training from the most eminent masters. Giardini himself gave her singing lessons and her voice, which was both exquisite and powerful, was cultivated to perfection; she learned to play various musical instruments well, and the harpsichord with remarkable distinction.

Her disposition was timid and Lord Sandwich was not a man to do away with other people's timidity; but it is clear that when she was not frightened or distressed, she showed a simple cheerfulness and a readiness to be pleased which made her society very delightful. She was spoken of generally as "the lovely Miss Ray", "the beautiful Miss Ray", but when the Press attempted to given an accurate description of her to a public which had become avid for every detail, the summing-up of the available information was that she was about five foot five inches tall, "of great elegance of person", with a fresh colour and a smiling face, and "great sweetness of manner". The portrait of her, said to be by Nathaniel Dance, shows a very slight figure, which gives the built-up hair and the great hooped skirt the exaggerated values they were meant to display. This portrait shows her with a conventional smile, but engravings of her that appeared in the Press suggest a strongly marked face stamped with care and large, troubled eyes. It seemed likely that her good looks were *journalière* and that they bloomed when she was happy and at ease. In the privacy of Hinchinbrook she was at ease, and there was a great deal in her situation to enjoy.

Hinchinbrook, a Tudor great house built on the remains of a medieval nunnery, was described by Horace Walpole as "most comfortable and just what I like, old, spacious, irregular, yet not vast or forlorn." Miss Ray appears in a flash in one of the Hon. Augustus Hervey's letters to Lord Sandwich, written in 1770: "My best compliments to Mademoiselle and all her parrots, dogs, etc." She was luxuriously kept and she occupied in some way, the position of the lady of the house; she was spoken of as a kind, considerate mistress to the servants and as very thoughtful for the poor of the neighbourhood. Much of her time was spent in pregnancies and lyings-in; in fifteen years she had borne nine children to Lord Sandwich, of whom, true to the infant mortality of the time, there survived only two sons and a daughter. But in spite of her long association with him and of her being the mother of his children, she had not learned to presume on her influence with Lord Sandwich. Her gentle, unassuming cast of behaviour remained unaltered. It may well have been one of her charms in Lord Sandwich's eyes, accustomed as he had been to the boldness of trollops and the assurance of women of fashion.

In Christmas week the musical parties at Hinchinbrook were devoted to oratorio, and the society of the neighbourhood was invited to hear them. Handel's *Jephtha* was a favourite, and though Giardini himself sang the title rôle, the foremost attraction was Martha Ray's singing of Iphis. Her rendering of the air:

> *Farewell thou busy world where reign*
> *Short hours of joy and years of pain!*
> *Brighter scenes I seek above*
> *In the realms of peace and love,*

thrilled listeners to the heart. But they were required to recollect themselves. "The elegant Mrs. Hinchliffe", the wife of the Bishop of Peterborough, understood this perfectly, and though she sat opposite to Miss Ray at supper, she knew that good breeding did not allow her to notice the young lady. She told Mr. Cradock: "I was really hurt—to sit opposite her...and yet find it improper to notice her. I was quite charmed with her." This "seeming cruelty" to Miss Ray, she said, "quite took off the pleasure of my evening." Not all the ladies behaved with Mrs. Hinchliffe's knowledge of the world. Between the acts of an oratorio "a lady of rank" who had been greatly moved by Miss Ray's singing went up and spoke to her. The young woman appeared miserably embarrassed and Lord Sandwich at once sought out a man in the audience, to whom he said: "As you are well acquainted with that lady I wish you would give her a hint that there is a boundary line drawn in my family which I do not wish to see exceeded. Such a trespass", his Lordship explained, "might occasion the overthrow of all our musical meetings." The man who could endure the awkwardness of such a régime without a qualm and could force it on other people, was not a person to be trifled with.

Martha Ray understood this thoroughly. It was true that her hold on Lord Sandwich was a powerful one. He was never contented to be without her. She was with him all the time at Hinchinbrook and when he went up to the Admiralty he took her with him, but she had no self-confidence in her dealings with him. As Cradock relates, "she was entirely dependent on him; Lord Sandwich gave her mother thirty pounds a year, but beyond the expenses of her education, dresses and the use of his house, Miss Ray had no provision or settlement whatever from his Lordship". And not only was this so: his influence on her affections and her fears was so great that it prevented her from achieving independence when it was within her reach. The management of Covent Garden Opera House, through Giardini, offered her £3,000 and a benefit performance if she would appear for a season. In modern money the £3,000 would be nearly the equivalent of £10,000. So far from accepting the offer, the terrified girl dared not even tell Lord Sandwich it had been made. He might think that even to consider it was ungrateful of her; if she accepted it he would become her enemy, and then—what would happen to her children?

She had never lost the remembrance of her humble origins, the poverty of her home with her disreputable father and her anxious, burdened mother, nor of that insight into the inferno of the London slums which no girl who had worked for five years in Clerkenwell could have failed to gain. She showed how vivid her recollection was in the intense anxiety she expressed for her children: her sons, Robert and Basil, her daughter Augusta. If she had been married to Lord Sandwich, she would have had no claim on the children except what he allowed, but since she was not, the possession of the children was entirely hers, and so was the responsibility. If their father chose to turn them off, the law as it then stood could not help her.

Though she had this underlying motive to make her contented with her position, there was much actual enjoyment in it, too. She had never had a passion for Lord Sandwich, but she had considerable affection for him and a great respect. She owed to him the things that made her life interesting. He was kind to her, and to someone who had not been born to it, it meant something to be treated with the deference that was considered due to a woman under Lord Sandwich's protection. In 1775 she was thirty-three and Lord Sandwich was fifty-seven. Of the two boys, Robert was twelve and Basil five, and between them came Augusta, the mother's favourite child. Martha Ray had lived with Lord Sandwich for fifteen years; there seemed no reason why she should not continue this remote, enchanted existence with nothing to break the spell. But life never stands still, even if it flows as slowly as a river under ice.

One October afternoon of 1775, Lord Sandwich was standing under the gate-house at Hinchinbrook when there cantered up his friend Major Reynolds and a young officer who was recruiting in the neighbourhood. His name was James Hackman and he was just over twenty. The value of agreeable visitors in the country was great and the military were especially welcome, as they knew the world and were reckoned to be good talkers. Lord Sandwich warmly invited both the officers to come in to dinner.

Captain Hackman did not live up to the military reputation as a talker but he made a very pleasant impression nonetheless. He was a slight young man with a long, pointed nose, and a bright, apprehensive look that conveyed a mixture of wildness and gentleness. He had not been bred as a soldier but had chosen the army as a more romantic calling than that of a tradesman. Beside the two visitors, the party at dinner consisted of Lord Sandwich and Miss Ray, Miss Ray's companion, Mrs. Berkeley, a native of Otaheiti called Omai, who was staying in England as a guest of the Government, and Mr. Cradock. After dinner coffee was drunk; then candles were brought and four of the company sat down to whist.

Lord Sandwich and Miss Ray played together and Major Reynolds partnered Mrs. Berkeley. Captain Hackman asked if he might sit and look on. He looked to some purpose; when the table broke up, he was deeply, helplessly in love, with the passion of a very young man which, like Romeo's, leads to a state of mind in which death is better than life without the desired object.

Lord Sandwich in the course of the evening had developed a severe headache, and now said he must go to his room. He regretted that he did not feel well enough to unpack the parts of a lunar telescope which Dollond's, the makers of optical instruments, had sent from London. He was anxious to make sure they had travelled safely. Mr. Cradock said he would unpack the telescope and put it together and the visitors offered to help him. When the ladies had retired, the three gentlemen went out on to the lawn in the light of a brilliant October moon. Here they stayed till late, looking through the telescope. The emblem of romantic love undergoes a startling change when so seen; it is no longer a radiant sphere, transforming the heavens with its light; it becomes a dead object of ghastly whiteness, borne in a sky of black.

For the events of the next three and a half years, the chief source of information is a series of letters written by James Hackman to Martha Ray and a few of her replies. These letters were published under unfortunate circumstances. Sir Herbert Croft, who though a clergyman was a person of doubtful integrity, gained possession of the letters at the moment when events had made a large public agog to read them. Croft had previously got possession by questionable means of letters and information concerning the poet Thomas Chatterton, whose suicide was still a topic of sensational interest, and determined to produce a best-seller, he interpolated the Chatterton matter, as well as an eye-witness's account of the execution of the notorious Dr. Dodd, into the collection of letters, pretending that Hackman had written the material to entertain Martha Ray, and sprinkling references to the events mentioned in the additions, in the letters leading up to them. This vexatious tampering gave the whole collection of letters the reputation of being forgeries; but from the similarity of many of them to the one which is indisputably Hackman's, as well as from other indications, it is now considered reasonable to accept the bulk of them as genuine, and indeed, it would have required much greater ability than any that Croft ever showed, to have invented them.

It is not easy to gain a clear picture of Martha Ray except obliquely, from the effect she had on two men as different from each other as Lord Sandwich and James Hackman. Her attraction for the former was easily understandable, but that she should have aroused an engrossing, a besotted passion in a youth thirteen years younger than herself shows that, quiet as she was, her attraction could be extraordinarily potent. Her own emotions were never as deeply stirred as Hackman's, but his youth and his passion created a feeling which she had never known before. Lord Sandwich's old black coachman, James, recalled long afterwards that for three weeks after the dinner party, whenever he drove Miss Ray out in the carriage, Captain Hackman was sure to be met with at some point on the road, waiting to bow to her. Nothing was thought of this at the time, and the matter was managed with such caution that the rest of the household knew nothing except that Captain Hackman was a frequent caller, at Lord Sandwich's cordial invitation.

In less than two months after their first meeting, Hackman was writing to her:

"Why did you sing that sweet song yesterday, though I pressed you? Those words, and your voice, were too much. No words can say how much I am yours."

His whole mind was bent on gaining possession of her, yet the thought of Lord Sandwich made him feel distressed at what he was determined to do. He did not admit that Sandwich had any right to her; the latter's age, the fact that the benefits he had given her were those of a father rather than a husband, the fact that he was not her husband and that Hackman himself meant to be, all this he firmly believed justified his own conduct, and yet he was sorry for the pain he knew he must cause. He determined that the laws of hospitality at least should be respected.

"You shall not make me happy (oh how supremely blest) under the roof of your benefactor and my host. It were not honourable. Our love, the inexorable tyrant of our hearts, claims his sacrifice but does not bind us to insult his walls with it."

Martha Ray, mindful of the thirteen years between them, replied that she would not take advantage of what might be only a youthful infatuation. She explained, too, the hold which Lord Sandwich had on her affection and her gratitude by copying out for Hackman Lady Ann Lyndsay's poem "Auld Robin Gray". It was one of her songs, but she had never sung it to him. She felt it strangely applicable to their case, as the young lover in it was called Jamie, and the young wife of Robin Gray says:

"He has been good to me."

But copying out verses was no defence against the passion of such a lover. Her reluctance, her compunction, her caution were swept away. A meeting place was devised outside the walls, and on 13 December Hackman wrote:

"No language can explain my feelings. Oh Martha, yesterday, yesterday! ... Oh thou, beyond my warmest dreams bewitching! What charms! ... Where, when? ... Yet *you* shall order, govern, everything.

"Are you now convinced that Heaven made us for each other? Whatever evils envious fate design me, after those few hours of yesterday, I will never complain or murmur."

On Christmas Day she wrote him a note, speaking of her social duties in a way that reminds one of Mrs. Hinchliffe's words. "I must do penance at a most unpleasant dinner." But, she added, everything was disagreeable where he was not. Shortly afterwards, a piece of unexpected good fortune fell to the lovers, which awed and almost alarmed them. The snow had begun in December, and in the second week in January it became so heavy that the roads were travelled with difficulty. Hackman, undeterred, had ploughed his way through them to call on Lord Sandwich, and the latter invited him to stay at Hinchinbrook until they were clear again. Hackman protested; then Lord Sandwich urged Miss Ray to add her persuasions, and the stricken, ecstatic Hackman gave way.

For three weeks the lovers were under the same roof, with the white, silent world outside, and inside their own fear and agitation and their secret raptures, for the vow not to injure Lord Sandwich in his own house could not hold good in such temptation. The only being who appeared to suspect them was Omai. The coloured man had a loyal devotion to Lord Sandwich. He spoke very little English but he put his small vocabulary to very good use; he once described a wasp that had stung him as "a soldier bird". The fact that he was silent for the most part meant that his observation was not interrupted, and though Martha Ray did not actually believe that they had betrayed themselves, some of Omai's looks made her slightly uneasy. Hers was the harder task. For an ingenuous young man like Captain Hackman to be sometimes inarticulate was not out of the

way, when he found himself for the first time staying in such a
house; but Miss Ray was expected to be always composed, agreeable
and sympathetic to Lord Sandwich.

"My poor, innocent, helpless babes!" she wrote, in a mixture of
self-contempt and despair. "Were it not on your account, your
mother would not act the part she does." What was Mrs. Yates's
acting to hers? she said. When the curtain fell the actress could go
home and be herself.

The thaw set in on 7 February and Hackman had no excuse to
linger. He left immediately, and from his lodgings he wrote to
Martha four letters in two days. He said in one of them, "Would I
might be in your dear, little, enchanted dressing-room when you
read it!" The last three weeks had made their present separation all
the harder. Martha wrote on 8 February:

"When again shall I enjoy your dear society as I did during
that—to me, at least—blessed snow?" But she feared he might be
less eager for her society now.

He answered:

"The bliss I have enjoyed with you these three weeks has increased, not diminished my affections. Three weeks and more in the
same house with M! It was more than I deserved. And yet, to be
obliged to resign you every night to another! By these eyes, by your
still dearer eyes, I don't think I slept three hours during the whole
three weeks. Yet, yet, 'twas bliss.... Would it had snowed till
Doomsday! But then, you must have been *his* till Doomsday. Now,
my happy time may come."

The weather remained cold despite the thaw. Martha wrote on 22
February:

"Where was you this morning, my life? I should have been froze
to death, I believe, with the cold, if I had not been waiting for *you*.
I am uneasy, very uneasy. What could prevent you?" She was in a
frame of mind when a missed appointment was more than dis-
appointing, it seemed ominous. She had begun to have frightening
dreams, and dreamed that Sandwich and Hackman were fighting a
duel. But her spirits rose the next day. She wrote a note to tell
Hackman that business had called Lord Sandwich to the
Admiralty. "I am to follow, for the winter." She said that Lord
Sandwich's own horses were to take her; therefore they would be
obliged to bait on the road and she would take care to stop for the
night at some place where she and her lover might conveniently

meet. "If I am not happy for one whole night in my life it will now be your fault. You *must* go to town. Though things can't often be contrived at the A., they may—they may?—they *shall* happen elsewhere."

Two days afterwards, however, these prospects were dashed. Lord Sandwich had decided she was to go post; with relays of horses, there would be no stopping on the road. She tried to soothe a little of her disappointment; "Will you?" she wrote, "bring me some book tomorrow, to divert me as I post it to town, that I may forget, if it be possible, that I am posting from you?"

And then, again, Lord Sandwich altered his arrangements. She was, after all, sent with his own horses and she spent one night on the road at the village of Hockerill, near Bishop's Stortford. When she had gone on the next day, Hackman stayed behind at the inn and wrote to her, writing down with all the needless repetition of a lover, the things they had already settled in conversation:

"Don't forget to write and don't forget the key. As far as seeing you, I shall use it sometimes, but never for an opportunity to indulge our passion. That, positively, shall never happen again under *his* roof." He went on, with considerable candour, to reproach himself because he had first vowed that he would never possess her under Lord Sandwich's roof and then his memory had dwelt with such rapture on the number of times the vow had been broken "during the time the snow shut me up at H! A snow as dear to me as to yourself." The sense of dishonourable dealing remained to gall him. "Though I had not the strength to resist when under the same roof with you, ever since we parted, the recollection that it *was* his roof has made me miserable."

He came to town in the wake of his letter and took a lodging in Duke's Court, St. Martin's Lane. His headquarters, his daily resort, was the Canon Coffee House at Charing Cross. The Admiralty, standing at the upper end of Whitehall, was just round the corner. And now the love affair entered its second phase. The lyrical rapture of the opening was past, but it gave place, not to a calmer state of mind and a more mundane sense of pleasure, but to a relentless, driving impulse; Hackman was now in the fearful grip of an obsession that engrossed him to the exclusion of every other idea. He had a sister living in Craven Street; her husband, a Mr. Frederick Booth, was also her first cousin. Booth, so closely connected with Hackman, was very sympathetic towards him, and the latter once told him: "You have been almost my only friend." He had one other friend, however, whose surname has not transpired. Hackman wrote to him on intimate terms as "My dear Charles", and he appears in the correspondence as "Charles —— Esqr." This gentleman lived some way out of London. To neither of them had Hackman so far confided his great matter. Conscious of an iron determination that would not let him listen to any contrary advice, he may have purposely refrained from confidences until he should have gained his object. This was to marry Martha Ray as soon as he could. On 17 March, 1776, he wrote:

"I shall never be happy, never be in my senses, till you consent to marry me, and notwithstanding the dear night at Hockerill and the other which your ingenuity procured for me last week at D. Street, I swear it by the bliss of blisses, I will never taste it again till you are my wife."

Martha Ray, as well as Hackman, had entered a new phase of emotion. She loved him both passionately and tenderly and her personal happiness would have been secured by a marriage with him. But whereas Hackman had one idea in his head and one only, she had several matters of great difficulty to consider. The security of her children was the first. Hackman had written: "Lord Sandwich cannot but provide for your boys, and as for your sweet little girl, I will be a father to her." But Hackman's knowledge of Lord Sandwich dated only from five months ago and she had lived with his Lordship fifteen years. It was not likely that any misgivings of hers about Lord Sandwich's probable conduct to her boys would be cleared away by Hackman's assurances. As for his promising to be a father to Augusta—everything that care and affection could do, he would perform; but what could they do, on the pay of a captain in the 58th Foot, for a child who had been brought up as a daughter of Lord Sandwich? And even this slender resource might be lost if Lord Sandwich were determined to pursue the lovers with hatred. He had great influence in military circles, and the career of an obscure young man would not be likely to survive his personal animosity. She might try to take advantage of the opening at Covent Garden which had been offered to her, but if the management knew that her engagement would displease such a powerful patron, would they renew the offer? The facts were harsh, but someone had to face them, and the retiring woman had a firmer grasp of economic realism than the soldier. As events turned out, it is reasonable to believe that such fears did Lord Sandwich a grave injustice, but his conduct to Martha Ray had made it impossible for her to know this with absolute certainty. All she knew was what happened to children when their parents had no friends and no means of making money.

She was now in a position not only acutely painful but dangerous. With Hackman stationed at the Canon Coffee House, haunting Whitehall in front of the Admiralty, and sometimes getting access to her own rooms by means of the key she had given him, she ran the risk of a discovery by Lord Sandwich. She had also to manage and to endure the sufferings and the impatience of the man she dearly loved. She told him, what she thought he had not realized till now, the actual discrepancy in their ages. He replied: "Nothing to the purpose. My mind is made up. Besides, I knew your age all along." Then she told him that not only had she no income or property, but that she was in debt. She did not say for what, or why it was that she could not ask Lord Sandwich to pay the bills. She may have incurred a liability by helping somebody of whom Lord Sandwich did not approve. She only said that she was in debt for an amount between two and three hundred pounds, and that she would not lay this burden on him. Whatever she urged the lover brushed aside and reproached her with not loving him because she would not immediately come to him. She wrote:

"If I do not marry you, I do not love you? Gracious powers of love! Does my H. say so? My *not* marrying you is the strongest proof I can give you of my love."

It is not clear how Hackman managed to combine so much waiting and watching and calling and writing with any military duties, but early in March of 1776 he was offered a commission in Ireland. There were some grounds for the idea that the matter might have been arranged through the agency of Lord Sandwich. The offer meant promotion and Hackman himself said he knew he ought to take it. Martha Ray implored him to do so. The separation would be temporary; she would write to him by every post; he must not refuse this opportunity to improve his position; he must rouse himself and not give way to despair. "There are joys, there is happiness in store for us yet, I feel there is." He admitted that he ought to go, he half-promised that he would go, but he stayed where he was, snatching every chance of seeing her and writing all the time. At last, she was almost beside herself.

Admiralty, 19 March.

"Why, why do you write to me so often? Why do you see me so often? When you acknowledge the necessity of complying with my advice?

"You tell me, if I bid you, you'll go. I have bid you, begged you to go—I *do* bid you go. Go, I conjure you, go! But let us not have any more partings. The last was too, too much."

He went. He remained in Ireland for two years, and he wrote to her on an average of twice a week. The letters are, as ever, those of a young man entirely absorbed by love.

"To talk of music is to talk of you. Martha and music are the same. What is music *without* you? And harmony has tuned your mind, your person, your every look and word and action." It was into this correspondence that Croft introduced the bulk of his matter on Thomas Chatterton. So far from needing any additional interest, any heightening, the story of Hackman's passion, reduced to a mere statement of fact, is astonishing. Two years' absence from a woman thirteen years older than himself had made no difference to his infatuation, and when he received a letter saying that she was ill he abandoned all his commitments and, in April, 1778, returned to England, to his old lodgings in Duke's Court and to his coign of vantage in the window of the Canon Coffee House.

He sent word of his arrival and a letter of farewell was brought to him which Martha had begun to write, thinking herself dying, and which her maid had finished. As doctors in the eighteenth century were not able to do very much for their patients, invalids frequently died from what seemed slight causes, but they sometimes appeared about to die and recovered suddenly. Martha Ray made such a recovery and wrote a short note to Hackman, who received it with ecstasy and described the agony in which he had hung about outside the Admiralty, on an evening in early May, watching lights cross the windows as they were carried from room to room and trying to determine if this meant that she were worse. But when the rapture of relief was over, he found himself dissatisfied, yearning, in despair. Lord Sandwich had engaged Signora Galli of Covent Garden to give Martha Ray some singing lessons, and Galli had made herself acceptable in the household; she now spent a great deal of time at the Admiralty, on the semi-official footing of a chaperone to Miss Ray. She appeared to have gained Lord Sandwich's confidence. What he told her did not transpire; but Omai had, it was thought, given his benefactor some warning hints before he himself was sent back to Otaheiti, and if Lord Sandwich had in fact taken the trouble to see that Hackman was posted to Ireland, the latter's return was not likely to be disregarded by him. There was never a suggestion at any time that Lord Sandwich was angry with Miss Ray; a man of great astuteness, he was no doubt satisfied that he had the situation under control; but a woman of the world, who was congenial to Martha Ray and at the same time devoted to his Lordship's interests, would be a very useful person to act as companion and chaperone in Lord Sandwich's household.

Hackman found that Martha Ray's objections to throwing in her lot with his were unchanged and that it was no longer so easy to gain access to her as he had found it two years ago. He began to decline into a state of solemn, bitter grief. In September, 1778, he followed the party from London to Huntingdon, and he wrote to Martha from the inn at Hockerill.

September 5.

"Here did I sit more than two years ago in this very room, perhaps in this very chair, thanking you for bliss, for paradise, all claims to which I soon after voluntarily resigned, because I hoped they would soon be mine by claims more just, if possible, than those of love."

His passion was becoming a standing matter for pain and reproach on his part, for grief and pity on hers; it was already a little in the background of her existence. She managed to keep up at least an appearance of being disengaged and gay. Mr. Cradock remembered an evening spent with her and Lord Sandwich at Vauxhall. The latter was to go on board the East Indiaman *Duke of Grafton* at Woolwich to receive a deputation and be present at a banquet, and he made plans for something rather more entertaining afterwards. "Cradock," he said, "you shall go with me. Miss Ray shall meet us in the coach and we will all pass the evening at Vauxhall." Then it turned out that business would detain Lord Sandwich at the Admiralty until late in the day. Mr. Cradock, he said, should represent him on board the East Indiaman and they would all dine afterwards at Deptford before coming up to town for the evening. Cradock was dismayed; he protested that he would not have an idea of what to say. Lord Sandwich told him he need not say anything much. Cradock got through the ceremony somehow and was much struck by the decoration of the ship which had been carried out in the oriental manner and included two elephants trapped in gold and scarlet. At the dinner party, there was placed before Lord Sandwich the largest rock cantaloup melon ever grown in England, but his Lordship did not care about such things. He would not cut the melon and said it had better be kept for another occasion. Then they drove up to London and took one of the boxes in Vauxhall Gardens. As part of the entertainment the audience were singing catches and glees. Miss Ray joined in the singing, and heads began to turn in the direction of the box. No one could make out "who it was that sung so enchantingly".

If things had remained as they were, Hackman must gradually have lost his hold on the situation and receded into the background. He might, at long last, have recovered, even; he was but twenty-four; then something which seemed at first a piece of wonderful good fortune gave matters a fatal turn.

A well-wisher presented him to the living of Wiveton, a village in Norfolk. A parsonage house and a modest but sufficient income were now before him; he sold out of the army and at Christmas in 1778, he was ordained. It now seemed to him that every difficulty was cleared, miraculously, from his path. In January, 1779, he wrote:

"I have ten thousand things to tell you. My situation in Norfolk is lovely, exactly what you like. The parsonage house may be made very comfortable at a trifling expense....

"Now my happiness can be deferred no longer.... Oh, then, consent to marry me directly! The day I lead you to the altar will be the happiest day of my existence!

"Oh, M., every day I live, I do but discover more and more how impossible it is for me to live without you."

Martha Ray was confronted, inescapably, with a choice of two actions; either would entail the most extreme agitation: the dismay and terror of leaving Lord Sandwich, the anguish of finally rejecting James Hackman. Whether she were in serious doubt as to what to do, and if so, how long it took her to make up her mind, must be uncertain, but she showed herself unusually troubled, and though he did not connect the episode with anything at the time, she astonished Mr. Cradock by something she said to him. They were sitting, at the Admiralty, "in the great room above stairs," and suddenly Miss Ray began, with an air of great distress, to talk to him about her own position. She asked Cradock if he would speak to Lord Sandwich about the possibility of making a settlement on her. Cradock was completely taken aback at the suggestion. He replied emphatically that no one but herself could make such a proposal to his Lordship.

Though Hackman found Signora Galli in the way when he wanted to be with Miss Ray, he also found her sympathetic. His youth, his romantic interest and his situation appealed to her, and he felt that she was his friend. So far as liking him went, she was, but her own interests were bound up in serving the interests of Lord Sandwich. The latter had now reached almost the highest pitch of his unpopularity. In the early months of 1779, ballads abusing him were hawked about the streets. At the end of February Admiral Keppel was court-martialled as a result, it was thought, of his victimization at the hands of Sandwich's party. When the tribunal acquitted Keppel, a hostile and triumphant mob stormed up Whitehall, tore down the gates of the Admiralty and hurled missiles through the windows. Sandwich hurried Miss Ray out of the back of the building and took her into the Horse Guards next door. He himself showed no alarm, but she was terrified, and in the course of the following weeks she was frightened whenever she saw or heard the ballad-mongers. Lord Sandwich regarded them with total indifference.

Meanwhile, Hackman was working to remove every objection which Martha Ray had produced. She had spoken of a debt of some hundreds. He had a little house property in his native Gosport and he was raising money on it to complete the sum he meant to use for clearing her. On 1 March, he wrote:

"Though we meet tomorrow I must write to you two words tonight, just to say I have all the hopes in the world, ten days at the utmost will complete the business. When that is done, your only objection is removed, along with your debts; and we may surely then be happy, and be so *soon*. In a month or *six weeks at furthest* from this time I might certainly call you mine. Only remember that my *character*, now I have taken orders, makes expedition necessary. By tonight's post I shall write into Norfolk about the alterations to *our* parsonage. Tomorrow!" he exclaimed.

And now from 1 March to 20 March the series of letters discloses an ominous blank. During those eighteen days, Signora Galli received "a hint" from Lord Sandwich to tell young Mr. Hackman that his hanging about had been remarked, that his attentions were annoying to Miss Ray and that his Lordship would be obliged to him to take himself off. She attempted to carry out these instructions, but against Hackman's vehement indignation and passionate assertion of his rights, she could make no headway. The difficulty in which she found herself led her to make use of a shocking deception. With all the theatrical ability she possessed, she told Hackman, and actually made him believe, that Martha Ray was tired of him and had taken another lover.

On 20 March, he wrote to his friend Charles:

"Your coming to town, my dearest friend, will answer no end. G. has been such a friend to me it is not possible to doubt her information.... What I shall do I know not. Without her I do not think I can exist. Yet I will be, you shall see, a *man* as well as a lover. Should there be a rival and should he merit chastisement, I know you'll be my friend. But I'll have ocular proof of everything I believe."

Hackman said afterwards:

"Cruel G! And yet I can excuse her. She knew not of what materials I was made. She was employed to preserve the treasure. And she suspected not that my soul, my existence, were wrapped up in it." He was now in the grip of an unrelenting agony. During the day, he longed for darkness; at night, sleepless, he longed for it to be day. By the first week of April he had formed a settled, implacable determination to kill himself, but under the long strain of his sufferings, the manly, protective instincts of his mind had given way, and he meant to commit the act before her eyes. To Charles he wrote:

"Death only can relieve me.... Often have I made use of my key that I might let myself into the A, that I might die at her feet." The language of love he meant now to translate into literal terms. "She gave it to me as the key of love. Little did she think it would ever prove the key of death." He asked himself: "What have I to do, who only lived when she loved me, but to cease to live, now she ceases to love?"

6 April was a Tuesday, and he determined the day should be his last. He watched and waited for an opportunity to force his presence on her, but he found none. The next day, 7 April, saw him some further degrees fixed in that awful solemnity of purpose, some steps forward on his unfaltering way to the edge of the abyss.

On this Wednesday there was a small dinner party at the Admiralty. Certain ladies were present whose rank did not preclude them from dining, in strict privacy, with Miss Martha Ray. One of these was the young, charming and sympathetic Mrs. Lewis, whose son afterwards became famous through his sensational novel *The Monk*. Mrs. Lewis thought that Miss Ray seemed in very low spirits. She spoke, however, with her usual sweetness and courtesy to everyone, and after dinner she said how sorry she was that she was engaged to go to the performance at Covent Garden. It was only the first part of the programme, Dibdin's operetta *Love in a Village,* which she had promised to hear; she would return after the interval and she hoped she might have the pleasure of finding the guests still there. She was in full dress and wearing jewels; a red rose was fastened to her bodice. Mrs. Lewis admired the beautiful flower and it crossed her mind that in certain districts of Italy the red rose is looked on as a symbol of early death. Almost as Mrs. Lewis spoke, the rose fell from Martha Ray's bosom. She stooped to pick it up, but the fall had shattered its petals, and she held only the stalk. "The poor girl," said Mrs. Lewis, "said in a slightly faltering voice: 'I trust I am not to consider this an evil omen!'"

Lord Sandwich's carriage stood at the gateway in Whitehall, from which the mob had torn the gates eight weeks before. The fragile, unhappy creature, splendidly dressed, crossed the forecourt and got in; the carriage drove away and Hackman, who had lain in wait, followed it. He saw it drive in the direction of Signora Galli's lodgings in the Haymarket. Knowing or assuming that its destination was Covent Garden, he went back to the Canon Coffee House, and presently from his window he saw the carriage making its way up the Strand.

He had plenty of time for what he meant to do. His lodging in St. Martin's Lane was near at hand. He had dined that evening with his sister and brother-in-law, who kept earlier hours than Lord Sandwich and his fashionable friends. He now wrote a long letter to Frederick Booth, thanking him for his friendship, blessing him and trusting, in what he meant to do, to Booth's understanding and compassion.

"When this reaches you I shall be no more, but do not let my unhappy fate distress you too much. I strove against it as long as possible but it now overpowers me. You know where my affections were placed; my having by some means or other lost hers (an idea which I could not support) has driven me to madness. The world will condemn me but you will pity me. God bless you, my dear F.... you were almost my only friend.... May Almighty God bless you and *yours* with comfort and happiness and may you ever be a stranger to the pangs I now feel! May heaven protect my beloved woman and forgive this act which alone could release me from a world of misery I have long endured. Oh, if it should be in your power to do her any act of friendship, remember your faithful friend J.H." This letter he put into his pocket, meaning to post it as he went. He then charged a pair of pistols. The bullets had to be wadded, and for this he tore up his most treasured of Martha Ray's letters to him. Then he set out on foot for Covent Garden.

Miss Ray had meant to leave at the interval, but for some reason she changed her mind. She sat with Signora Galli in Lord Sandwich's box on the Grand Tier, and throughout the evening "gentlemen of the Admiralty" kept dropping in to pay their respects to her. Perhaps her mind was soothed by the music and she was finding pleasure and relief, as she was particularly able to do, in an evening at the Opera. Hackman did not know what the programme was; he thought of it as a play. He went to the Bedford Coffee House which stood on a side of the square next to the piazza of the Opera House. Here as he sat drinking brandy and water and longing "for the play to be over", he saw one gentleman point him out to another, with the remark that he looked as if he were out of his senses.

At eleven o'clock the foyer of the Opera House was already thronged, and the audience was still streaming down the staircases. Hackman, watching above the heads with frantic intensity, saw Martha Ray come down the stairs, with young Lord Coleraine, attractive and handsome, beside her. He had said that he would have ocular proof of everything he believed—was this it? He shouldered his way through the crowd and came up to her, holding a pistol to his forehead, but there were still people between them. She did not see him, and so dense was the crowd that no one else noticed his behaviour. Driven farther from her by the press, he put the pistol back into his pocket and in a momentary reaction to sense, he was about to make his way out of the foyer by another exit. Unhappily, before he did so, he looked over his shoulder.

Lord Coleraine was not attending Miss Ray. She stood in her conspicuous finery, with no one but Signora Galli to protect her from the jostling of the crowd. Young Mr. MacNamara of Lincoln's Inn, who was acquainted with Lord Sandwich and knew Miss Ray by sight, went to her assistance. He called out to the link boys and footmen to send up Lord Sandwich's carriage, and making his way to Miss Ray and her companion, offered her his hand to guide her through the mob. Hackman saw it all, and the grateful smile with which she took the stranger's hand made him feel that "it was received with peculiar pleasure". In his own words: "The stream of my passions which had been stopped now overwhelmed me with redoubled violence." The strip of pavement between the doors of the Opera House and the row of arches before it was known as the Stone Passage, and here Hackman overtook the three as the footman opened the carriage door.

A fruit-woman and a chair-man who were standing in the passage saw two ladies and a gentleman approach the carriage, followed by "a gentleman in black". Signora Galli got in first, and as she did so, Hackman laid hold of Martha Ray's gown. Her hand still on MacNamara's arm, she turned and looked Hackman full in the face. In that instant, it came to him that it would be best for both of them to die. He drew the pair of pistols. With the right-hand one he shot her through the head, with the other he attempted to do the same to himself. In the words of the fruit-woman, "the bodies fell feet to feet".

So instantaneous was it that MacNamara, feeling Miss Ray fall from his arm, thought that she had fainted at the sound of a shot. Then he saw that a bullet had rebounded against his cuff, and stooping to lift her, realized that he was covered with blood. At the sound of the shots, the crowd had dispersed like hares and the small group about the carriage had the Stone Passage to themselves. Hackman, ill-starred to the last, had failed to shoot himself; he lay in the gutter striking his head with the pistol and crying: "Kill me! Kill me!" Martha Ray was dead.

A doctor named MacMahon joined MacNamara. He wrenched the pistol from Hackman and led him off to dress the wound in his head. MacNamara had the body of Martha Ray carried down Russell Street to the Shakespeare Tavern and there laid on a table. The doctor came back with Hackman, and word was sent to Sir John Fielding, the blind magistrate. MacNamara, who found himself feeling sick at all the blood on him, went home.

Sir John Fielding was roused, and at five o'clock in the morning

Hackman was brought before him. The magistrate committed him for trial and he was lodged in the prison at Tot-hill Fields.

Meanwhile, at almost midnight, the carriage returned to the Admiralty and James, the old black coachman, had to break the news to Lord Sandwich. The old man was overwhelmed with grief; his emotion and the awkwardness of his language at first prevented his master from understanding him. Lord Sandwich thought that James had something more to tell of demonstrations and ballad-mongers. He exclaimed impatiently: "You know that I forbade you to plague me any more about those ballads! Let them sing or say whatever they please about me!" "Indeed, my Lord," cried the poor man, "it is not any ballads! It is all true!" And he managed at length to get out the words.

Lord Sandwich stood absolutely still. Then he seized a candle-stick, ran upstairs and threw himself on his bed. To the terrified servants who followed him, he said: "Leave me to myself." They heard him say, groaning: "I could have borne anything but this."

From his prison next day Hackman wrote to Charles:

"I am alive—and she is dead. I shot her and not myself. Some of her blood and brains is still upon my clothes. I don't ask you to speak to me. I don't ask you to look at me. Only come hither and bring me a little poison. Such as is strong enough. Upon my knees I beg, if your friendship for me was ever sincere, do, *do* bring me some poison."

But the following day, 9 April, he no longer wanted to commit suicide. He now welcomed the idea of death at the hands of justice. It was suggested to him that he might plead insanity, but, he said, he would not allow the plea to be used on his behalf. His case was to be heard on 16 April and, awaiting trial, he was committed to Newgate.

The body of Martha Ray was kept in the room where it had first been carried. At the street's end, on two adjoining sides of the square, were the Piazza where she had met her death, and St. Paul's Church, Covent Garden, where she had been christened. As Cassius said of himself:

Time is come round,
And where I did begin, there shall I end.

Lord Sandwich did not come to the Shakespeare Tavern: he was not a man to find comfort in attending a corpse. The necrophilous George Selwyn, whose fondness for witnessing executions and gazing on dead bodies was well known, was out of London at this time, and his friend the Rev. Mr. Warner tried to send him a description to atone to him for his missing the sight, but was obliged to write confessing failure. "I called today in coming from Coutts' at the Shakespeare Tavern in order to see the corpse of Miss Ray and to send you some account of it, but I had no interest with her keepers and could not gain admittance."

It would have soothed Hackman to know of this; while he was detained in another room at the Shakespeare he had implored Dr. MacMahon to keep out the sightseers who were already coming to gape at the body. He inquired what undertakers were employed and when he heard, some passionate exclamations of his were carried to them in the form of a message, begging them to use every decency and tenderness. When the post mortem had been done, the jewels were removed from the corpse, but no other preparations for burial were made, and it was coffined in the rich dress it was wearing. The coffin was carried down to Elstree, where old Mrs. Ray was still living, and buried in a vault under the church pavement.

Hackman's trial at the Old Bailey was heard before the great Sir William Blackstone. He appeared dressed in black, the wound on his forehead covered with a round, black patch of plaster. Though the verdict was never in doubt, the effect he made on the court was one of awed and solemn sympathy. It was explained on his behalf that he only refrained from pleading guilty so that a full process of trial might not be prevented. He felt that such a process was due to the justice of his country. A speech which he had written in Newgate was then read aloud:

"I stand here the most wretched of human beings and confess myself criminal in a high degree; I acknowledge that my determination against my own life was formal and complete. I protest ... that the will to destroy her who was ever dearer to me than life, was never mine until a momentary phrenzy overcame me.... I have no wish to avoid the punishment which the laws of my country appoint for my crime, but being too unhappy to feel a punishment in death, or a satisfaction in life, I submit myself to the disposal and judgment of Almighty God and to the consequences of this inquiry into my conduct and intention."

MARTHA RAY

She was about five feet five inches tall, "of great elegance of person", with
a fresh colour and smiling face and a "great sweetness of manner".

ELIZABETH TUDOR

Elizabeth in her thirties, the last phase of her youth, and before the
excellent outline of Tudor dress had become blurred by preposterous
exaggeration.

The witnesses were few: the fruit-woman Mary Anderson, the chair-man, Dr. MacMahon and Mr. MacNamara, and they repeated a short and graphic tale. The letter which Hackman had written to Mr. Booth and forgotten to post had been found in his pocket when he was arrested, and it was read as evidence that he was of sound mind when he committed the act. The Judge's summing up contained a memorable passage; the prisoner had said: "I had no intention against her until the *very instant*," but his lordship directed the jury that where the determination to murder had been formed, it did not matter how short an interval separated the determination from the act. The jury did not retire but returned the verdict—guilty—without hesitation. Those watching the trial, among whom was Boswell, were struck by the gentleness and compassion which all the members of the court displayed in their manner towards the prisoner. Though the verdict was against him, it was clear that he aroused the sympathy of everyone from the Judge downwards. The newspaper account said: "The murderer was forgot in the lover. One fact is indisputable—that he loved her to distraction and that the death of both parties was the consequence of that love." Boswell told Dr. Johnson that he had attended Hackman's trial and Johnson listened with deep attention. When Boswell told him that the prisoner had prayed for the mercy of heaven, Johnson said, "in a solemn, fervid tone: 'I hope he *shall* find mercy'." But the most remarkable evidence of this sympathy came from the most unlikely quarter. There was brought to Hackman in the condemned hold a note addressed:

To Mr. Hackman in Newgate.

It said:

17 April, 1779.
"If the murderer of Miss Ray wishes to live the man he has most injured will use all his interest to procure his life."

Hackman was moved to the soul, but he sent Lord Sandwich an immediate answer, saying he wished only for death, and imploring Lord Sandwich not to leave the children unprovided for. There was not the least sign that Lord Sandwich had ever intended to do so. His daughter grew up to be eligibly married; of the two sons, Robert became an admiral, and Basil, who took his father's surname of Montagu, had a distinguished career as a lawyer and a man-of-letters. But that issue had had too dreadful an importance in Hackman's life for him to be able to leave it, as he should have done, in silence.

An awful calmness settled on him in the condemned hold, though it was shivered by transitory storms of emotion. He told his friend Charles after the trial that "the only painful part of his time was now over, and that he was rejoiced to think what a short time he had to live". His execution was to take place on Monday, 19 April.

During the last two days he wrote a quantity of short letters and fragments, chiefly addressed to his friend Charles. These fragments were added by Booth to the collection of Hackman's papers in his possession, which consisted of the copies of his own letters kept by Hackman, in the manner of eighteenth-century letter-writers, and the originals of Martha Ray's. The whole were afterwards given by Booth to the publisher Kearsley, who allowed them to be edited and garnished by the Rev. Herbert Croft.

Some of Hackman's most moving words were written in the condemned hold:

"My God, my creator, my first father! Thou who madest me as I am: with these feelings, these passions, this heart! My father who art in heaven. I bow before thy mercy and patiently abide my sentence."

The dreadfulness of his situation did not dismay him as it would have dismayed many men. He had always had a turn for melancholy. He spoke of the gloominess of Young's "Night Thoughts" as "congenial to his soul", and being in the condemned hold at night, instead of driving him to an extremity of fear, raised his imagination. During the night of 17 April, he wrote:

"My dear Charles,
"The clock has just struck eleven. All has for some time been quiet within this sad abode;...it is an awe-inspiring experience to hear St. Paul's clock thunder through the still ear of night in the condemned walls of Newgate. The sound is truly solemn, it seems the sound of death."

At four in the morning of the day before his death, he dashed down a horrible dream from which he had just awakened. He had dreamed that he saw her as an angel, but resting on the bosom of another angel. "Charles, she saw me where I was, steeped to the lips in misery. She saw me, but without one tear, without one sigh....

Oh how I rejoiced, how I wept, sobbed with joy, when I awoke and discovered myself in the condemned cell of Newgate!"

On the morning of the 19th, at 7 a.m. he attended the service for the condemned in Newgate Chapel. Boswell, with insatiable curiosity, was among the congregation, and got himself a place in one of the mourning coaches that followed the prisoner's coach from Newgate, through Holborn and down Oxford Street to Tyburn. In the coach, Hackman wrote a last word to his brother-in-law. He used a pencil and when Booth received the note it was largely indecipherable but so much was plain:

Tyburn.

"Would it prevent my example having any bad effect if the world should know how much I abhor my former ideas of suicide, my crime...will be the best judge...of her fame I charge you to be careful...your dying H."

At the gallows' foot he asked for time to say his prayers and said he would drop his handkerchief when he was ready. His bearing was abstracted and calm. When after ten minutes he dropped his handkerchief it fell from the cart in which he was standing to the ground. The executioner scrambled down after it; the handkerchief was his perquisite and he did not mean to see it snatched by the crowd. Even this abominable delay did not daunt the prisoner. He remained standing in steadfast composure. The halter which the sheriff's officer had put round his neck before he left the jail was at last tied to the gallows, the horses that drew the cart were whipped up, and they rushed forward, dragging the cart from beneath the prisoner's feet. The yoke of inauspicious stars had been shaken off.

Lord Sandwich's unpopularity was so great that in many quarters his sufferings were treated merely as new material for squibs.

> *When Lords turn musicians to gather a throng*
> *And keep pretty Misses to sing them a song . . .*

began one such. Another said:

> *Our Navy Board seems hastening to decay*
> *Since our First Lord has lost his brightest Ray!*

But Lord Sandwich had never cared about such things. His agony of mind was too great for him to feel them now. He left

London for some time and when he came back, Cradock called on him at the Admiralty. Lord Sandwich was in his private room, and Cradock, who had begun on some indifferent topic, stopped in spite of himself. He had caught sight of "an excellent resemblance" of Martha Ray over the chimney-piece. The portrait had been brought up from Hinchinbrook. Lord Sandwich followed the direction of his eyes. He looked so ill that Cradock made some hasty, awkward excuse, and left him to himself.

For a long while Lord Sandwich made himself a recluse, and then kind, open-hearted Admiral Walsingham persuaded him to come to an evening party. After coffee, Mrs. Bates was asked to sing. Mr. Bates, on the other side of the room, saw to his horror that his wife was preparing to sing a song which was a favourite of Lord Sandwich's and which Martha Ray had often sung to him. Bates attempted to warn her, but he could not reach her in time. The song was begun. It was:

Shepherds! I have lost my love.

Lord Sandwich got to his feet. He apologized to Mrs. Walsingham, but said he had suddenly remembered some pressing business which required his return to the Admiralty. He bowed to all the company and hurriedly left the room.

When the church at Elstree was undergoing some repairs, the coffins in the vault were reburied in the churchyard. Beside the churchyard path a tombstone now stands with the inscription: "Sacred to the memory of Martha Ray, died 1779." The neighbourhood is famous today for the manufacture of synthetic romance. Do any of the stories it has produced compare with hers?

CHAPTER 2

Elizabeth Tudor

Intellect is usually thought to detract from a woman's charm. The young Elizabeth Tudor is a very rare instance of a woman whose dazzling intelligence was recognized as a chief element in her power of attraction. Without the intellect that irradiated her youthful personality in its cold and brilliant light she would not have inspired in the men who threw in their lot with her that intense confidence and enthusiasm which were responsible, among the violent dangers that surrounded her at its outset, for launching her on her tremendous career.

Many very clever women have gained an ascendancy over men by dissembling and concealing their mental superiority; Elizabeth never did this and the men who, in her young years, committed themselves to her cause, did not find their emotion chilled by her amazing cleverness; she inspired in them a high-pitched admiration for the woman she was.

Elizabeth had, it is true, neither of the drawbacks which are supposed commonly to afflict intellectual women. She was attractive to look at and she had an innate sense of dress. Her figure was a little above middle height, slender and upright; her face was oval, the nose slightly aquiline and she had a superb carriage of the head. She had the very pale skin that goes with red-gold hair; her brows and lashes were so fair as to be almost invisible and her lips and cheeks were nearly colourless. This whiteness was particularly noticed in her hands with their preternaturally long and slender fingers. Their frailness gave them a translucence like alabaster.

One of the most speaking of Elizabeth's portraits shows her in her thirties, the last phase of her youth, and before the excellent outline of Tudor dress had become blurred by preposterous exaggeration. This picture shows still the natural waist, the moderately rounded skirt, the long tight sleeves and the head dressed small. The dress is of black and gold brocade, embroidered with large pearls and slashed with white; the bosom is covered by a black lace

yolk, a small ruff of black and white lace underlining the characteristic lift of the chin. The light-red hair, framing the pale face, is
crowned with a small coronet of pearls and black ribbon, from
which a transparent gauze veil flows over the shoulders. The regal
poise of the head and the expression—undaunted and astute, concentrated on some immense task—contrast strikingly with the
hand, whose tenuous fingers are holding, lightly and precisely, a
pale-pink rose.

Elizabeth herself was one of the most remarkable women who
ever lived, and it is interesting to see among her immediate fore-
bears vivid gleams of the different qualities which united in her,
as a whole of such complexity and power. A wonderful tapestry
in the parish church at Lyme Regis shows from where the
Tudors got their red hair. The tapestry depicts the wedding of
Henry Tudor and Elizabeth of York. All its tints are ash grey,
sepia, indigo and green, except for those of the central figure: the
bride wears a chaplet of white roses and beneath it the hair flowing
down her shoulders is flame-coloured. This hair she gave to her son,
Henry VIII, and her grand-daughters, Mary and Elizabeth. A great-
grandmother gave Elizabeth a gift which sounds ordinary enough
but without which no mind can be eminent. Memory is the basis of
intellectual power and Henry VII's mother, the Lady Margaret
Beaufort, was famous for "a very holding memory".

Henry VII himself was distinguished by an unsleeping caution
and a first-class financial sense. He knew that without economy you
cannot have financial stability. His grand-daughter knew it too and
the lengths to which she carried parsimony and the ends for which
she practised it made it appear alternately a disease and an inspiration. The leading qualities she inherited from her father, Henry
VIII, were those obviously associated with kingship. Henry VIII
possessed, for good or ill, an overwhelming force of personality, and
an instinct for popularity that amounted almost to a sixth sense.
The famous portraits of him are all taken in late life and show what
must be without question the most frightening face recorded of any
English monarch. The gross figure and the bull neck, alarming in
themselves, are made hideously terrifying by the small slits of eyes,
narrowed to a stare of cunning and cruelty and bright with lust.
But the ruthlessness that Henry showed to everyone who stood in
his way, the cruelties he practised on Roman Catholics and
Protestants alike, his abominable tyranny in private life, had little

or no effect on his reputation as a king. In that relationship, he had the confidence of the majority of the people and he took care to do nothing seriously to disturb it. He had also the advantage of great physical magnetism. Henry VII had been impressive in private conversation but seen in public he was a weazened elderly man. Henry VIII drew the eye and held it. In his prime, tall, large, fresh-coloured and radiant with vitality, it was natural that his presence should be commanding, but he never lost this attribute even when corpulent and diseased. The force of personality which not only displays itself on occasion like a set piece of fireworks, but has always something in reserve that can out-do and out-last everybody else, was as strong in the elegant young woman as in the boisterous and over-bearing man. So, too, was the inexplicable genius for popularity. Elizabeth had little cause to love her father, but she took with extreme seriousness the task of being a popular sovereign and she admired her father for the way he had done his part. When she was being carried to her coronation through the streets of London the tribute that made her smile and blush with pleasure was a voice bawling: "Remember old King Harry the Eighth!"

Elizabeth's father beheaded her mother. Perhaps no other fact about Anne Boleyn has so much significance in connexion with her daughter's emotional history. The event took place when the child was two years and eight months old and we have been taught that what happens around us has more, rather than less influence on us if it happens while we are still too young to grasp it with our conscious mind. The effect must have been vast, but it is incalculable. There are, however, traits inherited from Anne Boleyn which proclaim themselves in Elizabeth with glittering distinctness. Anne Boleyn had neither intellect nor self-control but she had an extraordinary power of sexual attraction. She was one of those women who dazzle without beauty and allure without being pleasant. The tart, witty, excitable creature who enthralled Henry for six years before marriage became the hysterical shrew who completely lost his affection two years later. Elizabeth had neither her mother's degree of fascination nor her mother's utter lack of judgment; yet she had something that recalled her. She showed the same susceptibility, the proneness to be excited in the society of men, and the same recklessness in allowing her feelings to appear. As a child of fifteen on her guard, her reserve and caution baffled ministers of state, but her wild amorousness had already brought

her within measurable distance of the block; as a queen she
manoeuvred in impenetrable secrecy in all respects but one: in any
amorous relationship she was so open and so shameless her well-
wishers were nearly beside themselves with dismay.

The feminine characteristic of her mother which she inherited to
advantage was Anne Boleyn's taste in clothes. Descriptions of royal
garments, however highly detailed, are often a meaningless
agglomeration of violent colours, but to read the descriptions of
Anne Boleyn's is to see how extraordinary was her talent for
presenting herself. In the period before her marriage when she had
already become the King's mistress, Henry paid the tailor's bills for
a cloak and a nightgown (or negligée) for her, both voluminous
and entirely of black: black satin lined with black taffeta and
trimmed with black velvet. On the last day of May, the eve of her
coronation, she was carried from the Tower to Westminster in a
litter hung with white shot with gold. She wore a dress of cloth of
silver and a mantle of cloth of silver lined with ermine. Her dark
hair was loose under a circle of great rubies. Behind her came ladies
in robes of crimson velvet, riding on white palfreys.

There is no record of Elizabeth's having uttered one word about
her mother to anybody, yet it is not perhaps altogether a coincidence that Katherine Ashley, the governess to whom she clung so
vehemently, was a connexion of the Boleyn family.

Even as a baby, Elizabeth showed unusual distinction and
charm. The sixteenth century was interested in children not as
children but as potential adults, and precocity was admired and
relentlessly stimulated. Lady Bryan, the kind and sensible woman
who had charge of Elizabeth at her mother's death, did her best, it
is true, to see that the child was not overstrained. Elizabeth, she
said, was as "toward" a little girl and "as gentle of conditions" as
any she had ever seen, and she wanted peace and quiet for the child
after the periods of rigid drilling which had to precede her public
appearances. She asked permission for the Princess, not yet three, to
have her meals in the nursery and not at table in the great hall,
where she would want to eat everything she saw and Lady Bryan
would find it difficult to be firm for fear of having a scene in public.
She said: "My Lady hath great pain with her great teeth and they
come very slowly forth which causeth me to suffer her Grace to
have her will more than I would." But three years later immense
progress had been made. When the King's secretary, Wriothesley,

told the six-year-old Princess that the King sent her his blessing, "she gave humble thanks, inquiring after His Majesty's welfare with as great a gravity as if she had been forty years old". The visitor found this both satisfactory and entirely charming.

Henry VIII married Jane Seymour the day after Anne Boleyn's execution, and in September the following year, at Hampton Court, the longed-for boy was born. In her brother's christening procession, the four-year-old Elizabeth carried the chrisom, but she was so small that she was carried herself in the arms of Lord Hertford. However, she walked, holding the hand of the Princess Mary, when the procession came back from the chapel to the bedroom of the dying Queen. Mary was seventeen years older than Elizabeth. Her deep loyalty to her mother had been profoundly outraged by her father's treatment of his lawful wife, and she had withstood, with implacable courage, the blandishments and the threats of Anne Boleyn. These experiences had made her warped and old at twenty. But Catherine of Aragon had been avenged in the shameful death of the woman who had injured her, and Mary allowed herself to have no grudge against her small, attractive half-sister. The gentleness, unselfishness and warm affection that contrasted so strangely with her terrible fanaticism made her ready to be a motherly elder sister to Elizabeth, now that the birth of a prince had so drastically reduced the importance of them both.

But Elizabeth acquired a new importance of her own. From the time of his being able to recognize anybody it was seen that the Prince was extremely fond of his little sister. From her nearness in age Elizabeth was his best companion, to help and play with him "from the first of his speech and understanding". The hardships young children experience in growing up, severe in that era of cumbrous clothes, rigid discipline and lack of medical comforts, led the precocious, sickly little boy to depend on his sister with concentrated affection. She was a child and therefore she shared his outlook, but her being four years older made her able to be a guide and protector, while her superior vitality replenished his and her affection was the dearest thing in life to a child whose mother had died when he was ten days old. Both of them were unusually intelligent and forward, and their tutors, delighted with such material, fanned the children's interest in their lessons to a shocking degree. "As soon as it was light they called for their books." The first hours were spent in studying the scriptures; some time was taken for breakfast and the rest of the morning was given to languages and moral science. Then the six-year-old Prince went to exercise in the open air and the Princess practised the lute and viol or took up her needlework.

When Elizabeth was ten, Henry VIII married Katherine Parr. This pretty, gracious and warm-hearted woman was very good to Edward and Elizabeth and the years of their father's last marriage were the only ones in which they enjoyed anything approaching normal home life. The fact that their rigid, ceremonious existence was now softened and made more gentle and interesting by the kindness of their step-mother did not take off from their intellectual enthusiasm. It was at this period that Elizabeth became recognized as a Princess of unusual gifts. The slender child, sober and pale, with smooth red hair hanging down her back, was as outstanding at twelve years old as she had been at three. In an age when the standard expected of clever children was dangerously high, Elizabeth astonished by her faculty for acquiring knowledge and for using it with judgment. She already spoke fluent French, Spanish and Italian; the famous scholar Dr. Grindal was "laying down the foundations of her Latin and Greek"; her other studies included geography, mathematics, architecture and astronomy. Her favourite subject, however, was history. She liked to spend two to three hours a day reading it and she would read the same period in books of different languages.

Towards the end of the King's life Edward and Elizabeth were established at Hatfield in the red brick palace, part of which still stands in the beautiful wooded park. The arrangement was broken up in December, 1546, on one of those sudden orders that frequently disturbed the children's lives, removing them arbitrarily, they knew not for how long, to this place or that. This time the brother and sister were separated, Edward being sent to Hertford and Elizabeth to Enfield. She wrote to him trying to console him for the abrupt dismissal from their happy place, and the nine-year-old Prince replied, in Latin: "I did not mind the change of place, dearest sister, so much as your going from me. Now, however, the pleasantest thing that can happen to me will be getting a letter from you, especially as you have written first and told me to write to you. Thank you for your kindness and for being so quick.... It is some comfort in my unhappiness that I hope (from what my chamberlain tells me) that I can come and see you soon (if nothing happens to either of us in the meantime). Goodbye, dearest sister."

The visit took place in an unforeseen way. In the New Year Edward's uncle, Edward Seymour Duke of Somerset, brought him to Enfield. The Princess Elizabeth was summoned and in the presence of both children Somerset announced the death of Henry VIII. They immediately burst into tears and cried for so long they aroused the pity and what almost seemed the admiration of the beholders. The following day Somerset, now Lord Protector of the Realm, escorted the ten-year-old King to London.

Before her marriage to the King, Katherine Parr had been about to make a love-match with Sir Thomas Seymour. This man was Somerset's brother, and a very awkward relation for someone as selfish and ambitious as the Lord Protector, whose situation demanded such tact and vigilance. Seymour was a soldier; he had been an ambassador and in the year of the King's death he had been appointed Lord High Admiral and created Lord Seymour of Sudeley. He has been shrewdly described by a contemporary as "fierce in courage, courtly in fashion, in personage stately, in voice magnificent but somewhat empty in matter". He was uncle to the young King; he now proposed to marry the Queen Dowager. With all his natural advantages, he had that form of recklessness and conceit which turns good fortune into a means of self-destruction.

His marriage to the Queen Dowager was performed secretly and with what was regarded as indecent haste. Katherine Parr had never ceased to love him; she was still pretty and attractive, but she was thirty-four and she felt she had no time to lose. Released from the laborious, indeed nauseating duties of attending to Henry VIII in his last illness, and from the perils of a marriage in which Bishop Gardiner, who suspected her orthodoxy, had nearly succeeded in bringing her to the block, Katherine gave herself up to long-delayed happiness. She made her house at Chelsea the scene of ease, pleasure and content and she took Elizabeth to live with her; she had always been fond of her younger stepdaughter, and she was glad to give her a share of this new, delightful existence.

Among those who criticized the Queen Dowager most harshly was the Princess Mary. The latter felt that by her conduct Katherine had proved herself an unsuitable guardian for the Princess Elizabeth, and she wrote to Elizabeth, urging strongly that the two of them should live together.

Elizabeth had now to write a very difficult letter. She did not want to offend Mary—nor did she want to go and live with her. She was very fond of the Queen Dowager and the household at Chelsea was the pleasantest she had ever known. It was the only one where ceremony was reduced almost to nothing and where she was entirely surrounded by indulgent affection. Besides her happy, tender-hearted stepmother, she had Mrs. Ashley with her. Kat Ashley, as the Princess always called her, had one desirable quality as a governess—a hearty love for her pupil. Unfortunately, she lacked discretion. Her darling's enjoyment seemed to her so important that it overrode any other consideration. So far was she from using restraint that the pupil sometimes showed more caution than the governess. To a child so much of whose upbringing had been severe, alarming, joyless, such conditions were irresistible; and there was something else. Lord Seymour was twenty years older than the Princess, but as he was still in his prime this meant only that he had the experience and maturity that impress a very young girl. Elizabeth, in the exquisitely beautiful handwriting that was afterwards so famous, thanked Mary with humble gratitude for her sisterly care, assured Mary that she assented to every one of her arguments, but explained with unmistakable clearness that she did not feel herself able to quit her stepmother's roof.

There would have been no danger if the only feelings to reckon with had been those with which Elizabeth regarded Seymour. The head of the household, absorbed in a newly married wife, could have discouraged or ignored the adolescent passion of his wife's stepdaughter. Seymour might have resisted the temptation to a flirtation with an attractive child if there had not been considerations attached to her state which made her very important. These considerations were precisely those which would have restrained a man of sense, but to Seymour they were an added incitement. In herself, Elizabeth was a powerful one. Her extreme youth contrasted with his wife's maturity; her royalty, as unmistakable as her red hair, added an exciting quality to the ardent affection he evoked, and it was highly diverting to him to turn the sedate Princess, cautious and watchful beyond her years, into an excitable little romp.

At first the Queen Dowager saw no harm in the skirmishing: in visits to Elizabeth's bedroom before she was up, when Seymour's antics drove her "to go further into the bed", or in the garden where Katherine herself held the Princess while Seymour, in outrageous horseplay, cut her mourning dress into a hundred pieces. But the Queen Dowager was not always present as a chaperone; one day she came into the room unexpectedly and found her husband and Elizabeth in each other's arms. Katherine was with child and the situation was a horrible one to people who were all three fond of each other. It was accepted immediately that the parties must separate, and Elizabeth and her household were transferred to Cheshunt in Hertfordshire. Elizabeth, ashamed, sorry and anxious about her stepmother's health, departed almost speechless. On her arrival at Cheshunt she wrote to Katherine: "Although I could not be plentiful in giving thanks for the manifold kindness I had received at your Highness's hands at my departure, yet I am something to be borne withal for truly I was replete with sorrow to depart from your Highness, especially seeing you doubtful of health, and albeit I showed little, I weighed it the more deeper when you said: 'You would warn me of all evilness that you should hear of me.' "

Katherine had sent her out of the house for everybody's sake, but she did not alter in her affection towards Elizabeth. When she made her will before her lying-in she left Elizabeth half her jewels. But three days after the birth of her child, as she lay dying, she complained that everyone around was unkind to her. Her husband, who was holding her hand, exclaimed: "Why, sweetheart, I would you no hurt!" "No, my Lord, I think so," she answered; then she turned her head and whispered: "But, my Lord, you have given me many shrewd taunts." When the news reached Elizabeth that her stepmother was dead, Mrs. Ashley told her that she should write a letter of condolence to the widower. Elizabeth replied: "I will not do it, for he needs it not."

Seymour lost no time in getting in touch with Elizabeth. He wrote to tell her that his affairs would bring him into her neighbourhood and that, going or coming, he would like to visit her. Elizabeth made Mrs. Ashley write a reply to the effect that if he came she would be glad to see him and if he did not she wished him a good journey. Mrs. Ashley and the cofferer of the Princess's household, Thomas Parry, were very intimate with each other and both of them were on highly confidential terms with Elizabeth. They spoke constantly and freely to each other and to her of Seymour's passion for her, Mrs. Ashley not hesitating to declare to

her that if he had been able, Seymour would have married her
instead of the Queen Dowager. Parry said on one occasion to Mrs.
Ashley that Seymour would be an ill husband for the Princess, for
he was a cruel, jealous man who had used his wife unkindly. Mrs.
Ashley replied: "Tush, tush, I know him better than you do, I
know he will make but too much of her and that she knows well
enough." It was plain to both of them that Elizabeth's feelings were
very much engaged; she blushed when Seymour's name was spoken
and could not conceal her pleasure when anyone praised him; but
the young Princess showed more discretion than her servants.
When Mrs. Ashley told her it was said in London that she would
marry the Lord Admiral, Elizabeth smiled and said that was but "a
London news". When one of the women of her bedchamber began
to talk of Seymour as a suitable husband for the Princess, Elizabeth told her that if she did not hold her tongue she should be
thrust out of the room.

But Elizabeth only reached her fifteenth birthday two days after
the Queen Dowager's death, and with her own emotions deeply
roused by Seymour, and Mrs. Ashley using all her efforts to connive
at indiscretion, it was next to impossible for her to avoid scandal
altogether. She was at her brother's court for a brief season and
Seymour was suspected of paying her several clandestine visits.
Then there was a night when Mrs. Ashley permitted the Princess to
go out in a barge on the Thames. This came to the ears of the
Protector's wife, an arrogant and disagreeable woman but not
without sense. The Duchess of Somerset declared furiously that
Mrs. Ashley "was not fit to have the governance of a King's
daughter".

The need for discretion was shown with startling plainness in a
warning given to Seymour by Lord Russell. The former, speaking
of the two Princesses, said it would be better for them to be married
to private gentlemen, and why should not he, Seymour, take one of
them himself? Russell replied in the most solemn manner: "My
Lord, if either you or any other within this realm shall match
himself in marriage with either my Lady Mary or my Lady
Elizabeth he shall undoubtedly, whatsoever he be, procure unto
himself the occasion of his utter undoing, and you especially, above
all others, being of so near alliance with the King's Majesty."
Words could hardly speak plainer, but Seymour's recklessness,
stupidity and conceit had put him beyond the reach of warning. He

busied himself in the matter of the landed property left to Elizabeth under the will of Henry VIII, discussing the possibility of its being exchanged for other estates in the neighbourhood of his own; he suborned the Master of the Mint at Bristol to coin a large sum of money; finally he boasted that he had but to say the word to raise ten thousand men. On 16 January, 1549, the Council, with his brother at their head, had him arrested on a charge of high treason.

Somerset was determined to get his brother out of the way. Seymour had presented him with a choice of material on which to do this, but the strongest charge, if it could be proved, would be that he had attempted without the permission of the Council to marry Elizabeth. As the latter stood second in succession to her unmarried brother, a clandestine marriage with her was tantamount to a threat to the existing government, in other words to the capital offence of high treason. Nothing could have showed in a clearer light Seymour's brutal lack of consideration for Elizabeth. His own death was decided before the inquiry began; it was more than possible that by the time it was finished, Elizabeth's death might be decided also.

The Council's first step after the arrest of Seymour was to put Mrs. Ashley and Parry into the Tower, and to take depositions from both of them as to the intimacy that had existed between Seymour and the Princess. Then Sir Robert Tyrwhit was given the documents and sent to Hatfield to extract a confession from Elizabeth that could, if the Council so decided, be used as her death warrant.

Elizabeth knew that Mrs. Ashley and Parry had been removed, but she did not know where they were. She knew that the man she loved was under arrest and facing certain death, that she herself was about to be interrogated and that as a result of the questioning, she, as well as her lover, might be charged with high treason. She also knew one other thing, the thing of which she never spoke: that high treason was the charge on which her mother had been beheaded.

When Tyrwhit told her that Mrs. Ashley and Parry were in the Tower, she was "marvellously abashed" and cried bitterly. Then she made her single mistake. She asked if either of them had confessed anything? Tyrwhit assured her that they had and that she had better do the same, trusting to the Council's mercy, and to their laying the blame on her elders who had led her astray. But Elizabeth had already recollected herself. Tyrwhit was obliged to tell the Protector as the result of his first interrogation: "She will not confess any practice by Mistress Ashley or the cofferer concerning my Lord Admiral; and yet I do see it in her face that she is guilty." The next day he wrote: "I do assure your grace she hath a very good wit and nothing is gotten of her but by great policy."

As the next move in the game, Tyrwhit placed before her the very full accounts of the goings-on in the Queen Dowager's household which had been extracted from the governess and the cofferer. Mrs. Ashley's contained the details of the freedoms in which Seymour had indulged and the embrace which had led to Elizabeth's being sent from the house. Tyrwhit told the Council: "At the reading of Mistress Ashley's letter she was much abashed and half breathless before she could read it to an end." But even in the shock of such an exposure, Elizabeth had the coolness to understand that the confessions did not contradict what she had always maintained: that neither she nor her servants had ever discussed the possibility of her marrying Seymour without the Council's permission. She drew up at Tyrwhit's direction a confession under eleven heads in which she put down, she said, all the occasions on which the matter had been spoken of between herself, Kat Ashley or Parry. They all tended to the same meaning: that it was common talk that Seymour was much attached to her, that if he could get the Council's consent he might propose to her, that her servants would be glad to see her married to him, provided the Council allowed it. She wrote a note at the end to the Protector, saying this was all she could remember at present but if she remembered anything more, she would be sure to let him know.

Tyrwhit wrote to Somerset saying that he enclosed the Lady Elizabeth's confession "which is not so full of matter as I would it were". He thought that the unanimity of all three statements was owing, not to their all being true, but to the three prisoners having concerted beforehand as to what they should say. "They all sing one song," he said, "and so I think they would not do unless they had set the note before."

Elizabeth had complained that owing to the bruiting abroad of this matter, there were rumours that she herself was in the Tower and with child by the Lord Admiral, and she had demanded to be allowed to come to court to show herself and give the lie to these "shameful slanders". The Council, who had now accepted the fact that they could not convict Elizabeth on any charge except impropriety, offered, if she would point out any of her numerous traducers, to have them severely punished. Elizabeth replied that she could easily do it, but that she was unwilling to have men punished in the cause of her own good name; such a course, she said, would get her the evil will of the people, "which thing I would be loth to have". But she suggested that the Council might issue a proclamation, forbidding the further spreading of these lies. She pointed out to them that this would make people understand that the Council were concerned for the reputation of the King's Majesty's sister. Her suggestion was so eminently sound that the Protector could not for very shame refuse to act upon it, however little he might relish being shown his business by the fifteen-year-old Princess.

The Council, however, could still make her feel their authority in a painful manner. Mrs. Ashley was removed from the Princess's household as having shown herself unworthy of trust and Lady Tyrwhit was appointed in her place. Elizabeth was furious at being parted from her governess. "The love she yet beareth her is to be wondered at," said Sir Robert Tyrwhit. The Princess's tears and sulks were so mortifying to Lady Tyrwhit that at last that good lady told her roundly that anyone who had tolerated Mrs. Ashley in her service had no call to object to an honest woman.

Elizabeth withdrew into herself. She knew that an uncontrolled display of feeling was a luxury she could not afford. While her eyes were still swollen she acquiesced in Lady Tyrwhit's presence; but she came out of her refuge of silence to make a rescue which after such experiences as hers, a less intrepid girl would have left alone.

On 4 March, a Bill of Attainder against Thomas Seymour was read in the House of Lords. In that matter the part demanded of her was to be completely still; but Mrs. Ashley was in acute danger as someone who had been in the Admiral's confidence, and Elizabeth wrote to the Protector, asking him to befriend her governess. The three reasons she urged were that Mrs. Ashley had been good to her and taken great pains in her bringing-up, that as the Admiral had been, himself, a member of the Council, Mrs. Ashley had assumed that whatever he did had been with the Council's knowledge and consent, and that if Mrs. Ashley were to be punished, it would be tantamount to a public declaration of

Elizabeth's guilt; people would suppose that she had been pardoned because of her youth, and that in her stead, "she that I loved so well is in such a place". The plea was successful and Mrs. Ashley, though not permitted to return to the Princess's household, was allowed to retire without further molestation.

Now there remained nothing to be done but to wait for the news of Seymour's death. Elizabeth knew not only that observant and hostile eyes would be trained upon her as she received the announcement, but that the moment would be one in which she was playing a part before a wide audience whom she could not see. In such moments she was never to fail. When the time came and the thing was said to her, she made her utterance: "This day died a man of much wit and very little judgment." Not the least astonishing aspect of the words was that they were quite true.

She had made a supreme effort and almost at once the signs began to show themselves of approaching collapse. Weakness and depression grew so pronounced that in the course of the year she was a helpless invalid. The Protector had succeeded to a certain point in alienating her brother from her, but her sickness alarmed Edward, and the Protector saw that it was time to show leniency. The most skilful doctors were sent to her and, possibly on their advice, the expedient was tried of restoring Mrs. Ashley to her. Mrs. Ashley and Parry were both reinstated in the Princess's household by the end of the year.

A man who had much to do with Elizabeth's recovery by turning her mind into directions of absorbing interest was the great scholar Roger Ascham. His book *The Schoolmaster* shows that, assuming his pupils were ready to devote themselves eagerly and wholly to their studies, he taught them in an unusually sympathetic way. The book does not say what he would have done with a pupil who did not want to learn. With the Princess Elizabeth, however, this question did not arise. While Grindal had been her tutor Ascham, who was Grindal's master, had been interested to hear of her studies, and now, Grindal being dead, he himself was appointed to Grindal's place. Ascham saw immediately that to teach this pupil was the experience of a lifetime. He wrote letters to other scholars, his friends, describing the qualities of her mind and begging them not to think he exaggerated, for he assured them that he put down nothing but from his own observation. Elizabeth, at the time he wrote, was just sixteen. She had, he said, the quickest understanding and the most retentive memory he had ever known. Her mind seemed to be exempt from any sort of feminine weakness, and her power of application was like a man's. Her handwriting was exquisite. Her manners he thought particularly charming, they were so courteous, grave and modest. She spoke French and Italian as easily as English, and Latin fluently. She did not speak Greek quite so well, but she was always willing to practise speaking it with him whenever he wished it. She read classical authors not only with intelligence but with a keen appreciation of the qualities of their style, and no striking use of words passed her without her either "rejecting it with disgust or receiving it with delight".

Ascham threw all his energies into the rewarding task. He chose the authors who would not only give her the finest examples of style but whose philosophy would help to form her mind and inspire her with courage and endurance. He apportioned the day between studies of the Greek Testament, of classical tragedy, history and philosophy, between the translation of works from one foreign language into another and conversation on intellectual topics in all languages in turn. He knew of many learned young ladies, he said, who were an ornament to the age, but never had he met with one like this. He determined that no efforts should be wanting on his part to educate her according to her deserts. It is not surprising that Elizabeth's letters to Edward VI at this time beg him to put down her silence "not to my slothful hand but to my aching head", or apologize for the fact that the pain in her head has prevented her from writing or even dictating anything.

Yet drastic as the treatment was, it calmed and strengthened her, and it was very useful, too, in repairing her reputation. When she came to court now she was recognized as a lady who could scarcely bear to be parted from her books. Her dress was noticeably plain, and though she was known to possess a quantity of jewellery she wore none of it. Edward VI was barely in his teens but he had developed a somewhat formidable character, reserved, unemotional, with more than a trace of harshness, and devoted, with an enthusiasm that increased for the short remainder of his life, to the Reformed religion. This had caused an entire breach of sympathy between him and the Princess Mary, and the unfortunate events of the previous year had a good deal altered the feelings he had once had for Elizabeth. Now, however, he was delighted by her reassuring manner and appearance; he called her his "sweet sister

Temperance", but time was not allowed them to regain their early
intimacy. In his sixteenth year Edward succumbed first to measles
and then to smallpox. The ravages made by two serious illnesses
allowed a latent and still more dangerous disease to show itself. The
King was hardly well again when he developed a racking cough
whose paroxysms were frightful to watch. In the summer of 1553
he died of a galloping consumption, and the unhappy, ominous
figure who had stood in the background for so long now moved
forward into the light.

Mary had one overriding aim, to restore Roman Catholicism in
England. Her devotion to the Roman Church coloured every aspect
of her life, settling the value of every relationship, dictating love
and hate. The sacramental nature of her passion for a bored,
impatient husband owed something to the fact that Philip was the
greatest Catholic sovereign in Europe, and if it were to be proved
openly, beyond doubt, that her sister were an irreclaimable heretic,
then nothing would stand between Elizabeth and the Queen's
determination, at whatever cost to her own feelings, to destroy the
enemies of the true Church. Elizabeth's situation was made the
more dangerous as her identification with the Reformed Church
made her a magnet to the discontented elements in the realm. It was
with the utmost difficulty that she dissociated herself from the
attempts at rebellion in Mary's reign, all of which, after the death
of Lady Jane Grey, were supposed to have Elizabeth as their object.
The overtures of the King of France were nearly fatal to her until
she could convince Mary that she had never listened to them.
Henry II was a Catholic, but Mary's match with Philip of Spain
was an alliance the French King did not care for, and he would
willingly have had a claimant to Mary's throne under his protection. Mary and her advisers—Cardinal Pole, the Bishops Gardiner
and Bonner and the Spanish Ambassador—all regarded Elizabeth
as highly suspect in her religion and her loyalty. But whereas the
counsellors were determined to get her out of the way, assuring the
Queen, time and again, that her guilt was proved and urging her
execution, Mary herself was always willing to give Elizabeth the
benefit of any possible doubt.

In the matter of political intrigue Elizabeth was never proved
guilty of anything against Mary, and she was in the last degree
unlikely to have been so. There was no doubt in the minds of the
English people that Mary was the lawful Queen and none in

Elizabeth's own. All she did in Mary's lifetime was to keep herself close and quiet, to test by almost imperceptible touches the bond between her and that growing part of the nation that was waiting for her. The question of religious observance, however, required an active policy and one of the utmost discretion. If she declared herself an obdurate Protestant she might lose her head; if she announced herself a thorough convert to Catholicism she might lose something that she valued as much—the support and confidence of those who were going to be her most valuable subjects. By now refusing to go with the Queen to Mass, and again, asking for instruction in Catholic tenets, she managed to maintain her precarious course. The one thing it never occurred to her to do was the thing Mary had always done—to declare herself for the truth as she saw it.

Her caution, her tact, her vigilance were extraordinary, but however discreet she was she could not be inconspicuous. At Mary's accession the Queen was thirty-seven, withered, unhappy and neurotically diseased. Elizabeth was twenty, no longer a precocious girl but a young woman of the most exceptional ability, and a personal magnetism which, like her father's, made everyone aware of her. Her paleness, her reddish hair, her beautiful hands, were described by their ambassadors to the courts of Europe. Her calmness and self-control were wondered at by onlookers who saw the odds against which she was pitted, but occasionally those nearest to her saw with fond admiration some look or gesture such "as left no doubting whose daughter she was". People who had seen her only at a distance felt the influence of her personality; indeed, it was felt by those who had never laid eyes on her. One astute man, however, had had the opportunity of a personal acquaintance with her, and had formed an admiration of her powers that a lifetime's experience was only to confirm. William Cecil, afterwards the great Lord Burleigh and Elizabeth's chief minister for forty years, had become known to her some years before she became Queen. The opportunity for such acquaintance was slight, but it told him all he wished to know.

The rebellion which attempted to put Lady Jane Grey on the throne had been quelled by the Queen's supporters and Mary had treated Lady Jane with remarkable gentleness. In February of the following year, however, a serious insurrection was raised in Kent under Sir Thomas Wyatt, who protested against the Queen's proposed marriage with Philip of Spain.

Two lesser outbreaks occurred at the same time, one of them headed by kinsmen of the Greys, and this wide revolt signed the death warrant of Lady Jane Grey. When Wyatt's correspondence was waylaid it was found he had written letters meant for Elizabeth, and Mary sent to Ashridge, ordering the Princess to come to London to give an account of herself.

Elizabeth was ill. Her face, arms and hands were swollen and her skin had turned yellow. It is said that the symptoms were probably those of nephritis. She replied to the Queen's summons that she was too ill to travel. Mary countered this by sending three commissioners to Ashridge accompanied by two doctors. The treatment prescribed for kidney trouble to-day includes rest and warmth, but Dr. Owen and Dr. Wendy saw no reason against bringing the patient to London by litter in the month of February. She became so very ill on the way that it took them eleven days to accomplish the journey. When the cavalcade was within the city of London and crowds were collecting in the streets Elizabeth made the attendants pull back the curtains of the litter, and she performed the last part of the journey sitting up. The Spanish Ambassador reported that she had looked deathly pale but had worn a haughty air meant to repel any idea that she was in disgrace.

For three weeks she was shut up in Whitehall while Mary and her council debated what to do with her. Catholic peers, including the Earls of Sussex and Arundel, declared that her complicity with Wyatt was unmistakable and urged her immediate execution, and they were supported by the Spanish Ambassador, who added that he thought it unlikely that Philip would consent to come to England until the danger of Elizabeth's presence was removed. The Queen longed for the accomplishment of her marriage but to this unscrupulous threat she replied calmly that she would act as the law decided. Meanwhile, some arrangement had to be made for the Queen was going to Oxford to open Parliament. Mary asked each gentleman in turn if he would undertake to be responsible for the Princess during her absence and one and all refused outright. After some argument it was decided to send Elizabeth to the Tower.

On the Friday before Palm Sunday a commission headed by the ferocious Bishop Gardiner and the Earl of Sussex, one of Mary's closest adherents, came to Elizabeth and announced to her that she was charged with complicity in the late rebellion and it was the Queen's pleasure that she should go to the Tower

Elizabeth had barely recovered from illness. Her death had been openly suggested by her sister's advisers and now she was to be put into the Tower where, a few weeks before, her cousin Jane Grey, had been beheaded. The scaffold and the stains of blood were still there, but even that execution was, perhaps, less dreadful to her mind than one of which all traces had been removed seventeen years before. That night all her servants were dismissed except a gentleman usher, three ladies and two grooms. Guards were stationed in the ante-room leading to her bedroom, the hall was filled with armed men and two hundred soldiers were placed in the garden beneath her windows. The next morning the commission, headed by Sussex, came to her and said that a barge was ready and that she must go, "as the tide served which would tarry for no man". Elizabeth implored to be allowed to speak to the Queen but this was refused. Then she begged leave to write to her. One of the commission told her roughly that they could not give the permission and added that in his view she ought not to have it. Then a surprising thing happened. The Earl of Sussex melted suddenly. He went down on his knee and told Elizabeth "she should have liberty to write her mind", and that he would deliver the letter and bring back an answer.

In her flawless hand Elizabeth then and there wrote the letter to Mary that one may still see, of which the middle lines show some agitation only because the letters are larger and more widely spaced than the rest. In it she begs that she may see the Queen face to face. "I have heard of many in my time cast away for want of coming to the presence of their prince." She adds that she had heard Somerset say that he would never have put his brother to death if he had seen him first, but evil-wishers assured him that he could not be safe while the Admiral lived. "I pray God the like evil persuasions persuade not one sister against another." She says that she would not be bold enough to ask to see Mary "if I knew not myself most clear, as I know myself most true". She was oppressed with terror of being hurried to her fate without being allowed the personal contact that would save her. After her signature she wrote: "I humbly crave but one word of answer from yourself."

Sussex took the letter, but the only reply the Queen vouchsafed was to ask him angrily why he had not carried out her orders? The next tide was at midnight, and the Council would not risk convey-ing the prisoner then as they feared an attempt at rescue in the dark. It was decided that she should go the next morning when the populace would be in church. At nine o'clock Elizabeth was led through the garden to the waterside. It was the morning of Palm Sunday and it was raining. She looked up at the windows of the palace, exclaiming: "I marvel what the nobles mean by suffering me, a prince, to be led into captivity, the Lord knows wherefor, for I myself do not." Having lost the tide once and incurred the Queen's severe displeasure, the commission had made such haste to be off that they were now too early. The boatman at first refused to shoot the current racing between the piers of London Bridge, saying they must wait for it to slacken with the rising tide, but the nobles forced them to attempt it. The stern of the barge struck violently against one of the piers and several people looking down from the bridge thought the boat-load about to drown before their eyes. The passage was made, however, and the barge was brought to an arched water-gate overhung by a grating. Elizabeth saw where she was and protested angrily against being landed at the Traitor's Gate. One of the lords told her that "she must not choose", and as the rain continued he offered her his cloak. "She dashed it away with a good dash," and stepping out over the shoes in water, she exclaimed: "Here lands as true a subject, being prisoner, as ever was landed at these stairs! Before thee, O God, do I speak it, having no other friend but Thee alone." A posse of yeomen warders was drawn up inside the gate, and when they saw her some of them broke rank and knelt down, saying: "God preserve your Grace," for which they were afterwards sternly reprimanded. Immediately under the arch was the entrance which would conduct her into the precincts of the Tower. Elizabeth's resolution gave way. She sat down on a damp stone and declared she would go no further.

The Lieutenant of the Tower was in a quandary. It was his business to get the prisoner under lock and key, but to use force would be very unpleasant, and, in the presence of the Earl of Sussex, very difficult also. He said: "Madam, you had best come out of the rain, for you sit unwholesomely."

"Better sit here than in a worse place!" she said. It looked like an impasse; and then the gentleman usher broke down and sobbed aloud.

Elizabeth stood up. She rated him for giving way to tears when he ought to be a comfort and support to her, and she added proudly that her truth was such as, she thanked God, no one had cause to weep for her. She walked boldly to the lodging prepared for her and entered it with her servants. At the sound of locks and bolts being made fast behind her, she showed a deadly pang of terror, but she recovered herself, called for her prayer-book and asked her servants to join her in a prayer for divine protection.

In a few days' time she was subjected to a searching examination; it was conducted by Gardiner, whose relentless hatred of her was shameless and unmasked, in the presence of the rest of the commission. The intercepted letters from Wyatt, said to be copies of ones actually received by her, had urged her to retire to one of her houses called Donnington. That she had been actually going there at the time was taken as a strong proof of her complicity, but Elizabeth said: "What is that to the purpose? Might I not, my Lords, go to mine own houses at all times?" Sussex had already showed himself teeming with sympathy and resentment, and now, to the general astonishment, Arundel went down on his knees and said that her Grace said truth and that "he himself was sorry to see her troubled about such vain matters". Gardiner reported to the Council his opinion that the realm would never be at peace while Elizabeth was left alive, and added that if everybody worked as willingly as he did matters would show a striking improvement. The Spanish Ambassador took a gloomy view of the proceedings. "The lawyers," he wrote, "can find no matter for her condemnation and if they release her it appears evident the heretics will proclaim her Queen."

Gardiner was of the same opinion. In April he took advantage of the Queen's being ill and sent a warrant from the Privy Council to the Lieutenant of the Tower, ordering Elizabeth's immediate execution. The Lieutenant saw that the warrant did not bear Mary's signature and he forbore to act until he had asked confirmation from the Queen. Mary then saw that it was not safe to leave her sister where she was; she summoned Sir Henry Bedingfield and sent him, with a hundred armed men, to take command at the Tower, with orders, as soon as arrangements could be made, to escort Elizabeth, under close arrest, to Woodstock.

When Elizabeth heard that Bedingfield and his troop had invested the Tower, she could think at first of only one errand that might have brought him. She asked her servants if the Lady Jane's scaffold were still standing?

The journey to Woodstock revived her spirits after their long strain, but it was extremely trying to Sir Henry Bedingfield. The populace showed such enthusiasm at the sight of the Princess, Bedingfield found himself taking her on a triumphal progress. When at one village the church bells were set ringing, he was so much rasped that he turned back and ordered the ringers to be put in the stocks. The seat of Lord Williams of Tame lay in their way and it had been arranged that the party should stop here for refreshment. When they arrived at Ricote, Bedingfield found that Lord Williams had interpreted this request for hospitality by convening the knights and ladies of the neighbourhood to a banquet in the Princess's honour. Bedingfield took the host aside and asked him if he knew what he was doing, to treat the Queen's prisoner in this fashion? Lord Williams replied that her Grace might and should be merry in his house.

When Bedingfield had got the party under way again, they met with a violent storm of wind and rain. The Princess's hood was blown off three times into the mud, and as her hair was now streaming about her ears she asked if she might go into a gentleman's house that stood near the road, to put herself to rights? But Bedingfield had had enough of that, and she was obliged to turn into a hedge for a little shelter from the wind and to put up her hair as best she could.

Once they arrived at Woodstock, the respite from imprisonment was over. Elizabeth was lodged, not in any of the royal apartments but in the gate-house, where sixty soldiers were on guard all day and forty all the night, and six gates were unlocked and locked after her when she walked in the grounds. She wrote with a diamond on one of the window panes:

> *Much suspected—of me*
> *Nothing proved can be.*
> *Quoth Elizabeth, prisoner.*

But the strain of imprisonment, to which she saw no end, was beginning to tell on her spirits. Fright and danger had kept them up better than this close seclusion, where she was hidden away from her supporters, deep in the countryside. She heard a milkmaid singing in the park and she sighed from the bottom of her heart; she wished she were such a one, she said, with a milk-pail on her arm. The peculiar desolation that can associate itself with late summer is conveyed in the words she wrote on the fly-leaf of a copy of Saint Paul's Epistles:

"August: I walk many times into the pleasant fields of Holy Scriptures, where I pluck up the goodlisome herbs of sentences... and lay them up at length in the high seat of memory... that so having tasted their sweetness, I may the less perceive the bitterness of this miserable life." Her existence was not really so disregarded and forgotten as she fancied. More than one curious incident had occurred since her being shut up at Woodstock. One night a fire was mysteriously kindled between the ceiling of a lower room and the floor of her bed-chamber. Fortunately it was discovered and extinguished before she went to bed. A man named Basset appeared in the neighbourhood, attended by twenty-five followers, and demanded to see the Princess on a mission from a high and confidential quarter. Only Bedingfield's refusal to allow any access to her prevented the man from coming into her presence: and Basset, it was discovered afterwards, was Gardiner's protégé.

One day when she was walking in the garden, the sight of Bedingfield locking the gate behind her as usual was too much for her overstrung nerves. She rounded on him, upbraiding him for the perpetual use of his keys and calling him her gaoler. Then one more of those sudden, surprising acts of homage was offered to her. Bedingfield knelt down and begged her in most moving tones not to call him by that harsh word. He was one of her officers, he said, appointed to serve her and guard her from the dangers by which she was beset. Elizabeth might give way to temper but her estimate of character was almost unerring. She became reconciled to Bedingfield himself if not to his laborious precautions, but she found her sequestration unbearable, and when Cardinal Pole renewed the attack on her religious opinions with fresh vigour she at last professed herself a member of the Roman Catholic Church.

The unhappy Queen now imagined herself to be with child, and as this fact diminished Elizabeth's importance, and as Philip wished to gratify the English nation, Elizabeth, having made her profession, was sent for from Woodstock to Hampton Court. For a week she was shut up in her own apartments, seeing nobody but Gardiner, who tried to harass her into confessing her guilt and admitting that she was there as a suppliant for the Queen's pardon. When he had failed completely in each assault, Mary lost patience and determined to try herself. Elizabeth was sent for at ten o'clock at night and conducted to the Queen's bedroom. It was said that Philip, whose marriage had taken place while Elizabeth was in prison, gained the first sight of his sister-in-law through a hole in a screen placed in his wife's bedroom.

Elizabeth knelt before the Queen and burst into tears as she asserted her innocence.

"Well then," said Mary, "you stand so stiffly on your truth, belike you have been wrongfully punished?"

"I must not say so to your Majesty," Elizabeth answered. Mary retorted that Elizabeth would no doubt say as much to other people. Elizabeth assured the Queen that she would not; whatever her Majesty was pleased to inflict, she would bear it patiently; but, she repeated: "I am, and ever have been, your Majesty's true subject." Mary turned her head away and said in Spanish, half aloud: "God knows!"

The words expressed no confidence, but neither were they a condemnation, and they marked an attitude to Elizabeth that did not alter for the brief remainder of the Queen's life, darkened as it was by her husband's neglect, her lost hopes of a child and the hatred aroused by those hideous cruelties for which she, Pole, Gardiner and Bonner were accountable but for which her name bore the horrible epithet. The murk and gloom, however, enhanced the admiration and hope which Elizabeth inspired. Conspiracies against Mary increased, and whenever one was discovered Elizabeth's name was dangerously connected with it; for the last three years of Mary's life she was never quite free from suspicion and seldom entirely safe, but her name was all of her that could be detected in compromising circumstances. She was not imprisoned again. Philip, whose ambassador had done his best to hound her to death, adopted a favourable attitude to her; in his repulsive manner he was even gallant. That he thought Elizabeth more attractive than Mary requires no explanation, but his protective attitude towards her was accounted for by something stronger than romantic leanings, even if he had had any. Since there was no hope of a child from Mary, her successor, if Elizabeth were removed, would be Mary Stewart, Queen of Scots. Mary Stewart was already married to the Dauphin of France, and if she acquired the English crown French influence in Europe would be increased to the detriment of Spain. Philip made vigorous efforts to secure Elizabeth's hand for an ally of his own, first for the Prince of Piedmont and then for Philibert of Savoy. Elizabeth was gratified by Philip's attentions, and though she refused all his suggestions of a foreign marriage that would take her out of England, out of the view of the English people, she made her refusals with consummate courtesy.

Her public appearances again figured in ambassadors' dispatches. In 1555 she appeared at the Queen's side at the Christmas festivities. Her dress was white satin oversewn with great pearls and the gentlemen of her household were attired in red and black. The Venetian Ambassador reported of her: "Miladi Elizabeth is a lady of great elegance, both of body and mind."

Her followers became increasingly confident, and took on themselves to exact respectful behaviour towards her. One of her servants heard a tradesman say: "That jilt, the Lady Elizabeth, was the real cause of Wyatt's rising." The man was so angry he accused the tradesman before the ecclesiastical court. He said that he himself, the day before, had seen King Philip, on meeting the Princess, make such obeisance that his knee touched the ground, and so, he declared, "methinketh it were too much to suffer such a varlet as this to call her jilt". The court was presided over by her enemy Bishop Bonner, but they agreed that it was too much, and told the tradesman he must not say such a thing again.

Elizabeth had the Queen's permission to live at Hatfield once more, always her favourite house. Her going down there in 1555 was like the prologue to some great play, a sunset that prepares the way for the sun's rising. The French Ambassador noted her departure through the London streets: "Great and small followed her through the city and greeted her with acclamations and such vehement manifestations of affection that she was fearful it would expose her to the jealousy of the court and with her wonted caution she fell back behind some of the officers of her train."

At Hatfield, old friends were gathered. Kat Ashley was there, and Parry, and Ascham had been engaged to read with her again. Ascham's praise sounded an even fuller note. He told his colleagues what the Princess was reading and added the strangely revealing comment: "I teach her words, and she me, things." His friend Metellus, he said, who had visited the country and been presented to her, came away saying: "It is more to have seen Elizabeth than to have seen England." Another of the visitors to Hatfield was William Cecil. The fruit of these unobtrusive meetings was shown in the words Elizabeth addressed to him when he was sworn as one of her Privy Council:

"This judgment I have of you: that you will not be corrupted by any manner of gift and that you will be faithful to the state; and that without respect to my private will you will give me that counsel which you think best; and if you shall know of anything necessary to be declared to me of secrecy, you shall show it to myself only, and assure yourself I will not fail to keep taciturnity therein."

She was in the park at Hatfield when the deputation arrived from London with the news that Elizabeth was Queen. "It is the Lord's doing and it is marvellous in our eyes," she said. No doubt she had the words ready but no one who thinks of what she had lived through from the age of fifteen can fail to see what she meant or doubt the sincerity of what she said. The portrait of her in coronation robes, now in Warwick Castle, is the most vivid, as it is the most touching, record, of this close of an era in her existence. At the moment of this portrait she had not adopted her new style, that spirited elegance and decoration that was to become famous. The gold tissue robe and the gold mantle are so straight and heavy they are almost sexless in form. Beneath the gold crown the thin gold hair hangs limply on each side of a face which looks scarcely man or woman so much as intelligence incarnate. The eyes are the eyes of the later portraits, of an unmoving watchfulness, but no other likeness shows the youthful face with hollow temples and transparent pallor, still bearing the stamp of near escape from death. One long, delicate hand holds the golden sceptre, the fingers of the other are stretched lightly over the gold orb resting on the gold-covered knee. So much gold is only a background to the arresting expression of the face, young, unself-conscious, intent. There we can see the rising of "that bright occidental star, Queen Elizabeth of most happy memory".

CHAPTER 3

Sarah Churchill,
Duchess of Marlborough

The best fairy-tales are psychological parables and one of them perfectly illustrates the life of Sarah Churchill. The good fairies gave her beauty, intelligence and many virtues; they added power, wealth, fame and a happy marriage with a husband she adored, who was a national hero. The bad fairy threw in an overbearing temper, which nearly undid the effects of all the rest.

Sarah Jennings was the younger daughter of an undistinguished country gentleman. Her looks were of the straight-featured, blue-eyed, flaxen-haired English kind, but her personality, apparent in her direct, eager, imperious gaze, made an even stronger impression than her beauty. Great as this was, she seemed to be unconscious of it. She was quite without personal vanity and when in her heyday she appeared at the court of Queen Anne among other women whose diamonds "brilled and flamed", as an onlooker said, she, the most important of any of them, was noticeably unadorned.

Her mother brought her at thirteen years old to the court of Charles II, for Mrs. Jennings wanted to look after her elder daughter Frances, who was already a Maid of Honour. Charles II had no legitimate children and his heirs were his brother, James Duke of York, and the latter's daughters, Mary and Anne. The Duke was a Catholic, and the King, knowing the violently anti-Romish temper of most of the nation, determined that James's children, at least, should not be unacceptable on the score of religion. He had the little Princesses carefully and thoroughly instructed in the tenets of the Church of England. The younger, Anne, was a child who was very deeply affected by early impressions. At nine years old she received two with a force that moulded the whole of her existence: one was devotion to the Anglican Church, the other an admiration and love for Sarah Jennings. The latter said, years afterwards: "We used to play together when she was a child, and she even then expressed a particular fondness for

63

me." Anne was weak and undecided, was fond of amusement but could not amuse herself, no talker but enjoyed listening to interesting conversation, without much attractiveness of her own but ready to give generous admiration to the attractiveness of others. Above all, though she had courtiers and servants "she coveted a friend". The brilliant, downright Sarah Jennings was exactly the friend she wanted. When Anne was eleven and Sarah fifteen, the latter was appointed as the Princess's Maid of Honour.

The Duke of York's mistress, Arabella Churchill, had a brother, John, whom the Duke had befriended and given a commission in the Foot Guards. John Churchill became thoroughly established in the Duke's favour, and when Sarah Jennings was appointed to the Princess Anne, she and young Churchill were under the same roof. He was ten years older than she, an enigmatic, and for all his quietness, a disconcerting character. Handsome and serene, with manners that were perfect to everybody, some odd things were said about him. The Duchess of Cleveland, who as Barbara Palmer had been the King's mistress at the Restoration, was a beautiful creature still but ten years older than Churchill. He became her lover and she made him a gift of five thousand pounds. If he had spent the money extravagantly no great surprise would have been felt at the transaction, but he bought himself an annuity with it. This handsome, tranquil and strangely provident young man was now shaken out of his calmness; he fell violently in love with a high-spirited, impatient girl of sixteen, who was entirely chaste. Churchill was hardly to blame considering the standards of the society in which he met her if he tried first of all to seduce her. He soon found, however, that this was throwing time away. She did not disguise the fact that she was attracted by him but she would not allow him the smallest familiarity of a disreputable kind. Sincere, earnest, unaccommodating, she was quarrelsome as often as not.

He could think of no-one else, longed to please her and implored her to be kind. "I cannot remember what it is I said that you take so ill", he wrote, in almost pitiable bewilderment. It was clear that she meant either to have nothing to do with him or else to marry him. "If it were true", she wrote, "that you have that passion for me which you say you have, you would find out some way to make yourself happy. It is in your power. Therefore press me no more to see you since 'tis what I cannot in honour allow of." This policy was

SARAH, DUCHESS OF MARLBOROUGH

The good fairies gave her beauty, intelligence and many virtues; the bad
fairy threw in an overbearing temper which nearly undid the effects of
all the rest.

ELIZABETH INCHBALD

She gained a reputation that was said to be "irreproachable", no small feat for a highly attractive woman living alone in the literary and theatrical society of London.

the effect of a disinterested, honest affection. She had no money but he had none either. His parents objected to the match for that reason; they wanted him to repair the family fortunes by a wealthy marriage. But Churchill redeemed the reputation he had lost over the Duchess of Cleveland. He determined to marry a beautiful, virtuous, penniless girl for the single and sufficient reason that he adored her. "Could you ever love me", he wrote, "I think the happiness would be so great it would make me immortal." In 1678, when Sarah was eighteen, they were privately married, and the Churchill family agreed to put a good face on it. Penniless as she was, the bride was not a young woman whom anyone could fail to admire, or with whom anyone wanted to try conclusions.

They had at first very little of settled married life. The Duke of York's unpopularity with the nation, who did not want a Catholic heir to the throne, caused the King to send his brother out of the country so that his presence should not undo the efforts the King was making on his behalf. Churchill accompanied the Duke to Holland and then to Scotland; the letters he constantly wrote to his young wife show not only his absorbing passion for her but a shrewd insight into her character. Sarah had a fierce reserve over emotional matters. She once said she disliked a particular fashionable church because she met there so many people she knew, and "if I could, I would always (go) to my devotions where I could meet no-one of my acquaintance". She made her husband promise to burn her letters as soon as he had read them, though this did not prevent her from keeping every one he wrote to her. But even so, her letters did not satisfy him and he told her with a blend of acuteness and tenderness that she was afraid to tell him how much she loved him.

The Princess Mary had been married to her cousin William, Prince of Orange, a strong Protestant, who had a distant claim to the English throne. It was now felt that no time must be lost in marrying the Princess Anne, who had been discovered in the one brief romance of her existence, a flirtation with the disreputable Earl of Mulgrave. Prince George of Denmark was fixed upon, a tall, fair, good-humoured man whose only serious drawback was that he drank on a scale that surprised even the age he lived in. He is remembered chiefly for the King's comment on him: "I've tried George drunk and I've tried him sober and there's nothing in him," but the fact that the Prince's conversation was not up to

C

Charles II's did not mean that Anne found it inadequate. She became very much attached to a kind, affectionate husband, but he did not introduce any element into her life that was likely to put Sarah Churchill out of her head; and the shocking tale of her motherhood, in which she bore seventeen children, every one of whom died in infancy except the son who just reached his eleventh birthday, so far from superseding the interest she felt in Sarah, left her even more in need of such a friend.

Anne determined that in her household as Princess of Denmark, Sarah Churchill must have a prominent position. Sarah herself suggested that the post of Lady of the Bedchamber would give her the most opportunity to "serve and amuse" the Princess, and the Duke of York readily agreed to the appointment. Anne wrote to her friend: "The Duke...has promised me that I shall have you, which is a great joy to me. I should say a great deal for your kindness in offering it, but I am not good at compliments. I will only say that I do take it *extreme* kindly."

What was perhaps the happiest period of the friendship now began. Anne suggested that, in a fashion of the time, she and Sarah should adopt names and use them in their letters to each other. In their correspondence Anne was Mrs. Morley and Sarah Mrs. Freeman. Years later the latter said that when Anne offered her her choice of the two names, she chose the one that she felt suited best with her disposition.

Though she had an unbounded influence over her mistress, Sarah Churchill's position was no sinecure. Anne leaned on her very heavily. The Princess required to be enlivened, soothed, interested, supported, hour after hour, day in, day out. Sarah afterwards said: "I often spent hours talking to her when I would rather have been in a dungeon." The strain of such demands on a woman so highly strung was severe, and Sarah had little incentive to restrain her natural impatience, for Anne could not be offended. Indeed, the fear that she herself might have offended Sarah would cause her painful agitation. The delight she took in a show of kindness or a little present was extraordinary. "Ten thousand thanks for the dear ring which methinks is very pretty ... oh that my dear Mrs. Freeman would imagine how much I value any mark of her favour—but that's impossible."

The events from the death of Charles II in 1687 to her own accession in 1702 were all of a kind to strengthen the ascendancy of the Churchills over Anne. The collapse of her father in the Revolution of 1688 made her feel that she must leave the capital and Sarah Churchill both planned and helped her to carry out her flight. They made their way to Nottingham, where the Earl of Devonshire welcomed Anne and held a banquet in her honour. The Earl had not enough footmen to wait upon the guests and impressed some young dragoons to eke out the numbers. Among these was the youthful Colley Cibber, who was soon to give up a military career for a theatrical one. In his reminiscences, written fifty years later, Cibber says that though placed so near the guests he remembered nothing of what was said at table except the words: "Some wine and water," for these were uttered by Lady Churchill; the whole evening he remained spell-bound "with the delight of gazing on the fair object so near me." And he added that twenty years after, "when the same lady had given the world four of the loveliest daughters that ever were gazed on, even after they were all nobly married ... their still lovely mother ... very often took the lead in those involuntary triumphs of beauty."

The accession of Mary and her husband provided fresh occasions for Anne's friends to prove their value. Churchill was created Earl of Marlborough in 1689 and it was as Lady Marlborough that Sarah began to play her rôle in English history. When Mary's death should occur, Anne would by rights succeed to the throne at once, but William's supporters in Parliament determined that if he outlived Mary he was to retain the Crown for his lifetime. The Marlboroughs persuaded Anne to acquiesce in this arrangement, for they saw it was better that she should grant the concession than have it wrested from her, and they threw themselves into the movement for forcing Parliament, as a reward for her submission, to raise her income from £32,000 to £50,000. The rift between Anne and Mary was already deep. "I hear", said Anne, "that my friends have a mind to make me some settlement." Mary exclaimed angrily: "Pray what friends have you save the King and me?" If the Queen did not know already, she soon learned. The increased income was voted and it was an open triumph for the Marlboroughs as well as the Princess.

Marlborough owned only two loyalties, to his wife and to the soldiers he commanded. He was not incommoded by scruples with regard to anybody else. As the banished James II had the support of the King of France and might therefore at some time succeed in regaining his crown, Marlborough felt that mere common sense required him to keep a foot in either camp. His negotiations with James were well known to William III; the King's patience at length ran out, and in February, 1692, he dismissed Lord Marlborough from all his offices.

In this situation, it seemed obvious that Anne, out of loyalty, out of common courtesy even, to her sister, could not retain Lady Marlborough as her Lady of the Bedchamber. That is to say, it seemed so to everyone except Anne herself. She regarded the mere suggestion of dismissing her friend as an outrage. The Queen held a Drawing Room in that month; Anne was far gone in one of her pregnancies, but she went to the ceremony and she took Lady Marlborough with her. If an appearance in these circumstances were an ordeal, it was an ordeal that Lady Marlborough was well fitted to sustain. She was at the height of her beauty. Her slight and graceful figure could look well even in the long, rigid bodice and the cumbrous skirts of the time, and her small head on its long neck was elegant even when enlarged by the masses of her fair hair spread out beneath her coronet. Her appearance was a sort of nine days' wonder. The Queen gave no sign of indignation at the time, but she afterwards wrote her sister a letter saying: "Though my kindness would make me never exact, I must tell you I know what is due to me and expect to have it from you." Anne refused stubbornly to give way. Prince George was called on to reason with her, but he said he had not the heart to urge his wife to do anything that would make her so unhappy. Sarah herself suggested that she had better retire, and Anne told her never to speak of such a thing again unless she wanted to break her poor Morley's heart.

At last a Royal command was issued that Lady Marlborough was to leave the Princess's house. Anne said, very well, then she would leave it too. They would go together. She asked hospitality of the Duke of Somerset at Sion House and here she lay in, attended by Lady Marlborough. The baby was already dead by the time the Queen came to visit her sister. Mary walked to the bedside; her only words were: "I have made the first step in coming to you and now I expect you should make the next by removing Lady Marlborough." Sarah saw Anne turn as white as the bed linen and begin a violent shuddering; she had strength only to say "No", but it was all she wished to say. The Queen was in such a passion she left the bedroom immediately, sweeping past the unfortunate Prince George, who was attempting to hand her to her coach. Her savage unkindness was inspired by her love for her husband, but Anne found it none the easier to bear for that: she and Sarah were accustomed to speak of William as the Dutch Monster or the Dutch Abortion. In any event, the scene was not one to make her give up such a friend for such a sister. The breach was never healed, for Mary fell ill with smallpox and died before any reconciliation was attempted.

In May Marlborough was put into the Tower. "For God's sake have a care of your dear self and give as little way to melancholy thoughts as you can", wrote Anne anxiously to his wife. Sarah's anxieties were harassing in the extreme; at their house at St. Albans the Marlboroughs' two-year-old son Charles was taken ill and died at the end of May. The nursery of four daughters and one surviving son never took the first place in Sarah Churchill's heart, but after her husband she cared for her children more than for anyone else. Though she could not get on with her grown-up daughters, all of whom quarrelled with her except the charming Lady Anne, small children found her delightful; her spirits and her vitality pleased them, and the servants of Anne's surviving child, the sickly little Duke of Gloucester, said that Lady Marlborough's visits to his nursery were always a great success. Though she allowed herself to be continually separated from her children, she was not neglectful. She wrote to one of her friends from St. Albans, where she had been called on what proved to be a false alarm of smallpox in one of the little girls: "I am very well content to have made an unnecessary journey, for when servants are so careful as to apprehend every little thing and give one notice of it, one thinks oneself very secure, though one is bound to be often from them." The death of her boy while her husband was in prison was a matter of such acute suffering, she rejected all consolation and could not endure to see the tender, anxious, grief-stricken Anne. All she wanted was her husband's presence. In spite of his loyal obedience to her commands, a scrap of one of her letters to him escaped destruction. It runs: "Wherever you are, whilst I have life, my soul shall follow you, my ever dear Lord Marlborough, and wherever I am I should only kill the time wishing for night that I may sleep and hope the next day to hear from you."

Marlborough was released before long. The situation between

himself and William III, always uneasy, was such as would have worn down two natures less cautious, frigid and astute. Marlborough knew that the King did not trust him an inch and with good reason. William in his state of unsleeping vigilance over the menace of French domination of Europe, was most keenly affected by it, King of England though he was, as a threat to the Netherlands. He had seen Marlborough at work in some minor ·military engagements in the Netherlands and he knew that if the deadlock became an active struggle, Marlborough's services as a general would be worth any shortcomings. The situation was potentially dangerous; the Marlboroughs' connexion with the Princess Anne made it openly offensive. Anne abated nothing of her fondness for them both. She pressed the King to appoint Marlborough as the Duke of Gloucester's governor. Reluctantly William did so. The ten-year-old Duke had a small boy's fondness for soldiers and Marlborough arranged that on his eleventh birthday he should review a regiment at Windsor. The child was wildly excited by his glorious birthday festivities and five days later he succumbed to an attack of water on the brain. His mother was a woman who cried readily and copiously as a rule, but now, to the dismay of everyone who saw her, she did not cry. The Marlboroughs came to Windsor. The child's coffin was carried by torchlight from Windsor to Westminster, and Marlborough rode beside it all the way. His wife remained with the Princess, and after two months at Windsor took her back with her to St. Albans.

The death of William III in 1702 ushered in not only the accession of Anne to the throne of England but of Marlborough to a military triumph which earned him the title of the greatest military genius since Julius Caesar. Louis XIV, in spite of an undertaking to the contrary, supported the accession of his grandson Philip of Anjou to the Spanish throne, to which was attached the possession of the Spanish Netherlands. When Philip entered Madrid, the King of France exclaimed: "There are no more Pyrenees!" The rest of Europe saw his point only too well, but even so England was reluctant to enter a long and costly war which, though to England's advantage in the long run, had as its immediate aim the safeguarding of William's Dutch possessions. Nevertheless William died within sight of his object, for Louis XIV, called to the bedside of the dying James II, assured him that James's son should succeed to the English crown. The English nation were roused to fury by this arrogance and the threat of a Catholic succession, and two months after Anne's coronation war was declared on France.

Marlborough, as Captain General of the English forces, embarked to dislodge the French and their allies from the chain of fortresses in the Spanish Netherlands which Louis XIV had garrisoned in his grandson's name. The series of spectacular victories which Marlborough gained broke the power of France; and considering the enormous nature of his triumph and the dazzling genius he displayed, both of which were at the time fully recognized by his own country and the whole of Europe, it is a significant thing that his mark on English history has been comparatively slight. The English know how great Wellington was without reading anything about him. It is not until the reign of Anne is studied that any just idea can be gained of Marlborough's greatness. Herbert Paul has said that this was because Marlborough inspired no moral confidence except in the field. Calm, enigmatic and treacherous, he was utterly unlike the popular idea of a great soldier. The one whose character was much more in accordance with it was his wife.

Anne could now hardly do enough for her Mrs. Freeman. She gave Sarah Churchill the offices which brought her most nearly into contact with herself: Groom of the Stole, Mistress of the Robes and Keeper of the Privy Purse. The two latter required a considerable amount of administrative work, the dealing with tradespeople and the keeping of accounts. Sarah, with her practical intelligence and her rigid honesty, discharged these duties with the most complete zeal and success, and when afterwards an attempt was made to discredit her by saying she had enriched herself at the Queen's expense, it was recognized as ludicrously unapt. In December of 1702, the Queen celebrated the first of Marlborough's victories by conferring a dukedom on him. "I know", she wrote, "my dear Mrs. Freeman does not care for anything of that kind, nor am I satisfied with it because it does not enough express the value I have for Mr. Freeman, nor ever can how passionately I am yours, my dear Mrs. Freeman." Sarah had now reached an apotheosis. Her own ascendancy over the Queen was absolute; her husband was the greatest man in the kingdom, and the most influential man in the Government, the Treasurer, Lord Godolphin, was their devoted friend and adherent. Except that it is the quality of the future to be unforeseen, no-one could have expected this state of things to end. The merest hint of any of her three servants leaving her threw the Queen into a panic. "We four must stay together," she said, "till mowed down by Death's impartial hand."

In an indirect fashion it was Death's hand that began the work. In 1703, the Marlboroughs' only surviving son, the sixteen-year-old Marquis of Blandford, caught smallpox at Cambridge; expresses were sent across the Channel and his father came home just in time to see him die. Though the grief of both parents was awful, Sarah's was almost dementia. Her attacks of sobbing were so violent and prolonged that it was feared she would go out of her mind. Marlborough was obliged to leave her and his anxiety was made worse by letters from Lord Godolphin describing her alarming state. He wrote to her saying: "If you think my being with you can do any good you shall quickly see you are much dearer to me than fame or whatever the world may say." The Duchess's answer must have been the one to be expected from a soldier's wife, for her husband remained in the field, but from this time her character appears to have become exaggerated in its foibles, as if this blow, falling upon her at the age of forty-three, had very slightly affected her brain.

If once her personal dominion over the Queen should fail there was plenty of ground for disagreement between them. Anne's attitude to her own position was clearly shown by her choosing to reinstate the custom of "Touching" to cure scrofula known, because of the monarch's healing power over it, as King's Evil. The rational William had discontinued this, and when a wretched man begged him so hard that he had not the heart to refuse he had laid his hand on him, saying: "God grant thee better health and better sense." But Anne felt that the sacred power might reside in herself. Samuel Johnson was a victim of the disease, and one of his earliest memories was of being taken up to "a lady in a black hood and diamonds." The Queen both supported and dearly loved the Anglican Church and she was a Tory in politics. The Duchess was a rationalist, she tolerated Dissent and was a violent Whig. At the opening of the reign the Queen had ventured to raise the latter point with her. "I cannot help being extremely concerned that you are so partial to the Whigs because I would not have you and your poor unfortunate faithful Morley differ in the least thing." Nor would the Duchess have it, if it came to that. She was fully determined that the Queen should share her views.

It is interesting to imagine how differently another woman with her gifts would have behaved in her place. Sarah was exacting and unreasonable but she had never given herself airs as a beauty or tried to impose her will by playing on the affection she inspired. She went an altogether different way to work. What she wanted was right, and anyone who could not see that it was right must be crushed or else spurned from the path. Tory aspirants were spurned aside; as the Queen could not be removed, it was necessary to crush her.

The Duchess could not invariably have her own way, for sometimes her instruments turned in her hand. Lord Godolphin was a nominal Tory; the Duke of Marlborough was anything. They could not always be made to see how essential it was that they should do as she told them, and in 1704 two appointments of strong Tories to high offices had been made. Robert Harley had been made Secretary of State and Henry St. John Secretary for War. The Duchess was so angry at this lack of judgment she poured out her wrath on her husband, who was just leaving her to return to the wars. Their parting was dreadful. When he had gone, she came to her senses and wrote him an endearing letter and the gratitude of his reply shows what her behaviour had been. "Love me as you do now and no hurt can come to me. You have by this kindness preserved my quiet and I believe my life: for till I had this letter I have been very indifferent of what should become of myself."

In the last resort, Marlborough could always manage her if he wanted to. The Queen was in a very different situation. If she and the Duchess disagreed, the latter made no move towards a reconciliation. She was content to wait for an overture from the Queen. It would come soon enough—too soon, for her feelings, for Anne now irritated Sarah almost beyond bearing. Sarah made no attempt at kindness or even at decorum in their private conversation. From the bottom of the stairs leading to the Queen's closet, behind the closed door, the Duchess's loud, exasperated voice could be heard: "Lord, Madam, it must be so!"—as she gave up the unequal struggle to make Anne see sense. But nothing Sarah did could alter their relative positions, it seemed. However unreasonable and outrageous Mrs. Freeman might be, it was always Mrs. Morley who suffered, besought, apologized and was, most passionately, hers.

Then in August, 1704, came news which would have caused Anne to forgo all resentment at the Duchess of Marlborough even if she had been capable of feeling any. Marlborough's tremendous victory at Blenheim was announced in England. Colonel Park, on his first halt in a journey of eight days, presented to the Duchess as she sat with the Queen in the library at Windsor Castle a leaf torn out of the Duke's pocket-book on which he had written the news of the victory, telling her to announce it to the Queen.

The public rejoicings included a service of thanksgiving at the still unfinished St. Paul's Cathedral, to which the Duchess of Marlborough rode beside the Queen, through streets garlanded with oak leaves, ringing with cheers and the pealing of bells. Parliament decided to present the Duke with a tract of land and bestowed the manor of Woodstock on him; the Queen determined that a palace should be erected on it at her own expense, to be called Blenheim, a dwelling that should be also a national monument. Great events as well as domestic ones seemed all to favour the Duchess. On the next occasion of her interfering in political appointments she was successful. She urged the Duke to persuade Lord Godolphin to deprive the Tory Duke of Buckingham of the Privy Seal and bestow it on the Whig Duke of Newcastle. Marlborough wrote in reply: "I have writ to my Lord Treasurer as you desire. . . . I can refuse you nothing."

Power tends to corrupt, it is said, and absolute power corrupts absolutely. For a long while Sarah had not behaved to Anne like a friend; now she scarcely behaved as the salaried official that she was. She was not there when the Queen wanted her. She had a great deal to occupy her: there was her establishment at St. Albans, her favourite seat of Windsor Lodge which went with the Rangership of Windsor Park the Queen had conferred on her, and above all the building operations at Woodstock, though these were a source of as much annoyance as pleasure. The Duchess had wanted Wren to be the architect of Blenheim but Parliament had given the commission to Vanbrugh, grandiose, exotic and impractical. "I never liked any building so much for show and vanity as for usefulness and convenience," said Sarah with her usual sense, "and therefore I was always against the whole design of Blenheim as too big and unwieldy." Still she had to be there to see what was going on. She had very little time indeed for Anne, who felt the lack of her society, rasping though it was, with a keen sense of loss.

The Queen was driven to beg her Mistress of the Robes for a little of her company. "I will not be uneasy if you come to me, for though you are never so unkind I will ever preserve a most sincere and tender passion for my dear Mrs. Freeman." It was of course out of the question that the Duchess should give her much time, but Sarah had placed near the Queen a relation of her own as Lady of the Bedchamber who, she thought, could take some of the dead-bore work off her hands, who could do some of the sitting and talking and card-playing and embroidering and tea-drinking. This young woman's name was Abigail Hill. Her family had been in poor circumstances and Sarah had been energetically kind to them. Abigail was a plain, silent girl with mild manners, and Sarah thought she would make an effective subordinate to herself. With all her quickness she was not gifted in assessing character, and she did not see that Abigail was a great deal cleverer than she looked.

The Duchess's behaviour was so high and her person so picturesque that she was the inevitable target for sensational stories which, though untrue, were possibly no more sensational than the truth. Anne was four years younger than the Duchess but while the latter still retained her active figure and much of her beauty—Colley Cibber said that she was a great-grandmother without grey hairs—Anne at forty-five was a pitiable wreck: stout, short of breath and tormented by a very painful gout, she dragged herself about swathed in bandages, priming herself with brandy which, as she drank it from tea-cups, was known as the Queen's cold tea. The one Stewart charm she had inherited, that of beautiful manners to her servants, together with her essential gentleness and goodness, the uncomplaining way in which she carried out the duties for which her health was quite unfit, the memory of her sufferings and her pathetic helplessness made most of those about her feel very kindly towards her. But with Sarah Churchill impatience had become a kind of nervous abhorrence. It was said that when she had to hand the Queen her gloves she turned her head away "as if the Queen had bad smells." Though the story was probably untrue the fact that it was told was startling.

With her husband away there was no-one to warn or check Sarah; and then suddenly she was brought up short. A flash of lightning showed her where she stood, and it was followed by a distant but ominous roll of thunder. She discovered almost by chance that her cousin, her protégée Abigail Hill, without saying one word to

her, had got herself married to an equerry, a Mr. Samuel Masham.
The Duchess contemptuously described this gentleman as "always
making low bows to everyone and ready to skip to open a door".
But Mr. Masham was there to open doors, and the fact that he
opened them with good will might make him compare favourably
with someone who, it was said, had once thrown down her gold key
of office on the floor and told the Queen that Her Majesty might
pick it up, for *she* never would. The Duchess overlooked Mrs.
Masham's secretiveness, hoping, as she said, that she might ascribe
it to mere lack of breeding, and offered to stand Abigail's friend in
telling the Queen of the stolen match. Then she received a second
and much more serious shock. Abigail said that the Queen knew all
about the marriage. In fact, Her Majesty had been present at the
ceremony.

At this, Sarah went to work and made up for lost time. Within a
week she had found out that Mrs. Masham now spent two hours of
every afternoon with the Queen in private, and that, worse still,
Harley, whom the victorious Whigs had driven to resign his office
and whom Sarah had thought a spent force, used often to join these
afternoon sessions. He was a distant connexion of the Hill family,
but this hardly accounted for so much attention to his rather
dowdy cousin. More disconcerting than all was a subtle change in
Mrs. Morley's behaviour to Mrs. Freeman. With her usual blunt-
ness Sarah asked Anne why Anne had not told her of the wedding?
The Queen merely answered that she had told Masham over and
over again that she ought to tell the Duchess of it. Once her
attention was aroused, Sarah saw the significance of many things
that had passed her by. One recollection particularly now presented
itself in a sinister light. She had been with the Queen, having gone
to Her Majesty's bedchamber by a secret passage. Suddenly, she said,
"this woman, not knowing I was there, came in with the boldest
and gaiest air possible, but upon sight of me stopped, and immediately changed her manner and making a most solemn curtsey,
did Your Majesty ring? And then went out again. This singular
behaviour needed no interpreter *now* to make it understood."

She was fired with impatience to have it all out with Mrs.
Masham, but in spite of repeated summoning, Abigail evaded her
formidable kinswoman. Very naturally, said the Queen, when poor
Masham knew that the Duchess was angry. This expression of
fellow-feeling was not lost on Sarah. Nothing was lost on her now.

She cornered Abigail at last and taxed her with slyness, treachery and ingratitude, in attempting to undermine Sarah with the Queen. Abigail, pale, insignificant and looking at the ground, had paused like a tennis player, who waits for the ball to descend before he hits it with full force. In Sarah's own words: "She very gravely answered that she was sure the Queen who had loved me extremely would always be very kind to me." For once in her life, the Duchess of Marlborough was rendered speechless. "It was some minutes before I could recover from the surprise with which so extraordinary an answer struck me." But she saw now how ill-judged she had been in bringing in Abigail to act as a deputy for herself: Abigail who was an Anglican and a Tory, who was quiet and soothing, and who was always there.

Sarah saw at once that she could not get rid of her cousin—Abigail was too firmly entrenched; but had she acted with only moderate tact and sense she could have regained her own position, for the Queen loved her still, and still suffered from her friend's unkindness. The Duchess now had a standing reason for being unkind, as well as those which presented themselves in the form of the Queen's reluctance to be guided entirely by the Whigs. The latter wanted her to resign to the Lord Chancellor the power of filling church appointments, and the Queen wanted to keep it in her own hands. Her contumacy in this matter as well as her stubborn defence of "poor Masham" infuriated the Duchess, who, though she could no longer please the Queen, could still hurt her. The poor woman wrote: "I cannot go to bed without renewing a request I have often made, that you would banish all unkind, unjust thoughts of your poor unfortunate faithful Morley, which I saw by the glimpse I had of you yesterday, you were full of. Indeed I do not deserve them."

But Mrs. Morley was no longer quite so unfortunate. She had the consolation now, and to her mind it was very great, of a sympathetic, attentive, kindly spoken companion, who never attempted to thwart her policy with regard to the Anglican Church, but, on the contrary, admired it warmly. For the first time in many years Anne felt comfortable and supported, for not only was Masham with her: behind Masham there was Harley.

The rift between the Queen and the Duchess was now public property, and this made the Duchess more angry than ever. In July, 1708, Marlborough's victory at Oudenarde called for another public thanksgiving, and once more the Mistress of the Robes attended the Queen to St. Paul's Cathedral. The occasion which should to some extent have repaired the Duchess's position, she turned to dire disaster. Sarah had laid out the jewels she thought proper for the Queen to wear and at the last moment the Queen had decided to wear something else. Sarah was outraged by this show of independence and at once assumed that the Queen had been put up to it by Masham. She exclaimed that the Queen had chosen a very wrong day to mortify her, when just going to return thanks for a victory gained by Lord Marlborough. She kept on with the quarrel as the royal coach drove through the cheering crowds, and when it halted in the forecourt of St. Paul's amid waiting dignitaries the Queen, painfully alighting, made some reply as she prepared to hobble up the steps. Sarah had driven her into such a state of wretchedness that she had become oblivious of her surroundings, but Sarah herself was aware of what was due to the occasion. She sharply ordered the Queen to be quiet.

The Queen was quiet; she was very quiet indeed, and when a few days later the Duchess sent her a communication from Marlborough to read, she returned it without comment, saying that she did so since she had received the Duchess's *commands* to say no more to her. The Duchess for the first time wrote what, if not an apology, was at least an explanation of her conduct. "I desired you not to answer me then for fear of being overheard." She went on in a strain to bring no pleasure to the Queen and a great deal to Mrs. Masham and Mr. Harley: "I should be much better pleased to say and do everything you would like but I should think myself wanting in my duty to you if I saw you so much in the wrong as, without prejudice or passion I really think you are, in several particulars I have mentioned and did not tell you of it."

The unkindness of her sister had once driven Anne to find all her consolation in Sarah Churchill and now the latter was driving her to rely more and more on Abigail Masham. Anne was worse than resentful of the Duchess; she was getting tired of her. On receiving a letter from the Queen containing a mild rebuke, the Duchess relates: "I immediately set myself to draw up a long narrative of a series of faithful services for about twenty-six years past." When the narrative was sent to her, the Queen replied as most people would have been tempted to do in her place, that she had received it and would look it over when she had time.

Like the tearing-up of some ancient-rooted tree the process of final separation was intermittent, painful and hard. The death of Prince George caused a temporary reconciliation. Sarah came at once to Kensington Palace and found Anne beside her dead husband's bed. She took her in her arms and led her away, but even her kindness was dictatorial. The Queen wanted to stay at Kensington with her husband's body. The Duchess felt that this was undesirable and transported her to St. James's Palace. Here, Mrs. Masham was sent for, and things were soon in their old plight.

At last it came to the Duchess's ears that she had been accused of speaking disrespectfully of the Queen and betraying details of her private affairs. The charge was so damaging and, moreover, so abhorrent to the Duchess, among whose many faults indecency was not one, that she determined to see the Queen face to face to assert her innocence. In the letter which she wrote, asking for the audience, she said that she wanted only the opportunity to clear herself; she promised not to press the Queen for any answer. Anne put her off several times but at last the Duchess was permitted to see her at Kensington Palace. It was natural, in spite of everything that had gone before, that Sarah should think that in a personal interview she stood a good chance of coming off best. The old habit of submission to her, the old dread of her anger, the old love which would surely rekindle when she showed herself as a suppliant, could not have entirely disappeared; for better or worse, the two of them were Morley and Freeman still.

In a personal crisis the Stewarts had a power of surprising people who thought little of them. Two of them had shown it at the block. Anne would never have emerged victorious from this ordeal if she had not had the coaching of Harley and the support of Masham, but old, fat, infirm, flustered as she was, that she could do it even with their help was astonishing. Thirty years later the Duchess wrote her account of that interview and thirty years had not abated its edge. The Queen heard her vehement protest and said merely that no doubt many lies were told. After that she made no comment. The masterly refusal of any argument astounded and at last terrified Sarah. "I begged I might not be denied all power of justifying myself. But still the only return was: *You desired no answer and you shall have none.* I then begged to know if Her Majesty would tell me some other time? *You desired no answer and you shall have none.* I then appealed to Her Majesty to know if she did

not herself know that I had often despised interest in comparison of
serving her faithfully and doing right? And whether she did not
know me to be of a temper incapable of disowning anything which
I knew to be true? *You desired no answer and you shall have
none.*" The Queen presently decided to terminate the audience. She
walked to the door. As she reached it the Duchess's overstrung
nerves gave way; in her own words: "Streams of tears flowed down
against my will." Two amazing things happened at once. Sarah was
reduced by Anne to floods of tears, and Anne left the room in
indifference.

Sarah had made too many enemies for this interview to remain
dark. The news of it spread like wildfire. Everyone who cared for it
now had *carte blanche* to abuse and vilify the Duchess; she had
already appeared as Zara and the Empress Irene in two scandalous
novels, *The Secret History of Queen Zara* and *The New Atlantis.*
Now she was attacked by name. The *Examiner,* under Swift's
editorship, accused her of peculation as Mistress of the Robes and
Keeper of the Privy Purse. When this article was brought to the
Queen's notice, she herself gave it the lie. "Everyone knows," said
Anne coldly, "that *cheating* is not the Duchess of Marlborough's
crime." But her crimes were very serious. In her fury she had
threatened to publish letters that Anne had written her long ago
full of indiscretions about William III, and this decided the Queen
to dismiss her from her offices. The prospect was grave indeed, for
if his wife were dismissed from the Queen's service the Duke of
Marlborough would be obliged to resign the Captain-Generalship,
and Marlborough had performed his great work so thoroughly that
an inimical Government could afford to see him go. The victory of
Malplaquet in September, 1709, had made his name so terrible that
the French generals no longer gave him battle. They retired at his
approach. It was an irony of fate that his brilliant achievement
abroad had lost him his power of bargaining at home. If anything
were to be gained now it must be by humble submission and suing
for it as a favour.

The Duchess wrote to the Queen to beg that, for her husband's
sake, she might not be dismissed. "I really am very sorry that ever I
did anything that was uneasy to your Majesty...I am ready to
promise anything that you can think reasonable...I will never...
do any one thing that can give you the least disturbance or uneasiness...I would not omit anything possible for me to do that might

save my Lord Marlborough from the greatest mortification he is capable of." Marlborough took this letter to the Queen himself but she would hardly read it and told him that she must have the Duchess's gold key returned in three days' time. Marlborough begged for a year's grace, a month's and then ten days', but what Sarah Churchill had done over the past eight years was now made plain. The once gentle, generous Anne, whose throne he had saved, whose country he had made supreme in Europe, allowed Marlborough to go down on his knees before her and then told him that the three days were reduced to two. When his wife heard how he had been treated, she sent back the key that evening.

In her rage, on her husband's behalf more than on her own, though her own claims were not forgotten and filled many foolscap pages of flowing and meticulous exposition, the Duchess, before she left her apartments in St. James's Palace, stripped them of everything she had brought there herself. As these included the elegant door-handles and finger-plates, the rooms were left by the outgoing tenant in a state that was, to say the least, unusual in palaces and her enemies put it about that she had carried away the marble chimney-pieces, leaving gaping walls behind her.

Apart from the injury and disgrace, their situation was not hard. Marlborough would have retired with his wife years before if she had allowed it. He was very wealthy. He had never much cared for the enormous project of Blenheim, only begging Sarah to hurry on the builders "that I may have a prospect of living in it", but he could live in it now, and for twelve years more he had the life with Sarah that he had looked forward to ever since he married her.

She had twenty years of widowhood, filled, as all her years had been, with quarrels and kindnesses, with hard work and vigorous interference, with griefs and pleasures and anger and satisfaction. But the years after Marlborough's death ceased to be forward-looking; they drew their inspiration from the past.

One episode seems to contain the quintessence of them both. Her husband had a lover's fondness for her long fair hair and once, after a quarrel in which she had failed to disturb his glacial calm, she rushed away and, wild to hurt him, hacked off the hair close to her head. She laid the sheaf on a chair in the ante-room through which he must pass and waited. Nothing happened. She found the hair gone and thought the servants must have taken it away. Her husband made no comment on her shorn head, and even she did not dare to provoke him to one. The incident was closed between them. When, after his death she opened his private secretaire, she found the coil of hair carefully laid away. She was an old woman when she told the story but it broke her down into a passion of tears.

CHAPTER 4

Fair Rosamond

The story of Rosamond Clifford rests on few undisputed facts, it is very far removed in time, and yet her image has an undamaged beauty like one of the gilded effigies lying on the tombs in the chapel of Edward the Confessor. Her own tomb was broken up at the Reformation, and of the retreat at Woodstock where she lived and the nunnery at Godstowe where she died the ruins can be barely traced; nearly nine hundred years have intervened since her death and yet her fame reaches us like ancient light from a star.

Rosamond is a name of Frankish origin, but the chronicler of her own time, Giraldus Cambrensis, turned it into Latin. He said sternly that her name should not be read as meaning Rosa Mundi, Rose of the World, as some foolish persons supposed, but rather Rosa Immundi, the Rose Unchaste. When he says what ought not to have been, he tells us what was. To the English people her name has always meant the World's Rose.

The story is a classical one, that of the unhappy husband finding secret bliss with a loving and beloved mistress and of disaster overtaking the lovers when they are discovered by the wife. In such a story it is usually the wife who assumes the dominating rôle : here the wife and the husband were equally formidable. The gentle victim was the victim of them both.

Henry II was one of the greatest English kings and two men who knew him well have left a vivid picture of his restless and over-whelming personality. One of these was Giraldus Cambrensis and the other the King's chaplain, Peter of Blois. They describe a vigorous, intellectual man of devouring energy, of great practical intelligence and very highly strung. His appearance was not attractive but it was striking. He had a face like a lion's, florid with bright grey eyes that were bloodshot. His red hair was cut in a square fringe, his head was remarkably round and he poked it forward. He was broad-shouldered, long-armed, and though he ate moderately and took violent exercise, he had a heavy paunch. He never wore gloves except when he was hawking, and his hands and nails were neglected; they were probably shapely, for his feet had very high insteps.

His acute nervous tension showed itself in all his mannerisms. He could scarcely bear to sit still but stood at council meetings and to eat his meals. As he talked he was constantly turning some object round and round in his hands, a weapon or a hunting-knife. He seldom spared time to come to Mass and when he did he whispered excitedly to the person next him, or looked at the pictures in his missal and scribbled on the margins of the leaves. In spite of this irreverence he had an implicit belief in God's existence, though he showed it in a way of his own. In the teeth of a bitter disappointment he once exclaimed furiously: "God shall never see *me* a good man, I've suffered too much at His hands!" In fits of passionate anger he would roll on the floor and gnaw the rushes, but he was capable, too, of an ominous self-control. "When he smothered his inward feelings he was second to none in courtesy." He had the preoccupations of an intellectual man—"in night watches and labours he was unremitting"—but he combined these with pleasures requiring hard physical endurance. He followed the chase like a man possessed, mounting at dawn, riding all day through woods and across the ridges of the hills, returning at nightfall to keep a weary court on its legs while he ate his supper standing up.

The chase was not the only thing that took him afield. Henry not only gave comprehensive orders as to what was to be done but he was constantly on the move to make sure that his orders were being carried out. His public journeyings were carried on in a perpetual uproar. "When King Henry sets out of a morning", said his chaplain, "you see multitudes of people running up and down as if they were distracted: horses rushing against horses, carriages overturning carriages, players, gamesters, cooks, confectioners, morris dances, barbers, courtesans and hangers-on making so much noise, and in a word such an intolerable, tumultuous jumble of horse and foot that you imagine the great abyss has opened and that hell has poured forth all its inhabitants." But there were times when the noisy retinue was left behind; some visits of inspection, the King felt, would fail of their object if it were known that he was coming; sometimes a small troop on bemired, exhausted horses would appear suddenly at the gates of a town, and it would be learned with uncomfortable surprise that the King was among them.

Henry was the son of the Conqueror's grand-daughter Matilda, whose supporters had failed to make good her claim to the English crown against that of her cousin Stephen. The latter had reigned rather than ruled, and while he was King the barons had made life so hideous for their weaker neighbours with robbery, imprisonment, torture and massacre that it was commonly said that Christ and His angels must be asleep. When, on Stephen's death, Henry took the Crown as his mother's heir, he set himself the gigantic task of overthrowing anarchy and bringing the whole country under the rule of law.

His achievement was stupendous. He quelled the barons' intolerable powers by main force and he established the foundations of the English legal system of the present day. His Curia Regis became the Court of King's Bench and his justiciars going on their circuits were the forerunners of the present-day Judges of Assize.

In his reform of the Church courts, however, he received a most unexpected setback. His friend and protégé, Thomas à Becket, whom he had made Archbishop of Canterbury so that he should have Becket's support in his plans, had no sooner become Archbishop than he declared that his loyalty was due to the Church rather than the Crown. The prolonged and raging quarrel that ensued was only ended by Becket's being murdered in his own cathedral, without the King's knowledge but by his supporters; the horror caused by this deed was such that Henry was obliged to leave the Church courts alone. What he did accomplish was so tremendous it could have been done only by a man of exceptional powers, whose energies gave him no rest. If such a man were to find happiness with a woman, it could be only with one who, by her affection for him, her sympathy and her unquestioned loyalty would create for him the serenity and peace that he could never find for himself. Such a woman was the wife he needed; the one he got was Eleanor, Duchess of Aquitaine.

This lady had succeeded at thirteen years old to territories that covered almost the whole of the South of France. The southern provinces had a civilization and even a language of their own; their climate was much warmer than that of Northern France and their people were like those of some separate race; they were so much gayer, more quick-tempered, more amorous than the inhabitants of the north. Eleanor's predecessors had established the strange institution known as the Court of Love, a reaction against the roughness and barbarity of medieval life as it was found outside the walled garden of a château. It existed to discuss problems of sexual behaviour, to define the nature of passion and to lay down rules for the behaviour of lovers in society.

The young Duchess gained great éclat from her presidency of the Court of Love. The troubadours who composed and sang the rhymed stories which supplied the place of novels to the twelfth century, paid a more than formal allegiance to her. They made songs on her bold, brilliant, voluptuous beauty; they boasted of her that their Duchess could read and write. When the new songs were sung before her, her critical opinion was considered of real value. The Court of Love would sometimes listen to a *tenson*, a sung dialogue which poses some sexual problem; sometimes it would listen to and debate some problem that was being encountered by an actual lady or gentleman who had submitted it anonymously to the Court's ruling. Eleanor took the lead in such discussions: "Whether it is better to hate when loved or to love when hated?" and when the Court drew up axioms on the lines of: "He that is jealous does not love," "Love is always either increasing or diminishing," or "True love cannot exist within the confines of marriage," the Duchess gave the benefit of her experience and advice. When it should be thought politically desirable to marry her, there would be no fear of her being too immature to face the ordeal.

Her territories were so great that she was an eligible bride for the King of France, and the young Louis VII was besides deeply enamoured of her. He was serious, high-minded and chaste, and the beautiful, vital and exuberant Eleanor had the influence over him of the woman who aroused his first passion. The influence was entirely disastrous. As a result of her insistent instigation the King decided to join the Crusade preached by St. Bernard in 1147. Against all advice Louis declared himself ready to set out for the Holy Land, and Eleanor, as independent sovereign of the south, announced that she was going too. This caused general surprise and consternation except in the Abbé Suger. As Suger was to be regent in the King's absence, that the Queen should be absent at the same time appealed to him as a highly desirable arrangement; not that his opinion would have made any difference to the Queen's plans if it had not. Eleanor and her ladies threw themselves into their preparations with pious zeal. They had dresses and armour made for themselves as for a troop of Amazons, and they sent presents of distaffs to such gentlemen as declined to join the expedition. With vast bales of luggage containing dresses, looking-glasses and everything else they could not possibly do without, the ladies embarked with the King and set sail for Thrace.

Any chance of success which the French might have had in the opening stages of the campaign was obliterated by the tactics of the Amazons which led to the crushing disaster at Laodicea. The Queen and her troop had gone forward with orders from the King to occupy bare rising ground overlooking a valley. Louis, coming after them, much impeded by their baggage, found no sign of them at the appointed place and was forced to enter a luxuriantly wooded and watered valley in search of them. As the French defiled along the valley bottom, Arab archers stationed on the heights shot them down at leisure. By the time the King had come up with the ladies and managed to interpose a line of defence between them and the gathering forces of the enemy, thousands of picked French troops were dying on the grass. The remains of the army, their baggage lost and cut off from supplies, retreated into Antioch. Here a splendid welcome met them. Prince Raymond of Antioch was the brother of Eleanor's late father and he treated the suffering French with lavish kindness.

Eleanor, to whose preference for romantic scenery the frightful catastrophe had been owing, did not allow such considerations to prey upon her. She rapidly recovered her spirits, and with them her great beauty and the epicurean relish for romance which had made her so distinguished in the Court of Love. Her uncle was forty-eight, handsome, polished, fascinating, and she fell in love with him. Beautiful, domineering and above all persistent, she did not fail to gain a response. It might be argued that in spite of their close relationship, since they had never seen each other, she and Prince Raymond met now as mutually attracted strangers. There was no positive proof of how far the intimacy went, but in such matters the French are not apt to give the benefit of the doubt. The King was at first uneasy then appalled. Eleanor attempted to turn the tables by a master-stroke of impudence. While the Court waited breathless for an unspeakable scandal to declare itself, she let it be known that she was considering very gravely whether she ought to have married a man who was her own third cousin.

Louis acted with more decision than had been expected of him. He made a sudden departure by night, carrying off the Queen before she had time to say good-bye to her uncle.

The enmity that now set in between Louis and Eleanor was never healed. When they reached the Holy City the French King joined his allies at the siege of Damascus and the Queen and her Amazons were required to remain shut up in Jerusalem. Eleanor, however, was seldom at a loss. In Jerusalem she began an intrigue with a Saracen emir of commanding handsomeness. Louis wrote to the Abbé Suger, discussing the possibility of divorcing his wife for adultery, but Suger replied begging him to think of no such thing. If Eleanor left him, the southern provinces would leave the French crown. Louis regretfully admitted the force of this argument.

On the return of the King and Queen from the Crusade, which had failed in every military objective besides losing the country thousands of soldiers and a huge quantity of treasure, it was noticed that the King was much sobered. He had cut off his long hair, wore very plain clothes and showed himself to be altogether under the influence of the Church. On the Queen's haughty, selfish and self-satisfied nature, the catastrophe had made no impression. She despised her husband's frame of mind and declared scornfully that she might as well be married to a monk. Louis had now no fear of her displeasure and he refused to trust her out of his sight. The Queen was forbidden to return to her southern provinces. It is strange to modern ears to hear of any Frenchman or Frenchwoman wanting to leave Paris, but Paris had not yet become the adored city of later centuries. To Eleanor, filled with angry resentment and longing for Aquitaine, Paris was merely a formal, sunless city of the north. The bereaved troubadours were as angry as she, but the King was unmoved. She beguiled her existence with violent fancies for men, one of whom was Geoffrey Plantagenet, who had married the Conqueror's grand-daughter Matilda. Geoffrey as Duke of Normandy came to Paris to do homage to his overlord the King of France. Two years later Geoffrey died and his son Henry came to do homage for Normandy in his father's place.

Henry Plantagenet was nineteen and Eleanor was now thirty. This difference in their ages did not prevent her from making advances to him as she had made them to his father, and it is only fair to add that it did not prevent Henry from responding to them.

Eleanor was still beautiful and if her aspect had in it something of the caged eagle, a young man of such abounding energy and strength as Henry Plantagenet did not object to this as more timid or more experienced men might have done. But Eleanor's chief charm in his eyes that she possessed great independent wealth and a fleet of thirty-six ships. When she pointed out to him that if she were his the money and the ships would be his, Henry did not need telling twice; the English crown he meant to claim as Matilda's son seemed almost within his grasp.

Eleanor now had an urgent incentive to gain the divorce she had airily spoken of five years ago at Antioch, and when it became known that she was pregnant by Henry Plantagenet Louis did not argue the matter with her. The usually long-drawn-out negotiations of such an affair were shortened to a matter of weeks, for if a boy were to be born before the marriage was dissolved, then, whoever his father were, the child would be heir to the French throne. Louis was obliged to acquiesce in the loss of the southern provinces; he was perhaps somewhat consoled by the loss of Eleanor at the same time. It was a tribute to his magnanimity that the grounds of divorce were said to be, not adultery, but consanguinity. The marriage of Henry and Eleanor was not delayed and four months after it their son was born. The sudden death of Stephen cleared Henry's path and in December, 1154, he and Eleanor were crowned in Westminster Abbey.

Henry's alliance with so great a wife had helped him to acquire his throne, but Eleanor's French possessions even more than his own duchies of Normandy and Anjou caused a drain upon his time, energy and resources that he could ill spare from his task of putting his English realm to rights. In the same way, Eleanor had married him in the teeth of formidable difficulty because she had a passion for him, but the hatred to which her passion turned was the cause of his bitterest misery.

Once the latent hostility between two such natures had showed itself she had neither the power nor the wish to keep his affection, and when his four surviving sons, Henry, Geoffrey, Richard and John were in their teens, their mother, playing on their ambition and their father's unwillingness to relinquish power, managed to raise them up in a combined rebellion against him. Henry attracted devoted servants throughout his life, but the two great crises of his reign were the outcome of personal disloyalty to himself, and they came close upon one another's heels; when the rebellion of his wife and sons broke out, the quarrel between himself and Becket was already raging; in these years he had gained a measure of brilliant success but the strain and suffering he had undergone, though they had not impaired his mental powers, had seriously threatened his nervous stability. Wounded affection, disappointment and a passionate sense of injury drove him into fits of almost insane anger. If such a man, so beset, had discovered a secret spring of happiness in his harsh existence, it would be something unusually precious and to keep it safe would be worth uncounted pains.

Of the three largest royal palaces, Windsor, Winchester and Woodstock, the third was Henry's favourite. Here he kept his menagerie of leopards and lions. In succeeding centuries much of the timber has been felled, but in the twelfth century Woodstock was a palace among deep woods, and the King was "a great lover of the woods". His justiciar Richard Fitzneal said of the royal forests: "They are the secret places of kings and their great delights." "There," he said, "renouncing the arduous inevitable turmoil of the court, they breathe the pure air of freedom for a little space." Secret joy and peace hidden in a wood is something that breathes the spirit of a fairy-tale.

Walter, Lord Clifford had properties in many countries but he and his wife lived in Oxford and their daughter Rosamond had been partly brought up by the nuns of Godstowe nunnery, an enlightened community where the ladies lived a life of elegant cultivation and innocent pleasure. Little description remains of Rosamond Clifford, but that little tells so much there is hardly need of more. The points repeated in every version of her story are that she was fair-complexioned, that she had bright gold hair and that she enchanted by her gentleness and sweetness. The great eighteenth-century antiquarian, Hearne, says of early poems and ballads that they are more to be trusted as information than later ones when versifying had become fluent and stories were often elaborated. Of the early verse-makers he says: "The poets of those times for the most part kept close to truth." The earliest version in poetry of Rosamond's story is Thomas Delone's, published in 1612, but Delone was drawing on much earlier sources, possibly handed down by word of mouth. Delone evokes the impression of fairness and radiance with such energy that light seems to stream from the page:

Most peerless was her beauty found,
Her favour and her face,
A sweeter creature in this world
Did never prince embrace.
Her crispèd locks like threads of gold
Appeared to each man's sight,
Her sparkling eyes like orient pearls
Did cast a heavenly light.

The blood within her crystal cheeks
Did such a colour drive,
Appeared to each man's sight,
For mastery did strive.

In another ballad, one of Rosamond's brothers is made to say in the King's hearing:

I have a sister, Clifford swears,
But few men do her know.
The skin upon her face appears
Like drops of blood on snow.

An early chapbook relating the story in prose says: "Her eyes sparkled like two twin stars, her forehead was like a heaven of crystal." Hearne himself, citing the medieval chroniclers, says that King Henry was devoted to this lady "not only on account of her exquisite beauty but for the sweetness of her temper."

There is no indication of where the two met or how they became lovers but that the Clifford family lived in the neighbourhood of the King's favourite retreat explains the acquaintance and the fact of the two figures being what they were explains the rest.

An element of the story which is found in every form of it is that Rosamond was kept at Woodstock in extreme secrecy. The concealment must have been thoroughly effective since, sometimes at least, the Queen must have been at the palace as well as the King. Some said that it was a hiding-place in the middle of a maze. The monkish chronicler Higden, who died in 1364, and who is therefore one of the authorities for the story nearest to it in time, said that King Henry made for Rosamond at Woodstock "a house of wonderful working; so that no man or woman might come to her

but he that was instructed by the King or such as were right secret
with him touching the matter. This house after some was named
Labyrinthus or Dedalus' work which was wrought like a knot in a
garden called a Maze." The Elizabethan historian Stowe, who
repeats this, says that the maze consisted of vaults underground,
arched with brick and stone. The tradition that a certain walk in
the park at Woodstock returns an uncanny echo may derive from a
walk over hollow ground.

In the early eighteenth century there were still shown the
remains of a large building that was called Rosamond's Bower, in
which had been collected fragments of brick, stone, marble and
glass. These were cleared away by the ruthless hand of the Duchess
of Marlborough when Blenheim Palace was being built. She did
not, however, interfere with a spring enclosed in masonry and
known as Rosamond's Well. In 1660 a pamphlet describing the
environs of Woodstock said that this well was traditionally used by
the members of the secret household when it was not safe to fetch
water from further afield.

One splendid object remained to be seen and described by the
early historians. Until Godstowe Nunnery was destroyed at the
Reformation, it housed a possession of Rosamond. The chronicler
Knighton wrote in the 1360s that King Henry's great affection for
Rosamond "made him so careful of her that he at once provided
her with everything she desired"; a proof of his affection, then in
the keeping of the nuns at Godstowe, was "a cabinet of such admirable workmanship that on it the fighting of Champions, the
moving of cattle, the flying of birds and swimming of fishes were so
exquisitely represented as if they had been alive." It is not easy to
decide whether this means a cabinet painted in so life-like a way
that the figures seemed to move, or whether it refers to some
miraculous feat of medieval clockwork, such as one may see in the
animated figures of knights on horseback who ride out of clocks at
the striking of the hour. The skill, brilliancy and minuteness of
medieval handicraft, in illuminations, gold and silver work and
jewellery would produce a gift worthy of a king, whether the figures
moved or not.

The nuns of Godstowe were attached to the Clifford family. The
nunnery received many gifts from Lord Clifford and as Rosamond
had been for some time with them, a usual arrangement in a period
when families often used a convent as a finishing school, it was

natural that there should be at least a tradition of their having reasoned with her on her perilous situation as King Henry's mistress. Hearne says that when the nuns expostulated with her "she always returned very pretty though by no means satisfactory answers." The phenomenon of a petrified tree in the grounds of Godstowe was explained in after years by Rosamond's having said: "If that tree be turned to stone after my death then shall I have life among the saints of heaven."

These anecdotes suggest that at times at least she went freely about the neighbourhood. It appears also that many people knew of the King's keeping her at Woodstock; the historian Fabyan, writing at the beginning of the sixteenth century but speaking of what was common knowledge of the time, says that Henry treated his Queen badly "and kept that wench Rosamond out of all good order." Giraldus Cambrensis says that Henry had always had women whom he kept secretly but that at this period of his life he became shameless and flaunted this beautiful creature before the world. Yet Rosamond is the only mistress for whose keeping elaborate precautions are related and the precautions, whether of labyrinth or vaults, are a part of the story wherever it appears. It must be supposed that they were meant as a defence against the Queen alone and considering the freedom with which kings have always been wont to keep a mistress, that Henry should have felt it necessary either to conceal Rosamond or to put her under a strong guard throws a truly sinister light on Eleanor.

The Queen's anger when the story of her rival reached her ears is no doubt a measure of the extreme seriousness of the King's passion. There was also something in the tale of Rosamond's beauty and her sweetness, and the anxious care with which the King preserved this treasure, that was a particular outrage to the feelings of an overbearing, vindictive woman. Eleanor had been accustomed to admiration from childhood. At thirteen she had commanded the homage of the troubadours; as a young bride she had had the King of France at her feet; she had been famous all over Europe for the succession of her lovers. Now she was over fifty and her husband, whom she hated, was twelve years younger than herself. The rancour of her married life for which she found relief only in tormenting her husband through his sons, had perhaps reached that pitch at which she would not endure his finding happiness with any woman. If so, Rosamond as a mistress would be to the last degree intolerable. With her shining, gold-haired beauty and her infatuating gentleness and helplessness, she was an image to rouse murderous fury.

The different versions all agree that the Queen discovered Rosamond's hiding-place in Woodstock by keeping a sharp watch and following a clue. Some translate the clue literally into a clue of thread which was caught, unknown to him, on the King's spur, and brought into the Queen's presence. It is said that when she followed it and found the secret door of the hiding-place, she returned later with men who overpowered the knight on guard, and made her way through the secret chambers till she came upon Rosamond, whom she took completely by surprise.

The common tale, which has crystallized itself into imperishable legend, is that the Queen murdered Rosamond, offering her the choice of death from a dagger or a cup of poison and that Rosamond chose the less dreadful way.

> *And casting up her eyes to heaven*
> *She did for mercy call*
> *And drinking up the poison strong*
> *Her life she lost withal.*
>
> *And when that death through every limb*
> *Had shown its greatest spite*
> *Her chiefest foes did plain confess*
> *She was a glorious wight.*

A medieval French work, *Les Chroniques de London*, gives a hideous account of the murder, in which the Queen makes two horrible old women before her eyes bleed Rosamond to death in a hot bath. The detail is circumstantial: when Rosamond saw two great fires lighted she thought she was to be burned alive, but the hags stripped off her beautiful clothes and having opened the veins in her wrists forced her into a bath, where they held up her chin so that none of the blood carried in the water should flow back into her mouth. It is a relief to learn that the writer is unreliable: he puts the events into the wrong reign and ascribes the deed to the Queen of Henry III, Eleanor of Provence, but the anecdote shows the popular idea of the Queen's savage cruelty.

Such evidence as there is, however, shows that Eleanor did not actually murder her rival. One of the few uncontested facts of the story is that Rosamond died in 1177. Henry went over to France in 1172; having quelled for the time being the insurrections of the Princes Henry, Geoffrey and Richard and having received ample proof that their mother was implicated in their treachery, he brought the Queen back with him to England as a close prisoner. That he had another cause of undying anger against her may be fairly conjectured; yet Eleanor cannot have seen Rosamond for three years at least before her death, for from their return to England in 1175 until his own death in 1189, Henry kept his wife imprisoned. She was shut up in the palace of Winchester under the personal charge of the King's great justiciar, Ranulph de Glanville. What she had done to Rosamond had not resulted in immediate death, and the historians, as opposed to the story-tellers, bear this out. There is complete agreement among them in what they say and what they do not say, and the grimness of their statement lies in what they leave out.

"Queen Eleanor found the way and came unto her and she lived not long after."

"The Queen dealt with her in such sharp and cruel wise that she lived not long after."

"The Queen upon Rosamond so vented her spleen as the lady lived not long after."

It can only be assumed that the shock of some terrifying experience broke Rosamond's nerve: that the sense of guilt which the nuns had tried to rouse and which the King's influence and his passion had kept in check, the intense religious convictions in which she had been brought up and had succeeded for the time in thrusting away, and the annihilating terror of the hunted animal when the killer suddenly bursts into its retreat, all combined in the terrible apparition of the Queen to bring on a prostration from which she never recovered. There is no record of Rosamond's living in retirement at Godstowe in a gracious atmosphere of penitence and good works. Nothing is said except that she died there. But we hear afterwards that Lord Clifford "gave to the nuns of Godstowe in the county of Oxfordshire for the health of Margaret his wife and for the soul of Rosamond their daughter his mill at Frampton in Gloucestershire, as also a little meadow lying near it called Lechton."

Rosamond was buried in Godstowe chapel; and two years after

Henry's death, in 1191, Bishop Hugh of Lincoln visited the nunnery and saw in the middle of the choir a very rich tomb covered with a pall of white silk and round it a great number of wax lights burning. He asked who was buried there in such state? The nuns told him: "It was the fair Rosamond whom King Henry had so dearly loved and for whose sake he had been a munificent benefactor to their poor house." The Bishop was very angry. "Then," said he, "take out of this place the harlot and bury her outside the church so that other women may be frightened from keeping adulterous company with men."

The nuns were obliged to obey him, but they showed their affection for Rosamond's memory in a truly feminine way. When the tomb was opened, they collected the bones in a bag of leather which was very strongly perfumed. Another tomb was erected outside the church precincts and by an extraordinary freak of fortune, a description of the second tomb survives. An old man of 90, Thomas Allen, who died in 1632, had had described to him by an eye-witness Rosamond's tomb as it was before it was broken up during the Dissolution of the Monasteries. Hearne, who had it from another antiquary, printed this description. It is said that on the tomb "were interchangeable weavings drawn out and decked with roses red and green, and the picture of the cup out of which she drank the poison given her by the Queen, carved in stone." This cup, which was probably a representation of the chalice, gave weight to the rumour of the murder.

Whatever the degree of Eleanor's guilt, she was severely punished. She had had two husbands and outraged both of them. From her struggles with the French one she had, at last, come off victorious; but now she had injured the English one, and past forgiveness. Her angry sons attempted to take her part; in Aquitaine the troubadours wrote songs about her:

"Thou weepest but none hears thee! The King of the North keeps thee shut up like a town that is besieged. Cry, then, raise thy voice like a trumpet that thy sons may hear it!" But in vain. Winchester was a palace but it was a prison, and with two short periods of freedom when a reconciliation was attempted and then given up as hopeless, the Queen was kept there for thirteen years. Ranulph de Glanville was the Chief Justiciar of England and one of the great lawyers of the Middle Ages, but Eleanor was not likely to appreciate the privilege of a close connexion with him.

On her husband's death, the Queen was set free by her sons and John, with the harsh realism of the time, made a comment on the remains of his father's mistress. He gave some endowments to the nunnery of Godstowe, but he also caused to be placed on Rosamond's tomb a brass border with this inscription:

Hic jacet in tumba, Rosa mundi non Rosa munda.
Non redolet sed olet quae redolere solet.

or

Here lies entombed the World's Rose
Not fragrant now but stinking, she who used to smell
so sweet.

But thanks to feminine devotion, the last word was not John's taunt at mortality. At the Dissolution Rosamond's tomb was broken up, and Leland, writing at the time, said: "Rosamond's tomb at Godstowe was taken up of late." Her bones, he said, were enclosed in lead, and inside the lead, in leather. "When it was opened a very sweet smell came out of it."

The tomb has vanished. Godstowe is a ruin in a field, at Woodstock the hiding-place has disappeared and the great woods themselves, "the secret places of kings and their delights." But the tale is undying. All down the centuries, stories, ballads and chapbooks have retold it. Addison wrote the words of an opera, "Rosamond," set afterwards to the plaintive, exquisite music of Arne. One of his verses sung by the lovers recalls the tradition of the echo in the park and it seems to describe the persistence of the story:

As o'er the hollow vaults we walk
A hundred echoes round us talk.
From hill to hill the voice is tossed,
Rocks rebounding, caves resounding,
Not a single word is lost.

The name evokes strange associations with unhappiness. There was, at the east corner of St. James's Park, a piece of water known as Rosamond's Pond. In Smith's *Antiquities of London,* published in 1791, there is an engraving of the pond with heavy trees around it, above whose branches the towers of Westminster Abbey rise into a clear evening sky. In 1770 the pond was filled up, because of the

D

number of suicides that had taken place in it. "The irregularity of the trees, the rise of the ground and the venerable Abbey afforded great entertainment to the contemplative eye. This spot was often the receptacle of many unhappy persons who, in the stillness of an evening, plunged themselves into eternity."

Henry had told God he would not be a good man nor was he, but he was great. To his genius and his determination we owe the foundation of the greatest thing in English life, the rule of law. The savage misery he endured was to a great degree the result of his own temperament, but was none the less pitiable for that. He had a brief halcyon spell of happiness. Of the other women with whom he enjoyed himself it would be a matter of some work to discover any of their names, but Rosamond's name is inseparable from his, like the red rose tree twined with the briar which, the ballad says, sprang from the tombs of two parted lovers and joined above them.

CHAPTER 5

Elizabeth Inchbald

Novels are considered primarily as works of feeling; this, perhaps, accounts for the distrust in which they have sometimes been held. Anyone addicted to novel-reading, it was thought, was liable to develop an over-romantic or impractical view of life. Since the connexion between the temperament of the woman writer and what she writes is very close, much closer or at least much more obvious than that between the masculine writer and his work, one would expect the woman who wrote one of the most successful novels of the late eighteenth century to be a romantic character in herself. She was. Her name was Elizabeth Inchbald and she called her novel *A Simple Story*.

Elizabeth was born in 1753, one of the family of a Suffolk farmer. She had no regular schooling, but her natural, ardent love of writing, and the fact that though in the eighteenth century a girl might get next to no education, the little she did get was good, allowed her to develop a clear, elegant way of writing that no governess or fashionable boarding-schools could have improved.

She grew up not only beautiful but enchanting. Erect and very slight, with a small bosom which the taste of the time called "None", she had the white skin that goes with tawny colouring. Her hair was straight and fine and in a favourite fashion of the day it was cut and curled in loose, separate locks all over her graceful head. Her features were delicate and sharp, her eyes surprisingly large and her expression was described as "full of sweetness and spirit, excessively interesting". The eagerness of her speech was checked by a slight stammer.

Living at home, near Bury St. Edmunds, she longed with all her soul to get to London. Meantime the most interesting object in her ken was the theatre at Norwich. Visiting companies came frequently from London to act in the market towns, but the Norwich theatre had a company of its own under the management of Mr. Richard Griffith. Elizabeth regarded this gentleman with intense devotion. At eighteen she already showed the curious division of mind which was going to account for her success as an artist and to be fatal to happiness in private life. This was her capacity to become absorbed in romantic attachments which not only could not result in marriage but which she herself hardly wished to do so. It was not, either, that she wanted a series of lovers, or any lover. She strenuously resisted all efforts to seduce her, from that of the theatrical manager who, when she was a girl, made advances to her over the tea-table, and received scalding water in his face, to that of Sir Charles Bunbury, whom as a mature woman she would have been very glad to marry but whom she sent from her door when his attentions took an unmistakable turn.

She gained a reputation that was said to be "irreproachable", no small feat for a highly attractive woman living alone in literary and theatrical society. What she enjoyed, to the deepest and fullest extent of her emotional powers, was an absorbing romantic passion for a man, a passion as innocent as a schoolgirl's. That she did not connect this intoxicating pleasure with the serious business of choosing a husband and settling herself in life is oddly shown by three entries in her diary for January, 1772. In this year she was nineteen and Mr. Inchbald, an actor, kind, respectable and some sixteen years older than she, had paid her a good deal of attention and was obviously working himself up to propose. Without altogether discouraging him, Elizabeth was secretly engrossed by a passion for Mr. Griffith. The entries in her diary read:

22 Jan.   Saw Mr. Griffith's picture.
28 Jan.   Stole it.
29 Jan.   Rather disappointed at not receiving a letter from Mr. Inchbald.

In June that year, the daydream gave place to the concerns of real life. She married Mr. Inchbald and began the life of an actress in a touring company. Her appearance and personality enabled her to find employment, untrained as she was, in a profession not then so overstocked as it is now; her stammer she found less of a drawback in stage speaking than in private conversation. In spite of reasonable success, she did not much care for acting. When their circumstances were good she was glad enough to let her husband act while she sat at home in their lodgings, reading solid books and learning French. She had never pretended to have any passion for Inchbald, but his for her was known to everyone who knew them. She had once warned a would-be suitor: "My temper is so uncertain that nothing but blind affection in a husband could bear with it." Inchbald sometimes found his blind affection called for. A visitor at their lodgings remembered an occasion when Inchbald sat copying a portrait of Garrick while dinner was put on the table. Because he did not come immediately Elizabeth seized his drawing and tore it to pieces. But between her committing these offences and her husband forgiving them they went on happily enough.

In 1777 they found themselves in Manchester and here Inchbald introduced his wife to the actress who was soon to be at the head of her profession and to become at last one of the greatest theatrical figures of all time. Sarah Siddons with her husband and her brother, John Kemble, was in theatrical lodgings near the Inchbalds', and in January, 1777, Mrs. Inchbald first saw John Kemble. In February she began the first draft of *A Simple Story*.

Kemble was a tall man who was said to have a beauty and grandeur like that of a classical statue. Byron said that he was "the most super-natural of actors". He had meant at first to be a priest and had studied at the Jesuit College at Douai. His temperament was graver than is usual in his profession. He had none of the actor's instinctive wish to display his art. If Kemble wanted to draw your attention to a passage in a play, he put the book into your hand and told you to read it for yourself. Boaden, who knew him well, said that he only once saw him mimic in private life. Kemble was describing to him a bust of Henry VII which he had seen at Strawberry Hill. "Stay," said Kemble, "I think I can give you an idea." The amazing countenance of leanness, avarice, anxiety and cunning which he then produced came vividly into Boaden's mind when he saw the bust himself many years later. But this was a solitary instance.

In general Kemble could be deduced as an actor only because in his capacity of scholar, philosopher and man of strong character he appeared slightly larger than life. He not only awed his fellow-actors; he could even awe a fashionable audience. In the theatre at York, Kemble's lines were once interrupted by the chatter of a young lady and her escorts. He advanced to the footlights and said he would wait for silence. He had not to wait long. Mrs. Siddons once said that the difference between her brother's style of acting and her own was typified by the way they used their stage clothes; she wrung and tossed her own draperies into utter disorder, but in the most passionate scenes his were never disturbed. The judgment of theatregoers who had seen them both was that Garrick's leading attribute was passion, and Kemble's dignity. If the attraction of opposites be believed, it seems inevitable that Kemble should have been a magnet to Elizabeth Inchbald's susceptibility.

The hero of her story is a young man named Dorriforth who is in training for the Catholic priesthood. His serious, not to say solemn cast of mind does not conceal the attractiveness of his nature, his uprightness, gentleness and the profound capacity for feeling which has not yet been aroused. He has also, as is shown by his treatment of relations with whom he had quarrelled, a vein of morbid implacability. Dorriforth's appearance is described: his height is emphasized, and the charm of his face which, though it has no striking features but dark eyes and white teeth, has so much countenance that it seems handsome. It is significant that the model for the portrait was an actor. "In his looks you beheld his thoughts moving with his lips."

Dorriforth on the verge of ordination is obliged to accept the guardianship of a friend's daughter. His household in London therefore consists of himself, his ward the beautiful, brilliant, generous but irresponsible Miss Milner, Dorriforth's Jesuit tutor Mr. Sandford, a morose, elderly man who conceives a violent hostility towards Miss Milner that he does not attempt to conceal, and Miss Milner's companion Miss Woodley, a plain, sensible, affectionate woman who does her best to restrain her flighty charge.

The character of Miss Milner, whose Christian name is never mentioned, cannot be equated with that of Elizabeth Inchbald, for it is without self-command and almost without sense; indeed it displays the sparkling, erratic firefly almost to the verge of lunacy. The character is a painful mixture of qualities, for with all its disastrous folly it is lovable. Miss Milner's vanity requires her to torment Dorriforth, but for the reason that she is deeply in love with him. She is at once generous and sweet-natured, overbearing and exasperating, and capable of such intensity of romantic passion that had it been thwarted she could have fretted herself actually to death. None of this is exactly Mrs. Inchbald, yet the qualities are an exaggeration of some of hers; the relative positions of the man and woman arouse in the latter that mixture of rebellion and submission which was her idea of passion, and there are gleams of revelation which recall her irresistibly. When Miss Milner is already completely captivated by Dorriforth, but is not aware of any return, the latter asks her to come to his library that evening to transact some business.

"She answered, 'I will, sir,' and her eyes swam with delight in expectation of the interview. Let not the reader nevertheless imagine there was in that ardent expectation one idea which the most spotless mind, in love, might not have indulged without reproach.... The height of her happiness was limited to a conversation in which no other but themselves took part."

Dorriforth succeeds unexpectedly to a family title and as Lord Elmwood he is released from his vows that he may be able to marry and continue a Catholic peerage in England. The mutual enlightenment between himself and Miss Milner results in their betrothal and the second phase of the affair is occupied by a tormenting struggle of wills. Miss Milner in her triumphant ecstasy is determined that Elmwood shall give proofs of his passion by ceasing to forbid or even criticize her wild gaieties and extravagances. She pushes him some way towards this state of spellbound subservience; meanwhile Sandford brings all his influence to bear on trying to break a connexion in which he can foresee nothing but unhappiness for Elmwood, and Miss Woodley, clear-sighted and apprehensive, does her best to control Miss Milner.

The break occurs at last, and Miss Milner is so stunned with shock and misery that her hopeless grief touches even her archenemy Sandford. All arrangements for the parting of the households have been made and Elmwood is to leave them after an early breakfast the next morning.

"'I was too weak to say I wished him happy,' cried Miss Milner, 'but heaven is my witness, I do wish him so from my soul!' 'And do you imagine he does not wish you so?' cried Sandford. 'You should judge him by your own heart and what you feel for him, imagine he feels for you, my dear.' Though 'My Dear' is a trivial phrase, yet from certain people and upon certain occasions it is a phrase of infinite comfort and assurance. Mr. Sandford seldom said 'my dear' to anyone, to Miss Milner never; and upon this occasion and from him, it was an expression most precious."

The climax is reached the next morning when Miss Milner, though unable to eat or drink, has crept into the dining-room to give the appearance of friendly farewell.

"Lord Elmwood now went up to Miss Milner and taking one of her hands held it between his but still without speaking; while she unable to suppress her tears as heretofore suffered them to fall in torrents.

"'What is all this?' cried Sandford, going up to them in anger. They neither of them replied nor changed their situation.

"'Separate this moment,' cried Sandford, 'or resolve to be separated only by—death!'" He admits he is now convinced that their marriage is essential to the happiness of both and taking a prayer-book from the shelves, marries them where they stand.

Mrs. Inchbald's imagination was a limited one but its power within its own confines is shown by the fact that this is not the end of her novel, but of the first half. Up to the marriage of Lord Elmwood and Miss Milner the book might be called a daydream, vigorous and objective in presentation though it is. In the second part it becomes detached from any possible imaginative connexion with the writer. The second volume is sometimes spoken of as a landmark in the development of the novel of "feeling", and is thought to have contributed inspiration to *Jane Eyre*.

It opens after a gap of seventeen years. Lord Elmwood's marriage, ideally happy for four years, has broken up; the faithlessness of his wife during his absence abroad has caused him to separate from her. The impossibility she found of living without emotional excitement and support during her husband's prolonged absence had not meant any lessening of her love for him, but she had enough sense to realize that the effect of her conduct on his love for her has been fatal. She fled from his arrival and in his annihilating anger he sent their six-year-old daughter after her, afraid of the agony of being continually reminded of the child's mother. The seventeen years since the marriage have brought Lady Elmwood to a last illness and at her death she sends their daughter back to her father. Lord Elmwood makes an establishment for the sixteen-year-old Matilda and the ageing and still faithful Miss Woodley in a wing of his country seat Elmwood Castle, on the strictest understanding that during his infrequent visits the girl is never to come in his sight.

Matilda, very much like her mother to look at but without her unfortunate temperament, with her father's seriousness but without his sternness, now leads the life of a romantic recluse, centring all her emotions upon her absent father. She fearfully obeys his orders to seclude herself during his presence in the castle and has never laid eyes on him. One day, however, Lord Elmwood, who has already left the castle, returns unexpectedly to deal with some papers.

"One beautiful morning about eleven o'clock seeing Miss Woodley on the lawn before the house, Matilda hastily took her hat to join her, and not waiting to put it on, went nimbly down the great staircase with it hanging on her arm." She hears, most unexpectedly, a man's tread on the stairs below her; before she can stop herself, she is round the bend of the staircase and Lord Elmwood is immediately in front of her.

"The authority in his looks as well as in the sound of his steps...but above all, her fears, confirmed that it was he. She gave a scream of terror, put out her trembling hands to catch the balustrades for support, missed them and fell motionless into her father's arms." Lord Elmwood, who has instinctively caught her, is about to lower her to the ground and leave her to other helpers, but she opens her eyes and utters: "Save me!" "Her voice unmanned him. His long restrained tears now burst forth and seeing her relapsing into the swoon he cried out eagerly to recall her. Her name did not however come to his recollection—nor any name but this: 'Miss Milner—Dear Miss Milner!'"

It would tax a novelist of major rank to continue, after such an episode, without anti-climax. Mrs. Inchbald's mechanical contrivance for forcing Lord Elmwood to give way to the feelings that have been so suddenly raised has at least the negative virtue of not being impossible. He banishes Matilda and Miss Woodley to a small cottage where Matilda begins to droop and become ill and this situation, which seems as if it might continue indefinitely, is abruptly ended by an alarm brought to Elmwood Castle that Matilda has been abducted by a titled hooligan in the neighbourhood. When her father has rescued her, he no longer thinks of parting from her. The marriage to her young cousin Rushbrooke who adores her and whom she has always angrily rejected because she knew his advances would displease her father, is a matter of slight moment only because it was out of the author's power to create another emotional situation which would compare in intensity with the scene on the staircase.

For the time being Mrs. Inchbald put the draft by. In June of that year she had much else to think about. She and her husband were at Leeds, in a company under the management of Tate Wilkinson. It was a fine Sunday morning and Mrs. Wilkinson called at their lodgings to invite the Inchbalds to Sunday dinner. Inchbald was not yet up. Mrs. Inchbald was looking particularly lovely. Mr. Wilkinson, who admired her extremely, said that on that day "she looked beyond herself, a goddess, not a mortal, and appears so languishly sweet as if secure of all beholders' hearts". The invitation was accepted, but while the guests were waited for, as Wilkinson was about to carve the duck, a message was brought that Inchbald had died suddenly in his bed.

Horrified by the appalling suddenness of the death, everyone was kindness itself to the widow. Her friends and well-wishers in the various towns where the company was known now expected that she would marry Kemble. It seemed like perversity on her part to disappoint these expectations, but no doubt the fault did not lie with her. Boaden said of them: "Kemble would never have borne with the independent temper of her mind."

She now settled herself in London, changing to various addresses in and around Leicester Square. London had always been the goal of her wishes; she said herself that she "could hardly bear to live out of it". Now she established that reputation for living in "poverty, elegance and cheerfulness" that never left her. However humble her surroundings, it was said, "she always knew either how to give some pleasant property to her abode or by her personal charm to render it of no moment". In the same idiom, her dress was described as "always becoming but very seldom worth as much as eightpence". Her reputation for chastity was current at the same time and though admired by many was thought by some to be the reverse of admirable. The satirist Peter Pindar addressed some verses to her which, though in a disagreeable version, give an interesting picture of her attitude to men:

> *Eliza, when with female art*
> *You seem to shun and yet pursue,*
> *You act a false, a soulless part,*
> *Unworthy love, unworthy you.*

Reluctance kills the rising bliss,
Half-granted favours I disdain.
The honeyed lips that I would kiss
Are gall unless they kiss again.

No passive love that silent takes
All I can give without return;
Be mine the frame that passion shakes,
The liquid eye, the lips that burn!

Most of the men whom she fascinated did not get near enough to
be able to make such complaints. When they did they were usually
sent packing. Dr. Brodie was forbidden to come to the house again:
this was natural enough, but Colonel Glover proposed marriage,
and a marriage settlement that included a carriage and £500 a year.
Even now, it arouses regret that Mrs. Inchbald would not have
him. But she was now impatient of any idea of marriage to which
she could not attach some romantic lustre of her own peculiar kind.
There were men whom she would have been glad to marry.
Kemble, with unerring perception, she had long put out of her
mind in that connexion; but Sir Charles Bunbury and Dr.
Gisborne, both of whom had pursued her, disappointed her: the
baronet because he wanted only to make her his mistress; Dr.
Gisborne because, after establishing himself on a domestic footing
with her, he wanted her to listen to his plans for marrying somebody else. But with neither was she so deeply engaged as she was in
those affairs completely divorced from any possibility of tangible
result. Her devotion to the famous Dr. Warren, all fire and air as it
was, engrossed her as she loved, as she lived, to be engrossed. "If she
hears but his name in company she is delighted with the word."
She described in her diary her practice of walking up and down
Sackville Street watching whether there were lights in his apartments, and following his carriage about town for the chance of
looking at him.

These schoolgirlish infatuations would have made most women
ludicrous, but her friends as a whole always treated Mrs. Inchbald
with a kind of indulgent tenderness. The absurdity was less keenly
felt in a woman so very pretty that she could, clearly, have had all
the success in the world if she would have been content to take it
where she found it. The morose Godwin felt her charm, and

described her as "a piquante mixture between a lady and a milk-maid". He told Mary Shelley that "when Mrs. Inchbald came into a room and sat in a chair in the middle of it as was her wont, every man gathered round it and it was vain for any other woman to attempt to gain attention". Few women can have gathered so many compliments while seeming to care about them so little. Sheridan said she was the only authoress whose society pleased him; Charles Lamb called her "the only endurable clever woman" he had ever known.

From the standpoint of earning a livelihood, however, none of this affection and admiration was turned to account. Her precarious gains as an actress united to her simple and strictly economical way of living were for the first seven years of her widowhood her only means of support. Then in 1784 she tapped a new source of income. She wrote a short farce, *The Mogul Tale*, which was at once accepted and put on with success. This began her series of highly successful short comedies, and soon she had given up acting altogether and was engaged wholly in writing. Besides writing comedies, she edited a series of plays in twenty-five volumes under the title of *The British Theatre*, and translated and adapted several works of the German dramatist, Kotzebue. One, *The Love-Child*, which she renamed *Lover's Vows*, has acquired a kind of adventitious fame, for it was the play chosen for the amateur theatricals in *Mansfield Park*. It is amusing to read, in view of Miss Crawford's objections to the part of Amelia, that Mrs. Inchbald was considered to have toned down this character already. It was said of her version: "She has rendered the character of Amelia more delicate. There is no reserve at all in German passion."

With her energies now devoted to writing it was natural that Mrs. Inchbald should remember the seven-year-old draft of *A Simple Story*. She revised it, how much we do not know, but the striking likeness to Kemble in the hero she left unaltered, and no reader of this novel can fail to be reminded of its scenes when reading accounts by playgoers of the impression made on them by Kemble in his great parts. She sold the novel to the publisher Robinson, who brought it out in February, 1791, and its success was immediate. A second edition was called for the following month, and the book enjoyed a celebrity which no woman's novel had met with since the publication of *Evelina* thirteen years before.

This success encouraged Mrs. Inchbald to write a second novel, and *Nature and Art*, which she published in 1796, was also highly successful with the public but the greater part of it now reads as very inferior to *A Simple Story*. There is, however, one part of it which is almost as good as the best of the earlier book: it is an episode formed in that medium which was so dear to her, of a romantic connexion between a man and woman in which there is inequality of some sort which causes perpetual conflict. In *Nature and Art* this inequality is of a realistic and painful kind: William, the son of a dean, a clever young man bred to the law, is an exceptionally cold and selfish character, but a subtly drawn one, for he is not destitute of human softness. He appreciates affection given to himself, and he is, at long last, capable of an agony of remorse. As a young man at his father's country seat he seduces a very charming, sensitive and innocent country girl called Hannah.

"Bred up with strict observance both of his moral and religious character William...never promised Hannah he would marry her;...he paid so much respect to the forms of truth that no sooner was it evident that he had obtained her heart, her whole soul entire—so that loss of innocence would be less terrifying than separation from him—no sooner had he perceived this than he candidly told her he could never make her his wife." His cousin Henry, who is honestly courting the parson's daughter, one evening sees William and Hannah together. "Henry observed his cousin's impassioned eye and her affectionate, yet fearful glance. William, he saw, took delight in the agitation of mind, in the strong apprehension mixed with the love of Hannah; this convinced Henry that either he, or himself, was not in love: for his heart told him that he would not have beheld such emotions upon the countenance of Rebecca, for the wealth of the universe."

When Henry speaks to William of the matter, the latter says:

"'I love her, but not enough, I hope, to marry her.'"

"'But too much, I hope, to undo her?'"

"'That must be her own free choice—I make use of no unwarrantable methods....If she should make me happy as I ask, and I should then forsake her, I shall not break my word.'"

Hannah finds herself with child and has no opportunity to tell William till the family come down to the country again. He has not conquered his passion for her but has already repented it. He visits her at dead of night, when "he grew so impatient at her tears and sobs, at the delicacy with which she with-held her caresses, that he burst into bitter upbraiding at her coyness and at length without discovering the cause of her peculiar agitation and reserve, abruptly left her, vowing never to see her again.

"As he turned away, his heart even congratulated him that he had made so discreet a use of his momentary disappointment as thus to shake her off at once without further explanation or excuse."

Hannah hopes for some time that he may find himself to blame, understand the cause of her behaviour and pity her. "In vain she watched, counted the hours and the stars and listened to the nightly stillness of the fields around; they were not disturbed by the tread of her lover.... She now considered his word, 'never to see her more' as solemnly passed, she heard anew the impressive, the implacable tone in which the sentence was pronounced; and could look back on no late token of affection on which to found the slightest hope that he would recall it."

Eighteen years later, William, who has condemned himself to the arid misery of a marriage with an eligible woman he thoroughly dislikes, has concentrated on his professional advancement as the only interest in his life and has become a High Court Judge at what Mrs. Inchbald admits is the unusually early age of 38. Hannah, whose career may be described as conventional merely because it was so true to the conditions of the time, has borne William's child, become outcast from her own circle and finally gravitated to London, where the harshness of the only sort of employment open to a woman who has lost her character eventually drives her into regular prostitution. With morbid tenacity she has never relinquished the memory of her lover:

"Day after day she watched those parts of the town through which William's chariot was accustomed to drive—but to see the carriage was all to which she aspired—a feeling, not to be described, forced her to cast her eyes upon the earth as it drew near to her—and when it had passed, she beat her breast and wept that she had not seen *him*."

The wished-for sight, however, is granted at last. Mrs. Inchbald seems to have been able to produce one outstanding scene in each of her novels: the scene in *Nature and Art*, though entirely different in circumstance from its predecessor, and being, if anything, even stronger in narrative power, nevertheless owes its inspiration to the same sort of romantic imagination; but in it the values are reversed; two scenes represent as it were the bright and dark sides of the moon. Hannah's lot has been cast in with coiners, and she as the weakest and most incompetent member of the gang is caught and prosecuted on the then capital charge of coining. The assize town in which she is tried is within fifty miles of London and no novel reader, at least, will find fault with the coincidence by which William happens to be the judge on that circuit. "She will now behold him, and he will see her, by command of the laws of their country. Those laws which will deal with rigour towards her, in this one instance are still indulgent." "Once a ray of hope beamed on her that if he knew her he might befriend her cause... but again, that rigorous honour she had often heard him boast, that firmness of his word, of which she had fatal experience, taught her to know he would not for any improper compassion, any unmanly weakness, forfeit his oath of impartial justice."

Hannah has become so altered that when she stands in the dock she is unrecognizable, but when she ventures to look at the judge: "She gave one fearful glance and discovered William, unpitying but beloved William in every feature! It was a face she had been used to look on with delight and a kind of absent smile of gladness now beamed on her poor wan visage."

"When every witness on the part of the prosecutor had been examined the judge addressed himself to her——

" 'What defence have you to make?' "

"It was William spoke to Hannah! The sound was sweet, the voice was mild, soft, compassionate, encouraging. It almost charmed her to a love of life! ... She did not call to mind that this gentleness was the effect of practice, the art of his occupation, which, at times, is but a copy by the unfeeling, from his benevolent brethren on the bench.... Again he put the question and with these additional sentences, tenderly and emphatically delivered: 'Recollect yourself. Have you no witnesses? No proof in your behalf?'

"A dead silence followed these questions. He then mildly but forcibly added: 'What have you to say?' Here a flood of tears burst from her eyes which she fixed earnestly upon him as if pleading for mercy, while she faintly articulated: 'Nothing, my Lord.' " The jury returned a verdict of "guilty" which Hannah hears with complete composure.

"But when William placed the fatal velvet on his head and rose to pronounce her sentence—she started with a kind of convulsive motion—retreated a step or two back, and lifting up her hands, with a scream exclaimed: 'Oh! not from *you!*'...Serene and dignified as if no such exclamation had been uttered, William delivered the fatal speech. She fainted as he closed the period and was carried back to prison in a swoon, while he adjourned the court to go to dinner."

The drawback to this scene is the same as that of its fellow in the previous novel: it creates an impasse from which the novelist of any but first-rate powers cannot go forward, and the rest of the tale is bathos. But though the part of the novel engaged with the adventures of William's naïve and upright cousin Henry is unconvincing and dull, the passages describing William himself and his psychological development are of a higher degree of insight and skill than anything in *A Simple Story*. The manner in which the softer and more human element in William's nature is introduced, making the rest not only credible but alarmingly real, has perhaps never been bettered in drawing a character of this unusual cast. The writer explains that though the judge as he sat down to his dinner had not the remotest idea that he had ever before seen the prisoner whom he had just sentenced, he had never forgotten Hannah. "In every peevish or heavy hour passed with his wife, he was sure to think of her—yet it was self-love rather than love of *her* that gave rise to these thoughts—he felt the want of female sympathy and tenderness to soften the fatigue of studious labour, to soothe a sullen, a morose disposition; he felt he wanted comfort for himself, but never once considered what were the wants of Hannah." When a letter from the gaol is brought to him after Hannah's execution he realizes who she was, and then discovers that their son whom she implores him to befriend is already dead.

"It wounded, it stabbed, it rent his hard heart as it would a tender one: it havocked on his firm, inflexible mind as on a weak and pliant brain....Robbed by this news of his only gleam of consolation, in the consciousness of having done a mortal injury for which he could never now by any means atone...he envied Hannah the death to which he had first exposed and then condemned her. He envied even the life she had struggled through from his neglect and felt that his future days would be far less happy than her former existence. He calculated with precision."

Even at the time the second novel did not equal the first in popularity, and during the last hundred and fifty years, while *A Simple Story* is remembered, *Nature and Art*, whose brilliant passages are not only painful but short in relation to the whole, has almost disappeared into oblivion. Nevertheless the success and fame of both were very important in Mrs. Inchbald's life; they heightened her importance with her already enthusiastic private circle and spread that importance through a large public. In all, she made something over £5,000 by her novels, her plays and her editing work, and this sum, unlike many people who suddenly make money when they have been accustomed to poverty, she did not spend carelessly. She invested the greater part of each sum as she made it and gained herself a small income in the funds.

She had that rare and charming combination of economy and generosity. She supported one of her sisters who was an awkward family encumbrance, and to do this she was obliged to carry her taste for simple living farther than even she could wish. She wrote to a friend after she had been obliged to increase her payments to her sister:

"I say no to all the vanities of the world. I have not been in bed these five nights; my bed-chamber, due north, has a chimney that will not draw up the smoke. This might be remedied by a brick layer, and I might buy a curtain to the window, and a carpet for the floor to keep me warm, but I am resolved to be at no further expense." Her method of living with simplicity and elegance, making an attractive appearance in the world and doing all her own housework, seems less extraordinary to the women of today than it did to those of her own. She said in a letter of May, 1800:

"I have been very ill indeed and looked even worse than I was but since the weather has permitted me to leave off making my fire, scouring the grate, sifting cinders and all the etceteras of going up and down three pairs of long stairs with water or dirt I feel quite another creature. ... I am both able and willing to perform bodily hard labour but then the fatigue of being a fine lady the remaining part of the day is too much for any common strength. Last Thursday morning I finished scouring my bed-chamber while a coach with a coronet and two footmen waited at the door to take me for an airing."

Most of her time since she had settled in London for good she had lived in the environs of Leicester Square, in Frith Street, in

Castle Street, Leicester Fields, and in Great Russell Street, Covent
Garden. In 1810, however, she removed to St. George's Terrace,
Regent's Park. Though it was here that the bedroom chimney
would not draw, the place enchanted her, for the outlook combined
just those elements that were essential to her happiness.

"The trees tipped with golden leaves and the canal peeping
through their branches which are half-stripped, with the grass as
green as in spring, all delight my eye and almost break my heart. I
must have London, combined with the sun, the moon and the stars,
with land or with water, to fill my imagination and excite my
contemplation." These are strange words to come from a woman
whose social life was a continual triumph, for they show a creature
whose keenest emotions were experienced in solitude. *A Simple
Story* and *Nature and Art* reveal the same temperament, and in
keeping, too, are a series of memoranda she made for herself alone,
showing how strong were the memories, even, of her private
feelings.

In her pocket-book, Boaden found a curious list of notes against
dates, headed:

Account of my Septembers.

Septembers since I married.

These notes are written opposite the month of September in each
year. There is no clue as to why she invested this month with
particular importance, for of what might be considered the
important events of her life: her marriage, her meeting with John
Kemble, the publication of her novels, all belong to other months.
There can be no doubt however that September meant something
extraordinary in her mind. It can hardly be a coincidence that it
was a morning in September that Lord Elmwood and Matilda
encountered each other on the stair.

The Septembers noted in the pocket-book from 1798, when she
was forty-five, onwards, almost all contain references to that frightening perception of losing beauty and youth which makes a
woman, in its early and still unfamiliar stages, feel a stranger to
herself.

1798. London. Rehearsing *Lover's Vows*. Happy but for a suspicion
amounting almost to certainty of a rapid appearance of age in
my face.

1799. London. After *Lover's Vows*. And after having just sold a new German play, going into rehearsal—extremely happy but for the still nearer approach of age.

1801. London. After the death of my best friend in the world Mr. Robinson (the publisher of her novels) and in the suspicion of never more being as a young woman again, very happy but for my years.

1802. After feeling wholly indifferent about Dr. Gisborne, very happy but for ill health, ill looks, etc.

1803. After quitting Leicester Square probably for ever, after caring scarce at all or thinking of Dr. Gisborne, entertaining some hopes on the publication of my Life and some fears of an invasion by the French—very happy.

Mrs. Inchbald was now valuable as a journalist's commodity. One day she was startled by a loud knock at her door, upon which "a tall, black, vulgar-looking man entered. It was Phillips. The bookseller of St. Paul's Churchyard, a total stranger to me. He came to offer me £1,000 for my Life, without wishing to read a line of it beforehand."

In the end, in spite of the high price offered for what would have cost her little labour, she decided not to write her memoirs. To put it out of her power to recall her decision, she destroyed a number of her papers, and Boaden compiled his biography of her from the remains and from his own and other people's personal recollections.

That the most important episode of her life was her passion for Kemble it is hardly possible to doubt; and it is a remarkable illustration of how existence can be maintained on different planes at the same time; for besides the unrequited, hopeless passion which dominated her heart and soul and from which she never recovered in spite of lesser, temporary infatuations, there was also a practical, good-natured friendship with a busy man who was full of gratitude for her kindness. A characteristic note from Kemble in their middle years says that he will be perfectly satisfied with some professional arrangement "if I have you to manage for me, dearest". There was also the admiring affection, tinged with gallantry, that Kemble paid her as other men did. "Mr. Kemble has the pleasure of Mr. Twiss's company today at dinner and will be infinitely charmed to find the Tenth Muse at his table also." The

most vivid picture connected with this romance is given by
Kemble's niece Fanny, who had it from her mother. Mrs. Charles
Kemble told her daughter that Mrs. Inchbald was sitting with
another actress by the green-room fire, and Kemble himself was
standing near-by, while Mrs. Inchbald was "comically energetic in
her declaration of whom she could or would or never could or
would have married". "My Uncle John," said Fanny Kemble,
"excessively amused, at length said jestingly: 'Well, Mrs. Inchbald,
would you have had me?' 'Dear heart,' said the stammering beauty,
'I'd have j-j-j-jumped to have you!'"

No mind is altogether tranquil and unclouded, and the life of a
being who lives intensely in the imagination must experience the
variation of dark and bright to a greater extent than the rest of
humanity. The impression that Mrs. Inchbald left on the generality
of people who knew her was that of a woman independent, lively
and sweet, but she knew disappointment and grief. She would not,
however, console herself with any happiness other than her secret
kind. She knew loneliness, but if she had been afraid of it she would
have married Colonel Glover. Living as she did among people
whose livelihood, like her own, depended on the cultivation of
emotion, her existence was bound sometimes to be darkened by
disputes and misunderstandings, by omissions that were felt as
slights and preoccupations that seemed like wounding neglect.
Samuel Rogers said that shortly before her death when she was
over sixty he met Mrs. Inchbald in the street and she complained
that none of her friends would see her. She had just been turned
away from Mrs. Siddons's door, she said, and she knew Mrs.
Siddons was at home. Rogers spoke soothingly to her and led her
back to her own house where he left her, somewhat comforted.
Such states of mind were not surprising in a woman who was old
and tired.

As Elizabeth Inchbald lived most intensely in the sphere of
imagination, it is reasonable to judge her by her achievement
in that sphere also. The one scene by which she is remembered
as a writer not only displays her own capacity to its fullest
extent: it images in its small compass that entire emotional
satisfaction which the human kind as a whole awaits in some
further state of existence,

Where the traveller's journey is done.

The medium of the scene may be exaggerated or far-fetched, but the medium itself matters little, it is only the currency in which the value is conveyed. That value has never been more completely given than in the scene on the staircase where, in a September morning's light, the man in Kemble's splendid likeness holds the unconscious woman in his arms and calls her by the name of the dead love that is more real to him than his own existence.

CHAPTER 6

Becky Wells

She was exceptionally pretty: airy, vivid, bewitching and slightly crazy. One fact explains more of her history than anything else: her father died in a mad-house.

In 1781 the manager of a provincial theatre wanted an actress to play "Becky Chadwallader", the beautiful little dolt married to an elderly husband in Foote's farce *The Author*. He offered the part to the twenty-one year old Mary Wells. She was doubtful if she could play it, but the manager assured her that she had only to put her thumb in her mouth and look as usual to be Foote's creation to the life. He was right. She was so successful that she was offered an engagement at the Haymarket Theatre, where *The Author* was put on again for her, and here in July, 1781, her success was so brilliant that the unknown young actress became famous as "the greatest simpleton of her time".

There is some magical box-office value in the pretty idiot, properly exploited. Wycherly had proved it ninety years before with *The Country Wife,* of which great and savage original Foote's little farce was a much diluted imitation. It was natural that once Mary Wells had made her name as Becky Chadwallader, another vehicle of the same kind should be found for her as soon as it could be put together. In the following September a comic operetta, *The Agreeable Surprise,* was put on at the Haymarket. Mary Wells's part was that of the lovely, absurd dairymaid, Cowslip; her opposite number, the pedantic but enamoured schoolmaster, Mr. Lingo. The exiguous plot turns on the rolling-snowball manner in which the wife of a wealthy cheese-merchant comes to be mistaken for a Russian princess. Cowslip, huffed by the suggestion that she is an ignoramus, exclaims: "I could learn *you* somewhat if I had a mind, Mr. Schoolmaster, but it is a great secret, or I could tell you the big lady in the little parlour is the Princess Ruskifusky, how she killed seven whole Roman Emperors and how she'll be hanged in chains if she's catched, and I could have told you every word if I pleased, but you shan't know a syllabub of it from me, that you shan't, Mr. Schoolmaster." Mary Wells's success as Cowslip equalled her success as Becky Chadwallader. From now onwards she was called either Becky or Cowslip. Becky Wells became her accepted name.

Her mother, left a widow when Becky was a small child, had set up a tavern in Birmingham used a great deal by actors. Here Mrs. Davis got to know the manager, Robert Yates. Some years later she asked him for an engagement. The manager saw at once that Mrs. Davis would not do but he inquired about her daughter, whom he remembered as a child of six, singing a song about a bird: "Little, foolish, fluttering thing." When he saw the daughter he engaged her for juvenile parts: the Duke of York in *Richard III*, Prince Arthur in *King John*, Cupid in *A Trip to Scotland*. When she was eighteen, she met an actor called Wells. By the time they were playing the name parts in *Romeo and Juliet* they were in love with each other. Her own description is idyllic: "We rose from the tomb of the Capulets, happy in the idea of having inspired a mutual attachment."

Within a few months of the wedding Wells deserted her with heartless impudence, but the reason he gave for doing so was significant. He left a letter for Mrs. Davis saying: "Madam, As your daughter is too young and childish I beg you will for the present take her again under your protection." He promised to return and was never seen again. That perhaps would not have mattered, but he left behind a very awkward and distasteful reminder of himself—his name, which prevented Becky from taking the name of anybody else.

By the time she was twenty-two however her career would hardly have left her much leisure for married life. The season at the Haymarket was followed immediately by an engagement at Drury Lane, in which she was dazzling once again as Harriet in *The Jealous Wife*. Then she suddenly reappeared at the Haymarket. A grotesque production of *The Beggars' Opera* was running there, with the women's parts played by men and the men's by women. The beautiful Mrs. Cargill, who played Captain Macheath, nearly brought it to a standstill by eloping with the manager's son, but Becky Wells was rushed on in her place. The incongruity of this fairy-like creature with the swashbuckling part only spread her fame and gained her new admirers.

She was now well off and supported not only her mother but her two sisters. The managers kept her in work the whole time; her popularity with audiences was remarkable. Her youthful brilliance, her sparkling absurdity, that kittenish idiocy which in itself is a sexual attraction made her the rage of London playgoers and this at a time when the stage was already held by actresses of enormous fame. The extraordinarily harsh treatment which Becky appeared to have received from them, when, by all accounts, she was in high favour with everybody else, may have had more reason for it than shows on the surface. Mrs. Siddons was entering on the great period of her career, and second only to her was Miss Farren, who had for several years been under the protection of Lord Derby, and married him as soon as his first wife was dead. Both these actresses were not only at the top of their profession; they were quiet and serious in their private lives, they were neither extravagant, vain, quarrelsome nor mean; yet both of them appear to have behaved to Becky Wells with inexplicable hostility.

When Becky came down to Drury Lane for the first rehearsal of *The Suspicious Husband,* Miss Farren stared at her. "Good God, ma'am," she exclaimed, "are *you* to play Jacinta?" When Becky said yes, Miss Farren at once told the manager that in that case, she herself resigned the part of Clarinda. Becky did not wait for arbitration. She threw her script on the floor and went home. The management sent word after her to come back, that Miss Farren was under contract and *must* play with her. Some people would have thought the situation too uncomfortable to be tenable but Becky was satisfied with the victory. A little later however she received a more serious rebuff. Mrs. Siddons told the Drury Lane management that she would not play leads if secondary parts were given to Mrs. Wells. In her memoirs Becky reproached Mrs. Siddons and Miss Farren for their unkindness to one who earned her bread and was the sole support of a mother and two sisters. But Mrs. Siddons was not primarily concerned with what people did off the stage, but with what they did or were likely to do on it, particularly what they might do on it in company with her. Though no records remain of Becky's bad behaviour on the stage, unreliability or playing the fool, Mrs. Siddons's attitude and the only less important one of Miss Farren are somewhat ominous. A third piece of indirect evidence against her comes from an equally surprising source.

Becky surmounted the obstacle of not being permitted to play secondary parts to Mrs. Siddons's leads, by inducing the manager to give her first ones. For her benefit night when she might choose her own play, she chose to appear as Jane Shore. Though it was her first attempt at tragedy her success with the audience was immense. The critics said that her rendering of the part was unequal, that if she had been able to keep up her standard all the way through she need have feared comparison with no one. This was enough to encourage the managers to give her serious rôles. While playing Lady Randolph in *Douglas* she was supposed to faint and to be caught in the arms of an attendant lady who was played by the charming Elizabeth Inchbald. One night Mrs. Inchbald was not attending to what went on, and Lady Randolph would have fallen to the floor if one of the actors had not caught her in the nick of time. As the fall was backwards, it looked as if an accident were about to happen and several people in the audience screamed. Behind the scenes Becky improved the occasion by becoming hysterical. Mrs. Inchbald was spoken to sharply and told that her fellow-actress might have fractured her skull; to the general surprise she replied carelessly: "Then we should have had the tragedy *realized*."

It was hardly to be expected that so dazzling a creature, unencumbered with a husband, should be for very long without a lover. Somewhere about the year 1786, at the age of twenty-five or so, she contracted a liaison with a character of considerable notoriety, a Major Topham of the Life Guards. Topham was a dandy, an eccentric, a sportsman, a bon-viveur and also a man of outstanding journalistic ability. Becky said that she was captivated by his superior mind, but it may not be irrelevant to add that he was tall and of a rugged, aquiline handsomeness. Topham might, at the beginning, have been prepared to marry her but her disastrous marriage to Mr. Wells prevented this. She went to live with him in his house in Bryanstone Square and the ensuing few years were probably the happiest of her life. She bore children of whom three daughters survived, named after parts in which their mother had excelled, Juliet, Harriet and Maria Cowslip. In the intervals of child-bearing Becky continued to act. Antony Pasquin's verses on her, dated 1786, give a striking impression of her attractions. He ushers her in to the poem exclaiming:

'Tis Wells the resistless that bursts ⟨n the sight! and sums up his tribute in the words:

When she laughs, she enslaves—for that laugh is divine!

A portrait of her by John Downman in the character of Cowslip belongs to this era; it shows a very slender figure, a face of vivid colouring with large, over-bright eyes, the lips ajar in an insane smile. Though she is supposed to be a dairymaid, the clothes are in the extreme of fashion; the hat has a high, cylindrical crown with bows at each side of it. Perhaps a suggestion of rusticity is intended by the moss rose and its bud tucked into her bosom. The portrait is not only interesting as a facial likeness but it shows how her admirers saw her; it is their favourite idea of her personified. Though Becky was her official name, she was just as often called Cowslip. When Topham bought a small country-place in Essex, he called it Cowslip Hall. The common cowslip is an enchanting flower, graceful yet sturdy, of delicate and thrilling scent. To be called after that flower with its pale gold coat and ruby spots would suggest a character of charm, innocence and strength. But Parkinson in his *Herbal* cites another variety, the Foolish or Franticke Cowslip. One cannot but think that this was Becky's emblem.

Eccentricity and extravagance may, up to a point, be of use in keeping an actress before the public eye. Becky spent a great deal on dress and though she could look well in the simplest clothes her flamboyant, unself-conscious air enabled her to carry off the most elaborate toilettes. She adopted the eye-catching device of dressing inappropriately to the seasons, which only a creature whose perfect circulation made her indifferent to heat and cold could have borne to do. When other women wilted in muslin dresses, Becky appeared gay and vigorous, trimmed with furs. When they shivered and wrapped themselves up, Becky came among them in diaphanous draperies with bare neck and arms, glowing and radiant.

Topham was at first devoted to her, filled with passion and gallantry. Presently he found that she had abilities unconnected with the stage that made her useful as well as ornamental. He started a newspaper called the *World* which from the sternness with which it was censured and the avidity with which it was bought, seems to have been the forerunner of some at the present day. Hannah More was disgusted by its reports of elopements, divorces and suicides, and its rapidly increasing circulation caused *The Times* itself to publish the following statement of its own policy: "*The Times* shall be literally a *newspaper* and convey impartially and honestly to the public every article of intelligence that may be authentic and worth their notice," notwithstanding that such principles might cause the paper to be looked down on by "some *worldly* people". Topham showed his flair for sensational journalism both by the people he got to write for him and the material he used. "Perdita" Robinson, a cast-off mistress of the Prince Regent, lovely, injured and resentful, was one of his contributors. He had been a friend of John Elwes of Meggott, M.P. for Berkshire, who was afflicted with miserliness to the point of mental derangement. When Elwes died the breath was no sooner out of his body than Topham began to serialize an account of his friend's almost incredible parsimony. It was said that these grotesque details sent up the *World's* circulation a thousand a day.

One of the trials of the century was that of Warren Hastings on charges of corruption and cruelty in India, which opened in Westminster Hall in 1788. The crowds at the opening session were enormous. Topham was ruralizing at Cowslip Hall and in his absence he gave Becky the extremely important assignment of "covering" several days of the trial. Her method was remarkable. Topham's reporters were posted at the doors of Westminster Hall and Becky came down to them at intervals, pouring out an account of the proceedings to which she had been listening which the reporters took down from her lips and which the *World* published next morning. Making her way among the crowded benches she broke a bottle in her pocket. She said it contained lavender water. The reporters of *The Times* said it was brandy, and *The Times* carried next day a column headed: "Westminster Hall: Brandy v. Becky."

These activities did not prevent her from continuing a successful career on the stage. It was improbable that the same *dramatis personae* should contain parts which would make a rapprochement between Mrs. Wells and Mrs. Siddons necessary, but Becky sometimes found herself in the same cast with her old enemy Miss Farren. Mrs. Inchbald said that leading actresses who preserved few remains of reputation were exceedingly tenacious of what they had. One night, she said, when the company were dressing, some accident happened to the dressing-room of an actress "of known intrigue"; pressed for time the lady rushed into Mrs. Wells's dressing-room to finish her toilette. Mrs. Wells, "shocked at the intrusion of a woman who had a worse character than herself", jumped up exclaiming: "What would Major Topham say if I were to remain in such company?"—and flew for refuge into Miss Farren's dressing-room. No sooner did she appear than Miss Farren flew out of the door, repeating: "What would Lord Derby say if I should be seen in such company?"

Though Becky was so scrupulous in her regard for Major Topham's honour she allowed herself a good deal of latitude at least as regards absurd behaviour. In the summer months she often had engagements at provincial theatres, at Cheltenham, Brighton, Weymouth, where it was a source of pride to her that she was now offered the same terms as Mrs. Siddons. At the latter resort King George III was taking sea air and bathing, recuperating from one of his fits of madness. The King used to sail in the bay, accompanied by Queen Charlotte, and Becky, hiring a yacht for herself, "attended him in all his excursions." The King was aware of her fame and at first it interested and pleased him to see her. He would exclaim: "Mrs. Wells—Wells—Wells! Good Cowslip—fond of the water, eh?" But Becky's attendance was so persevering that he began to be alarmed by it. "Wherever His Majesty cast his eye over the blue element, there was the barque of Becky careering in pursuit of him", with Becky "reposing on the deck in all the languor and sumptuousness of Cleopatra." Things came to such a pass that whenever the King saw a sail he would say eagerly: "It's not Wells, is it?" or if it could not be mistaken he would exclaim in dismay: "Charlotte, Charlotte! Here's Wells again!" The story is related by the manager John Bernard, who got to know it himself all too late. Bernard was managing the theatre at Plymouth when the King was expected in the neighbourhood. Becky, "in flying finery of dress and buoyancy of person" a fit comparison with the pleasure yacht that bore her, sailed into the town and offered Bernard her services. The delighted manager, thinking that the presence of Mrs. Wells would be sure to draw the Royal party, went to great expense to enclose the pit as boxes. When he was commanded to submit his programme to Queen Charlotte, he mentioned that the company had received the addition to Mrs. Wells of Covent Garden, whereupon it was intimated to him that the Royal party would not be visiting his theatre. Bernard then heard, too late to do him any good, that Becky's foible was to imagine that any man who saw her, loved her, and that she had frequently insisted on Topham's calling out noblemen and ministers six at a time to avenge the insulted dignity of her feelings. But, added Bernard, "this depopulation of all the squares at the West End was a task he declined."

Lovely as she was, she had, probably, never been easy to live with, and growing abberation may have made her impossible. Perhaps the great affection for his daughters of a man who becomes a father late in life made Topham decide that he must consider their future before their mother's. Becky exclaims in the opening pages of her *Memoirs:* "That woman who can confidently listen to the empty promises of *man* deserves every misery the world can inflict." It is next door to impossible to assign dates to the events in her life for which her *Memoirs* are the only source, for she avoids dates almost altogether and introduces each fresh episode by "Now": but for whatever reason and however long it took to conclude these arrangements, Major Topham left town with Juliet, Harriet and Maria Cowslip and established them in Yorkshire at Wolds Cottage near Thring under the care of their grandmother, Mrs. Davis.

Becky meanwhile had accepted the protection of Topham's friend, Frank Reynolds, a lawyer manqué who had become a most prolific and tolerably successful dramatist. This gentleman had enough sensibility to be charmed by the Foolish or Franticke Cowslip, and sufficient coolness not to mind very much what she did. The trouble that dogged her steps was a heavy load of debt, made worse by her having rashly stood surety for a man called Samuel who had married one of her sisters. The pair had gone to India, Samuel promising to send back the money, no penny of which was ever received. Reynolds could not clear Becky but he hid her away in the country and took her over to France when creditors became threatening, while Topham arranged with them to accept instalments of her future salary. He pointed out that she could earn money as soon as they allowed her freedom to do it. She spent two periods at least in the care of Dr. Willis, who had a lunatic asylum run on enlightened lines, and who was said to have been successful in his treatment of the King. Her own pathetic explanation of the time passed in Willis's establishment is that Topham wanted to place her there so as to negative her accounts of his ill-treatment of her and that she consented to go there as a means of evading her creditors.

The saying that birds of a feather flock together is justified by the next chapter of her adventures, for she now connected herself with a person so preposterous that her worst enemy must have thought even Becky Wells outmatched. A young Moorish Jew called Joseph Sumbel had inherited, with his two brothers, a large fortune from their father, one-time prime minister to the Emperor of Morocco. Sumbel had calmly appropriated his brothers' shares of the money and his flight from the gorgeous East had brought him to Willesden Green, where he concealed India bonds to the amount of £5,000 in the hollow of an old tree, "which he could never afterwards find out". His extraordinary appearance and the fact that his pockets were inconveniently crammed with diamonds soon attracted public notice, and before long, his brothers having got a judgment against him which he refused to obey, he was put into the Fleet prison for contempt of court. He came into its confines with a train of menials bringing clothes, dishes, furnishings, wine and food for his use and his entrance naturally made a stir among the other prisoners. Seeing among them, staring at him, a woman of uncommon beauty, elegantly and fancifully dressed, Sumbel graciously invited her to dine with him. His guest was Becky Wells, detained in the Fleet by the creditors of her odious brother-in-law.

The acquaintance of these two brilliant and exotic figures, conspicuous against the murky background of the Fleet's precincts, developed rapidly and in a few days' time Sumbel asked her to marry him. Becky may have confused herself with the heroines of *The Mourning Bride*, *The Fair Penitent* or *Venice Preserved*, whom she had often played upon the stage, with Almeria, Calista or Belvidera who, lovely as angels and in full court dress, are discovered in a dungeon or a vault, plighting themselves or reaffirming their vows in torrents of blank verse. It looked at first, however, as if the absent Wells might deter her from assuming this rôle in real life, but she took advice—from whom she does not say—and was assured that if she became a Jewess her previous marriage need not stand in the way of her marrying Mr. Sumbel. Becky accordingly embraced the Jewish faith as rapidly as the process could be put through and was married under the name of Leah Sumbel.

The wedding, celebrated in the Fleet prison, reads like some episode from the *Arabian Nights*. A huge silver-framed mirror surrounded by sparkling masses of wax lights was set up in a gallery which led to a room, entirely draped in pink satin. The bridegroom wore a European suit of white satin with a turban, plumed with white ostrich feathers and enriched with diamonds. One of his brothers, sinking the cause of disagreement for the time being, appeared beside him in pink satin. A profusion of food and drink was served on silver dishes. One incongruous note was struck by the appearance of some guests of the bridegroom's party, who turned out to be old-clothes men from the neighbourhood, hastily convened. A strange old character called Abbo who had proposed to Becky at the time Mr. Sumbel had made his addresses, and been refused, had brooded over his repulse in silent malignity and now reappeared, meaning to assassinate the bride, but in this he was happily prevented. The festivities lasted a week. At their conclusion, Mr. Sumbel handed over to his brother the sum of £20,000 and the couple were released.

They at once set up house in splendid quarters in Pall Mall. Here Becky, surrounded by fantastic luxury, might have enjoyed herself had it not been for Sumbel's domestic behaviour, which was both despotic and half-witted. The advantages of the position were not ones which meant very much to her once the novelty had worn off and the disadvantages were those which a wild, eccentric nature like hers found increasingly irksome. The house was over-full of rich, luxurious things, many of them in the oriental taste, but the doors were locked and the windows shut and she was never allowed to have a shilling in her pocket, in case she ran away. She was given magnificent diamonds to wear when they went out, but deprived of them as soon as she and her husband returned home. One night she demurred at this. Sumbel was maddened by the least opposition, and as she was not quick enough to suit him in taking off a diamond ear-ring, he tore it through the lobe of her ear.

His ridiculous arrogance and his violent temper led him into such outbreaks against all and sundry that he felt obliged to leave his house to avoid being arrested for assault and Becky persuaded him to take a journey up to Yorkshire so that she could see her children at Wold Cottage. The miseries of the long, uncomfortable, freezing journey were deliberately prolonged to torment her impatience by the abominable Sumbel, who, to make up for having to wear European clothes in the carriage, had all his trunks unpacked at every inn so that at night he might sit cross-legged on the floor in the splendour of an Eastern potentate. At length she could endure no more but set off on foot for the last stage of the journey. Her daughters were wild with delight at seeing her. The eldest came out of the barn carrying a sieve of grain to feed the fowls, and screamed at the sight of her: "Our mother! Our mother!" And Becky had "six little arms round her neck at once." Their father might think her an unsuitable parent but she had sent them three little hats wreathed with cowslips and in their eyes she was a creature of visionary brightness.

After innumerable sufferings, humiliations and mishaps at the hands of Sumbel, who seemed to be animated by a mindless ferocity, Becky found herself in London once more. Sumbel now determined to go back to Morocco, where he thought he would follow his father as prime minister. He nearly succeeded in carrying her off in a ship bound for Mogadore, by taking her, as she thought, to dine on board while it lay at anchor. She overheard by chance that the ship was about to sail and got herself rowed to shore just in time. Sumbel came after her; his anger was so great that he bought a case of pistols and fired them over her as she lay in bed. She had him bound over to keep the peace and he retaliated by refusing to pay the rent for the house in Pall Mall because the original negotiations with the landlord had been conducted by her. When the landlord sued him, Sumbel thought he could evade his obligation by declaring that he was not a Jew but a Mohammedan. As this consideration was deemed irrelevant by the court and judgment given for the landlord, Sumbel drew all his money from the bank and without a word to Becky, quietly left the country and was said afterwards, for she never saw or heard from him again, to have spent the rest of his life in Denmark.

The relief of his absence was great, though it meant that the creditors were at her again and she dropped into an existence in and out of jail. She had not lost all her charm. A Captain Blackwood saw her in the King's Bench Prison, released her and took her to a cottage at Merton. When his regiment was posted to the West Indies he begged her to accompany him. She refused; she says she did so, not wishing to leave England on account of

BECKY WELLS

She was exceptionally pretty: airy, vivid, bewitching and slightly crazy.
One fact explains more of her history than anything else: her father died
in a madhouse.

HARRIETTE WILSON

She went on from conquest to conquest. Men pursued her headlong; they
worshipped her, but neglected their obligation to see her provided for.

her daughters, and adds that it was a decision she had cause to repent long since.

The little creatures who had screamed with delight at the sight of her were now young ladies. Their father had had them most carefully brought up and had at last forbidden their mother to have any connexion with them. Becky had no idea of being dictated to on such a matter. When her circumstances allowed her to be at liberty she determined to make another journey into Yorkshire. She arrived at Scarborough and set out to walk sixteen miles to Wold Cottage. She had not gone many miles when she saw approaching three ladies on horseback followed by a groom; they were her daughters coming into Scarborough to order their ball dresses. The blank young faces looked down in dismay at the wild, unkempt figure who hailed them from the road. The eldest took command and told her sisters to ride on with the groom. Then she told her mother that if Becky would walk on, another thirteen miles, to an inn, and wait there, they would stop and see her on their way back. Becky, burning with anger, scorn and wounded affection, walked on and gained the rendezvous; presently the eldest daughter arrived, dismounted, and in embarrassment, perplexity and emotion, spoke to her mother and then took her in her arms. Becky was obliged to relinquish her, but the girl promised to return next day. But their father meanwhile had heard of Becky's arrival in the neighbourhood, and he absolutely forbade his daughters to see her again. She found humble lodgings at a farmhouse. The shoes had worn off her feet and she walked barefoot about the wolds, hoping for a sight of her children which was never realized. A kind woman gave her a pair of shoes and in them she made her way back to London.

In the last years of her life she provided the material for her *Memoirs,* which someone else wrote down for her. Occasionally she gave an evening of her Imitations, when a ghost of the famous gaiety and charm was called up that could draw an audience still. She was allowed relief from the Theatrical Fund. It was said that she drank. If she did, one can but hope that drink drowned the memory of the Yorkshire wolds.

Her spirits were unquenchable and the last sight of her that was transmitted to the public was almost worthy of her brilliant past. The John Bernard who had suffered from her at Plymouth had been to America for several years. He returned to England in 1821,

E

and he suddenly encountered Becky in a street leading to Westminster Bridge. "Though old and faded she was still buoyant and loquacious." A rough-looking young man was with her, and after a few minutes, Bernard said he must not keep her friend waiting. Becky exclaimed: "Friend! He's no friend, he's my husband!" She took the young man's hand, singing:

> *And haven't you heard of the jolly young waterman*
> *That at Westminster Bridge used to ply?*

Then, like a piece of flotsam, bobbing up and down through the streams of coal-heavers, porters and passengers, she disappeared over the bridge.

CHAPTER 7

Harriette Wilson

When people threatened to publish anything scandalous about the Duke of Wellington, the Duke's stock reply was: "Publish and be damned." To Harriette Wilson, he said: "Publish and be hanged." The language was a little softened to a female, but it meant the same thing. Harriette took him at his word; in 1825 she published *Harriette Wilson's Memoirs of Herself and Others*.

Harriette had had a brilliant career as a courtesan, but she spent money as fast as she got it and she was now forty and in want of funds. She had declined in beauty, celebrity and success, though not in spirits, for hers were always high; she saw that the future did not offer her much and she decided to coin the past. Her lovers had almost all been men of rank and distinction; they were not particularly ready after an interval of ten or fifteen years to contribute to Harriette's support, but neither were they, in most cases, indifferent to the idea of seeing episodes of their past described in a *chronique scandaleuse* that was bound to have an enormous sale. Harriette had always taken a severe view of men who refused her requests for money, and over the past years her resentment against them had been rising. Henry Brougham, who was always kind to her, told her that she must not write this book. She replied: "Why don't my old friends keep me among them? They are all rich. I have applied to them and they refuse me the bare means of existence. Must I not strive to live by my wits?" When Harriette let it be known that she was writing her memoirs and that it was open to any gentleman to buy himself out of them, several were found amenable to the threat, but she should have known better than to approach the Duke of Wellington with any such proposal. She had proved his kindness and generosity many times in an acquaintance of twenty years: it appeared she still had something to learn about his other characteristics.

The book she produced is so full of entertainment that from the reader's point of view it would have been a loss if anything had prevented her from writing it. Her portraits are so vivid, we feel, as we read, that they must be first-rate likenesses. It is afterwards that we begin to ask ourselves how far she ought to be believed. Fortunately there exists a means of testing the accuracy of some at least of what she says, and of getting into clearer focus her own figure, which she presents to us as a wild, unaffected, generous, careless and astonishingly lovely creature. In the complexity of human nature it might even be allowed that she was all this, though she had also a side so grim and terrifying it recalls those pictures in old-fashioned moral works that represent vice as something hideous.

Harriette was born in 1786, so that when she burst upon the demi-monde of London it was the London of the Prince Regent. We may see its beauties in aquatints, where the pale, stuccoed house-fronts with their pillared porticos are uncontaminated by smoke and grime, and ladies trail nymph-like dresses of pale pink, lilac and sky-blue unconcernedly across the pavements. The aquatints do not show the slums with their ferocious horrors of disease and death by starvation, but they were there like an abyss beneath the feet of the prosperous classes and people who lived by their wits knew where failure would lead them. The struggle for survival in the face of such a menace was one that left no room for quarter.

Harriette was born in a small house in Queen Street, Mayfair. Her father was a clever, bad-tempered Swiss mathematician called Dubochet who practised as a watchmaker. Her mother, the illegitimate child of a country gentleman, was a great beauty but worn down by the cares of fifteen children and too timid to assert herself against an overbearing husband. From her, however, the daughters of whom we hear anything, Fanny, Amy, Harriette and Sophia, inherited not only beauty but elegance and taste; they received from her also a knowledge of good manners, if they did not invariably put it into practice.

Harriette says with startling frankness that she was lovely and fascinating, but pictures bear her out. She was small and slight with a full bosom and a very slender waist. Her black hair hung round her head in a curtain of ringlets. Her face was oval, her nose short and slightly aquiline. Her hazel eyes ringed with long black lashes were very fine but their expression was disconcerting; there was a stare in them, bright and stony. In her manner she was the graceful hoyden, wild and excitable. She galloped on horseback with her feathers and her hair blowing about her ears, and thought nothing, when no carriage was available after the theatre, of walking from Pall Mall to Camden Town in full evening dress with her shawl over her head. Scott said he had once had supper in her society, "when the company was more fair than honest." He denied that she was beautiful, but said she had black hair and fine eyes, "a smart, saucy girl with manners like a wild schoolboy."

At fourteen, her father, hearing of the opening, sent her to teach French and music in a girls' boarding-school in Newcastle. It was freezing cold in Newcastle, the day began at 6 a.m., the meals left her always hungry and in the evening perpetual shirt-making was on hand. The headmistress "took in" the work, for which she drew the pay while her assistants did it for nothing. After a brief but impressive experience of Miss Kittredge and her establishment, Harriette returned home avid for pleasure.

Queen Street is modest in itself but it lies between Berkeley Street, Piccadilly and Park Lane, what was then the most aristocratic residential neighbourhood of London. A near neighbour of the Dubochet household was Lord Craven, to whom Monsieur Dubochet's crew of lovely daughters had long been known. Harriette's *Memoirs* opens with the words: "I shall not say how or why I became at fifteen the mistress of the Earl of Craven." Lord Craven was an elderly man who wore a cotton nightcap and was fond of drawing pictures to illustrate his military exploits. "'Here stood the enemy,' he would say, 'and here, my love, are my fellows, there, the cocoa-trees.' It was, in fact, a dead bore. All those cocoa-trees and fellows, at past eleven o'clock at night." Nevertheless, this irksome liaison launched Harriette on her profession. From thenceforward, calling herself, why, she does not say, Harriette Wilson, she went on from conquest to conquest in what, if the rebuffs and failures and shifts and misfortunes are suppressed, and only the successes, the enjoyments and the brilliant public appearances dwelt on, seems a triumph of beauty and the power of captivating men. Not that Harriette ever wishes to conceal the financial hardships she suffered, but quite the contrary. Her account of her affairs is apt to follow a formula: men pursued her headlong, they would not take no for an answer, and while they worshipped her they neglected their solemn obligation to see her properly provided for. She was too childishly careless and disinterested to attend to financial matters and they took advantage of her. In a word, she never cared about money and she ought to have been given a great deal.

Lord Craven turned her off in virtuous dismay because he found her intriguing with Fred Lamb, Lord Melbourne's second son. Fred Lamb, though agreeably young, proved alternately ardent and neglectful and was mean with his money, but in his company she was able to attract the Duke of Argyll. As Argyll's mistress she entered the most brilliant phase of her career. Nineteen years old, in the height of youthful beauty with a child's powers of enjoyment, she was so irresistible that she met with many more advances than she chose to accept, and for the time being the passion she aroused was much stronger than any that she felt. She was one of the brightest stars in that peculiar society which in its freedom and its segregation was unlike anything today. It was frequented openly by men of the highest fashion and distinction and completely closed to their wives and daughters and to respectable women in general. Harriette felt herself immensely superior to the women who looked down on her but their position vis-à-vis her own gave her a sense of galling inferiority. She can scarcely mention a woman in society without uttering a slander or a sneer. She perpetually derides her sister, the blonde young Sophia, for her lack of intelligence and lack of temperament. Sophia at sixteen became the Viscountess Berwick.

With her other two sisters Harriette had a more intimate relationship: Fanny she loved dearly, with Amy she was always quarrelling. Fanny lived quietly; she had been the mistress of a Mr. Woodcock for seven years until his death; she was now living with Colonel Parker. Fanny had the family beauty, but unlike her sisters she was calm and radiant, with a seraphic sweetness of nature. In company, Harriette said, Fanny was a Refuge for the Destitute, always taking under her protection any man who was ugly or unattractive or unfortunate. Lord Hertford, the original of Lord Steyne in *Vanity Fair*, was one of Fanny's admirers. He wanted her to be painted by Lawrence. "That laughing, dark blue eye of hers is unusually beautiful," he said.

Amy was entirely different: good-looking as her sisters, but dark and fierce, with a jealous disposition, and always, so Harriette said, on the look-out to annex Harriette's men. Amy was under the protection of a Mr. Sydenham. She was fond of giving parties: her tray-suppers of cold chicken and claret after the opera were famous, and it was felt to be something of a grievance that Mr. Sydenham insisted on having the house cleared by three in the morning. It was at one of these parties in Amy's drawing-room— "the room was very full"—that Harriette gives a conversation-piece of the Three Graces at their most brilliant. These were not the three sisters, but Fanny, Harriette and their friend Julia Johnstone. Harriette was living in Somers Town when she discovered this lady, whose beauty was of a dark and melancholy cast, in deep but elegant retirement in Primrose Cottage, Primrose Hill. "There was something dramatic about Julia," Harriette said. "I often surprised her hanging over her harp so very gracefully, the room so perfumed, the rays of her lamp so soft, it appeared arranged for a purpose, like a scene in a play." Julia turned out to be a niece of Lord Carysfoot. Her family had thrown her off because she had been seduced by Colonel Cotton, under whose protection she was now living, by whom she had six small children. Unlike Harriette, who despised and kicked against the social conventions, Julia accepted her outcast state while she mourned over it. She was, to begin with at least, very glad of the friendship of the Dubochet sisters; rather older, not so beautiful or so magnetic, yet she was found fit to make a third with Fanny and Harriette and their frequent appearances together earned them their title.

On the occasion of Amy's party which Harriette describes, Fanny was wearing a pale-pink crape dress, her bare arms decorated with bracelets of plaited hair, clasped with rubies. She was the most unselfconscious of professional beauties. "Fanny would lay her laughing face on her folded arms, reclining on a table, while she made some odd reflections," never giving a thought to how she looked, in a company whose every glance and movement was calculated. "With her unadorned auburn curls waving carelessly round her dark-blue eyes and beautiful throat, she seemed the most desirable object in the room." Julia wore a silver lamé dress with large transparent sleeves and a Turkish turban of bright blue fringed with gold. "There was a voluptuous and purely effeminate languor about Julia's character which was well adapted to the Eastern style of dress." Harriette says in one page of her *Memoirs* that she herself never cared for anything money could buy except bread and milk and clean linen, but here she says in some detail that her evening dresses were always white, white gauze over satin, and that though she never wore ornaments in her hair because she was so proud of it, her earrings on this occasion were unusually long and made of rubies, diamonds and turquoises.

She never gives a date: "Ladies scorn dates," she says. "Dates make ladies nervous," but this picture of the Graces is probably contemporary with her connexion with Argyll, who, according to Harriette, resented the frequent visits made to her by the Duke of Wellington when the latter was in London from time to time during the Peninsular War. One night Wellington came to her house when Argyll was already with her. Argyll put on Harriette's dressing-gown and a cap and pretended to be her housekeeper, poking his head out of the window and crying shrilly: "Sir, you must please to call out your name or I daren't come down." Wellington took off his hat and held up his face under the street lamp. "While the rain was trickling down his nose, his voice trembling with rage and impatience cried out: 'You old idiot, do you know me now?'" Argyll began to quaver out that they were frightened of thieves, as the new water-butt had already been stolen out of the area, and Wellington went off with imprecations. Harriette says of her method of writing: "I neglect dates and relate anecdotes together which happened at different times, but happen they did." Taking her own description as accurate, we may credit this incident but decline to believe that it happened as she said it did on the very evening of Wellington's return from Spain (possibly in 1808 after the Battle of Vimiero) while cannon were firing salutes and illuminations blazing in the streets.

Apart from the affection she shows for Fanny, the most sympathetic part of Harriette's *Memoirs* is her account of her passion for Lord Ponsonby. The three years which this liaison lasted belong, again, to her early years, probably her early twenties. She had become infatuated with Lord Ponsonby from seeing him riding about Hyde Park followed by a large dog. Ponsonby, the eldest brother of Lady Caroline Lamb, was nearly forty, pale, grave and very handsome, dressed always in black. In the, then, almost rural quiet of Hyde Park and Park Lane, a striking girl who was constantly in his path, gazing at him with adoring wonder, could hardly fail to attract Lord Ponsonby's attention in the long run. Her youth and beauty, the admiration she aroused in other men and her passion for himself created a response, for though he had a young wife to whom he was very much attached, Lady Ponsonby was more like a child to him than a companion. The mutual passion, the tenderness, the absorbing happiness of his affair with Harriette are described with a moving simplicity. She never, even, makes her usual complaint about money. Ponsonby was not well-to-do for a man of his rank and he did not surround her with luxury but, she says, he always "took care" of her.

After three years of ideal happiness, without one word of warning or one sign of declining affection, one evening when she was expecting him, a letter was brought saying that they must part for ever. The thing had happened to her which women would say could not happen, were it not that it happens so often. She became ill, exhausted with crying and unable to eat. One bright moonlight night at nearly one o'clock, haunting the street in front of his house, she saw him suddenly turn the corner out of Park Lane into Upper Brook Street and rap at his front door. She tried to cross the street to reach him but an iron bar seemed before her breast. The collapse which followed this scene was the prelude, she says, to an attack of scarlet fever. When she was recovering she promised Fanny and the family doctor that she would take care of herself for the future; to herself she promised never to love again.

She went back to the old round. Amy's parties continued and Amy's snatching of Harriette's men. One of these was Argyll. Harriette was so exasperated that she locked the door, and exclaiming: "You deceitful, disgusting creature!" advanced on Amy with such an air that Amy was panic-stricken and shouted into the street for help. The young Sophia declared that she could not endure Lord Berwick but consented to marry him and thereafter appeared at the opera as Lady Berwick, in superb diamonds. Harriette was anxious for Fanny's happiness with Colonel Parker, who could have married her but did not, and both of them were anxious about Julia, who was distracted over the scornful Sir Harry Mildmay but whom they persuaded and shepherded into the keeping of the long-backed but wealthy Mr. Napier. And then, one evening as the Three Graces sat in their opera box, outfacing the haughty obliviousness of respectable ladies and their gentlemen's raking stares, Lord Deerhurst introduced to Harriette the Marquis of Worcester, a tall, pale, long-nosed boy of nineteen, tongue-tied with shyness and admiration.

Worcester was already longing for the introduction and he fell at once head over ears into a young man's infatuation, violent and exalted. Harriette could not be expected to forgo such a conquest.

She never pretended to return his passion, but she said that Worcester's extraordinary passion for her, his devotion and generosity, awakened her affection and gratitude. For the two years they were together his passion remained engrossing. He took a house for Harriette near Gloucester Place, and another at Brighton when he was obliged to be there with his regiment, the 10th Hussars. In this lodging he got up to make the toast for Harriette's breakfast with his own hands, he kept her side-saddle in his room that no one might touch it, and turned pale with anger when a groom offered his hand to help her to dismount.

Harriette was six years older than Worcester, but at twenty-five she still had her irrepressible spirits. She was not only the angel whom he adored to such an extent that no man had loved or ever could love any woman so much; she was also an exhilarating companion to a young man who was still little more than a schoolboy. Irksome scenes and boring persons she turned into hilarious jokes. Her presence had at first a deleterious effect on his military duties: Worcester was arrested and deprived of his sword for failing to attend parades. She made him get up in time by getting up herself and attending the parade at a discreet distance, the jacket of her riding habit trimmed like the uniform of the 10th, a grey fur stable cap on her head. When his parents, the Duke and Duchess of Beaufort, insisted on his remaining at Badminton, he besought Harriette to dress herself as a country girl and, in the protection of this disguise, to come alone by coach to Oxford, to meet him at the Crown Inn. Harriette entered into the scheme with a will; her theatrically pretty costume, the story she made of her adventures in the stage, the ecstatic delight of their reunion at the Crown, where she arrived soaked to the skin by a tremendous downpour, and went to bed at once, while Worcester ordered dinner to be brought to the bedside, made the escapade one of their most charming experiences.

His parents were beside themselves. Worcester was still a minor, but he threatened that if, at his majority, they would not consent to his marriage with Harriette, much as he loved them he would separate himself from them entirely. The family agitation resolved itself into a standing quarrel. Harriette says that she continually refused Worcester's vehement pleas for a marriage and invariably told him that he must not cross his father in this important matter. If she did, it was no comfort to the Duke, for his Grace did not believe one word of it. At last, although the 10th Hussars remained at Brighton, he succeeded in getting Worcester appointed to Wellington's staff in Spain. Worcester with extreme reluctance agreed to the year's separation involved, on condition his father made Harriette an allowance, which the Duke agreed to do. Harriette, to soothe the distracting jealousy and apprehensions of the lover, promised to leave London and bury herself in some remote village. She actually removed herself to Charmouth, but she had already become conscious of the attractions of a Mr. Meyler, a small, quiet, bland young man with a fortune of £30,000 a year derived from sugar-baking.

The Duke had promised her an annuity of £500 if she undertook to break off her connexion with Lord Worcester and it was not long before Harriette said she was ready to take the money. The Duke then beat down the sum to £200 and made it conditional on her not having any further communication with his son. There were rumours that Worcester was intriguing with a lady who was following the British army and Harriette accepted the reduced figure and the conditions with it. One half-year's instalment was paid her by the Duke's lawyer, who then attempted to get the money back, on the ground that the Duke had been told by Lord Worcester himself that Harriette had written him a letter after she had accepted the conditions of the allowance. Harriette's bosom swelled with generous indignation and when the Duke, foiled in his attempt to get back the first £100, refused flatly to pay over any more, she, on the advice of several lawyers, including no less a one than Brougham, sued the Duke of Beaufort in the King's Bench. The Duke's representatives offered to compound with a payment down of £1,200, and it was accepted. Lord Worcester arrived in England with Wellington's dispatches just as this conclusion was reached. He made no attempt to see Harriette, but he paid several visits to Fanny, telling her gloomily that he hoped Harriette would be happy with Mr. Meyler. Fanny tried to persuade him to make some provision for Harriette, but Worcester, perhaps understandably, declined any such thing. In relating his refusal, Harriette exclaims that he had "lost every atom of feeling in the war and from a shy, sensitive, blushing, ardent boy, had returned a cold-blooded and most shameless profligate". It does not seem to have crossed her mind that some of the blame for this alteration might have been laid at her door.

When the Duke of Beaufort's £1,200 was put into her hand, the turning-point in Harriette's success had been reached. Her affair with the cold-hearted, smug, sadistic Meyler was a long-drawn-out struggle of quarrels, reconciliations and more quarrels in which she held her own but barely; she was never in the ascendant. The later chapters of her *Memoirs*, though rollicking, loud and high-coloured, are full of complaints. She complains of the tormenting nature of Meyler: "'Can't you enter into the secret of my temper?' said this most provoking little man in his usual impressive, slow way. 'Can't you understand that were you to make it your particular request that I should sit down on that chair at the very moment when I was about to do so, it would be the very reason why I should determine against it?'" She complains, too, of the insulting manner in which a woman of her standing was treated when she was no longer the desired herself: Prince Esterhazy suggested that she should procure some girls for him. Above all she complains of the refusals of men to send her money when she wrote for it.

She had, however, a grief with which it is impossible not to sympathize. Colonel Parker, she said, announced abruptly to Fanny that he was going to be married. According to Harriette, the shock to her sister brought on a species of heart disease. "Fanny forced herself to go into society as usual, but her lips now assumed a bluish tint whenever she made the slightest exertion." Before long she became extremely ill. Lord Hertford had straw put down in front of the house, and when Harriette asked for eau-de-cologne to bathe Fanny's temples, instead of sending a servant he rode into town for it and rode back with it himself. He stood at Fanny's bedside and said, "God bless you, poor thing." Harriette describes Fanny's last moments poignantly but with a conscious, conventional elegance, like that of some funeral monument of the period where marble figures with veiled heads and bared arms and feet mourn over an urn. "She crossed her hands on her breast and there was something sublime in the stern expression her features assumed. She appeared a martyr, severe in virtue, almost masculine in fortitude." In Harriette's recollection, it was a June evening and the air was full of the scent of honeysuckle. "Fanny's cheek, still warm and lovely, rested on her arm. The expression of pain and agony was exchanged for the calm, still, innocent smile of a sleeping infant." The phrases describing the death are conventional, but not the simple words in which she summed up her loss: "Fanny was my only friend on earth. I had no sister but her."

Harriette speaks of Fanny as having died before she herself went to Paris with Meyler—"France being now open to us." Since the Duke of Wellington was in Paris at the same time, this was, presumably, 1814, the year of the meeting of the Allied sovereigns. She describes herself as passing frequently between Paris and London in the years following Fanny's death, and on one of her returns to London, she records the death of Julia. She says that she visited the latter in her last illness, which was a disease of the heart like Fanny's, and that afterwards Julia's bereaved lover Napier came to see her and broke out into exhibitions of violent despair. "'O Julia! Angel Julia! I cannot bear it!' he added, pulling his hair and throwing the handsome pillows of my new sofa all about the room." Napier, she says, told her that he had had Julia laid out in state with wax candles burning round her coffin for a fortnight. "'And I paid half of all her debts.'

"'Suppose you had paid the whole?'

"'Nonsense! They were very thankful for half.'" Napier then explained, she said, the arrangements for Julia's children. "'A noble relative has taken one, and Lord Folkestone another, and Mrs. Armstrong is consulting me about the rest.'"

Harriette decided, somewhere about 1820, to live in Paris altogether and took a lodging in the Rue du Faubourg St. Honoré. Here, after she had given everybody his chance, she wrote the *Memoirs*, and sent them over piece by piece to Mr. J. J. Stockdale, who kept a bookshop with an assortment of books of a somewhat risqué character, in the Opera Colonnade, Covent Garden. As chapter after chapter reached him, the enraptured bookseller estimated that a small fortune was coming into his hands. Nor was he mistaken. On the book's appearance, the crowds that stormed his shop obliged him to put up a barrier. Thirty editions were sold in the first year and it was said that Harriette and Stockdale netted ten thousand pounds between them.

The success was immediate but the trouble started nearly as soon. The original edition included a letter, supposedly written to Harriette by Fanny, saying: "Apropos! Talking of vulgarity, I have had a proposal of marriage since I saw you from Mr. Blore the stone-mason who keeps a shop in Piccadilly. Parker says it is all my fault for being so humble and civil to everybody." There followed an account of a blundering and absurd proposal which sounds, it must be admitted, much more like Harriette's than anything Fanny would have written. Mr. Blore, a well-known tradesman and a married man, secretly supported, it has been thought, by some of Harriette's more august victims, brought an action for libel against Stockdale in the Court of King's Bench.

The case is an interesting one for the details it brings to light about the Dubochet family, but even more for a clash of opinion represented by Blore's counsel, Mr. Scarlett, and a passage in Harriette's own book. Scarlett in his contention that Harriette is not fit to be believed, says: "Of course such a person would be perfectly indifferent to any censure which might attach to herself in the course of her real or pretended disclosures. It is a fact that in the virtue of chastity is bound up nearly all the moral feeling, the principle, the gentleness and the rectitude of women, and that when once she loses that gem there is scarcely any degree of vice and degradation to which she might not be, and probably would be reduced." One cannot but remember Harriette's exclamation: "She is a bad woman the moment she has committed fornication, be she generous, charitable, just, clever, domestic, affectionate and ever ready to sacrifice her own good to benefit those she loves. . . . All are virtuous who are chaste, even when chastity is to their liking, or when they are entirely destitute of affections or natural passion—the selfish, hard-hearted, cruel mother, the treacherous friend, the unfeeling mistress—all! all! are called virtuous who are supposed chaste."

The matter of the trial, however, was damages for libel, and after Stockdale had made a jaunty, unrepentant appearance in the witness-box, he was ordered to pay £300, which he could comfortably afford. Mr. Scarlett's opinion of Harriette would probably have been what it was in any case, merely from the fact that she had been the kept mistress of several men, but between the publication of her *Memoirs* in January and the action against Stockdale in July, something had happened which tended to put her character in a much more ominous light than that in which she saw it herself. In March, there came out: *Confessions of Julia Johnstone, written by Herself, in Contradiction to the Fables of Harriette Wilson.*

Julia wrote to say, in the first place, that she was not dead, and considering the circumstantial account Harriette had given of her death and obsequies and the arrangements for her orphaned children, when the question arises of which to believe on other occasions, it must be allowed that Julia's claims are strong. Julia was a woman who lived according to a picture of herself as elegant, pensive, delicate and of a moral sensibility that made her submit to social ostracism as a just punishment. Harriette allowed that she was graceful, attractive and interesting (though of course less so than herself and Fanny) but she added a few strokes to the portrait which turned it into just the thing that Julia abhorred to see associated with herself; Harriette said: "Her features were not regular nor their expression very good. She struck me as a woman of very violent passions." "Young and beautiful," she says, "her passions, like those of a man, were violent and changeable." Julia's passion for Sir Harry Mildmay, according to Harriette, "regularly increased, though it was unmixed or unpurified by the least atom of affection".

"Why does she publish—is a very natural question and very easily answered—because I have a character to vindicate," Julia begins, but the most interesting part of her book is not the vindication of her character, nor yet is it the instances she gives of Harriette's inaccuracy, and untruthfulness; it is not what she exposes and destroys, but what she adds of her own that, though composed on a principle diametrically opposite to Harriette's, yet fits in with it, like buhl with anti-buhl, to form a solid whole.

Julia and Harriette had lived in the same house at various times; when they had been on confidential terms, they had discussed and written their letters together. Julia still had some of Harriette's correspondence, among the rest a letter from the Duke of Wellington in answer to a request of hers for money for herself and for promotion for a Sergeant Porter. Harriette knew the man was a procurer: it turned out that the Duke knew it too. After the picture in Harriette's book of one of the greatest Englishmen of his time, disagreeable, doting and absurd, it is significant to find this letter brought out from its forgotten hiding-place.

"Strathfieldsay.

"Miss Harry—I had just prepared for a shooting excursion when your letter came and spoiled my sport. I know not what sort of opinion you must have formed of me to make such a *silly* application as your letter conveys. The man for whom you require my

influence is a bad character, and were he a good one, I could receive
no testimonials in his favour from *you*; whatever I can oblige you
in as a private gentleman I have always been ready to do, more
than becomes me; but let me never hear from you again on anything that concerns my military capacity, for I never will suffer
private friendship to interfere with my public duties. As a proof
that I am not offended and that I believe you only erred from want
of thought, I enclose a cheque for double the amount you ask, and
beg you to economize a little.

> "Yours,
> "Decimus."

Julia's hoard disclosed a few of Worcester's letters, too. She
admits: "Lord Worcester was very silly about her," but is able to
produce two scraps of writing of a tone which, from Harriette's
account, one would never imagine Lord Worcester to have used
to her. They date from that period of distraction when Worcester
was being forcibly appointed to Wellington's staff in Spain.

"You should not now pester me when I am assailed on all sides
on your account. My uncle only this morning read me such a
lecture—and they all insist on my marrying immediately. I hardly
know how to put off the evil day."

And again, on the eve of his departure:

"My best and favourite charger has been killed by accidentally
falling out of the slings in hoisting him into the transport. This
mishap at such a juncture almost transports me with madness—it
will take 250 guineas to replace him which should have been yours."

Julia often describes Harriette in an idiom which, though hostile,
allows the essential attractiveness to appear. Even her statement
that Harriette was "all paint and perfume, with what looked like
the contents of a hairdresser's window dangling round her head",
allowing for its spite, conveys a certain alluringness when it is
applied to a woman still very young. Her complaints of Harriette's
way of getting ready for bed show the latter in almost a sympathetic light. "Harriette was a perfect nightmare in the same
room with you, taking as much pains in doing up her fine hair
and folding her laced nightcap and gown as if she were preparing
for a ballroom. I once remonstrated with her on the folly of spending two hours thus and then waking me out of my sleep to give
my opinion of how her nightclothes became her, whether she

looked more like Cleopatra waiting for Antony or Potiphar's wife when trying to seduce Joseph. . . . Her reply was: 'Suppose there were to be a fire. I should so like to be admired as I descended the ladder.'"

Such sidelights on her vanity, her extravagance, her boisterousness: "With her own sex she was not at home, her manners were too bold and her temper too overbearing"—do little more than emphasize what Harriette had already disclosed. Julia says: "She would destroy ladies of rank and title in particular, who never did her any harm or scarce even heard her name," and Harriette's own pages are filled with sarcastic comments on respectable women. Julia prints a letter of Harriette's to Mr. Simpson, a creditor whom she was encouraging with a cheerful account of her finances, and even this only confirms the words to Brougham which Harriette had already printed: "My book has sold well but I get more for suppressing than for publishing and I will keep no one's name out for less than £200." "Julia's contribution to the picture is a turning-round of the dark side of the moon whose existence is not suspected from the bright face Harriette shows. The ominous note is sounded in such passages as that apropos of the Duke of Beaufort's disputed annuity: Lord Nugent observed "that with Meyler she could not want for pension." "But," says Harriette, "it is my right and I will have it and I will see Worcester tomorrow on the business and expose the family if I have not justice done me." "If you had justice done you," said Lord Nugent, "you would have neither annuity nor pension from anyone. I know you, my girl."

Julia's narrative perpetually fills in the gaps in Harriette's between those spirited or romantic adventures with distinguished lovers, with notes of small, sordid escapades, for mere animal pleasure, or a trivial reward, a day's excursion, an evening's entertainment, a meal or a guinea. Harriette says that a young Mr. Freeling, afterwards Sir George Freeling, Commissioner of Customs, began to haunt her with a sort of respectful, growing passion. She was obliged to tell him it would not do. The young man not only accepted the rebuff without complaint but, she says he had "the good heart to do me a very essential service some months afterwards". She leaves it at that. Julia says that Harriette was arrested on Westminster Bridge for a tavern bill of a large amount which she had run up at the Southton Arms in Camden Town, where she had been entertaining a young man in the Guards.

Freeling, riding by, saw her plight. He stopped, went with her to the sponging house in St. Martin's Lane and bailed her out, and afterwards paid the debt. The general effect arouses uneasiness, which increases to something, even, of pity and terror, in her version of Fanny's death.

Of Fanny's character Julia says: "A poor, good-natured thing, incapable of doing either harm or good, she scarcely knew the distinction between virtue and vice . . . she had a vacant, see-saw way of thinking that everything happened for the best. If you could not love her, it was impossible to hate her." It is just possible to recognize in this version the character displayed by Harriette in such tender, glowing colours, and to see that the latter might have, inherent in it, the weakness Julia so harshly describes. It is with a shock, but granting that Harriette's claim to accuracy has been exploded, a shock of horror rather than of incredulity that one reads Julia's account of Colonel Parker's separation from Fanny. His marriage, she says, did not take place till three years after Fanny's death. His parting from her was caused by the fact that on the evening of his return from Spain he followed Fanny and Harriette to Drury Lane Theatre, where he watched them throughout the evening and afterwards saw them set off in a hackney coach for a house of ill-fame. At parting he made Fanny an allowance of £50 a year, and at the end of two years, drunkenness and disease had brought her down to the edge of the grave, "her frame a mass of disorders, her intellect deranged". Lord Hertford had her removed from a Lock Hospital and put into lodgings in Brompton kept by a man who had been his cook. This was the dreadful scene which Harriette transformed into one of such marmoreal elegance. It is with a thrilling sadness that one sees Lord Hertford's remark: "God bless you, poor thing," put into its proper context.

Since Julia's book came out only three months after Harriette's own, Harriette can have been only forty when Julia, unseen herself, saw her for the last time. Harriette had come to London to see to her affairs, and Julia after an absence of ten years caught sight of her in the street, "a little woman in a black beaver hat and a long grey cloak—her figure at a short distance like a milestone with a carter's hat resting on its summit. Her once little feet now covered with list shoes to defend them from attacks of a desultory gout, her face swollen. A dingy lilac spreads all over her once bright countenance and appears burnt into her lips. The crows' feet are wide spreading beneath her eyes which though sunken still gleam through her long dark eyelashes. She bears the remains of what was once superlatively lovely. The wreck of the angel's visage is yet seen . . . in decay. Not the decay brought on by age and infirmity, but beauty hurried away prematurely from the practice of a licentious and dissipated life.'

Stockdale's thirtieth edition of the *Memoirs* in four volumes is illustrated by engravings of a remarkable life and depth. The small, full-length figures of Harriette that illustrate the story are clearly likenesses, but they have an exaggerated beauty of shape, and an almost maniacal stare. The two most interesting are those illustrating the episode of her affair with Lord Ponsonby. These have an uncanny degree of atmosphere. In one, she sits in a small room furnished in the manner of the Regency but a little garish; in her hand is the letter announcing the separation; the clock on the wall says a quarter to twelve. The bright-lit, empty room, the expression of her face, stunned, staring yet wide-awake, belong to one of those arid tracts of misery where realistic acceptance is unsoftened by any romantic shade. The other picture has all the relief of chiaroscuro. It is bright moonlight; at the end of Upper Brook Street, Hyde Park lies behind the palings of Park Lane. At the corner of the street Lord Ponsonby stands on the doorstep of his house, waiting for admittance. In the dark well made by the shadow of the houses opposite, Harriette hovers, trying to force herself towards him. She looks like a beautiful witch, wicked and sad.

We never conquer our astonishment that the good and bad related of the same person can be equally true. Probably we shall never be all agreed as to whether Mr. Scarlett was right in what he said about women's conduct or whether Harriette's vehement defence confutes him. It cannot be denied that with all her attractions she was mercenary, sensual and deceitful, and that her brilliant enjoyments led her straight to that terrifying condition in which Julia last saw her, the more hopeless because she herself saw nothing more in it to lament than the loss of beauty which meant the loss of lovers and their money. But in spite of our difficulty in knowing whom or what to believe, one unmistakable and undeniable good thing can be said about her. Twice in her life, when she lost Lord Ponsonby and when poor Fanny died, she was able to suffer.

CHAPTER 8

Lady Blessington

The drawing-room in Seamore Place was all ruby and gold. The walls, covered in crimson damask, supported constellations of miniatures between gold-framed looking-glasses, the carpet was crimson, the gilt chairs and sofas were upholstered with crimson satin. In the day-time the windows looked out to Hyde Park; at night they were covered with ruby velvet curtains fringed with gold. The light of candles in gold sconces and in a crystal chandelier sparkled on a wealth of small treasures, all of historic interest: a gold knife and fork that had belonged to Madame de Maintenon, a crystal smelling bottle of Madame de Sévigné's, an enamelled watch bearing a portrait of Madame de Pompadour with a diamond star on her forehead. The clock in the corner on its ormolu stand had been Marie Antoinette's; the firelight was reflected on the backs of brass eagles, for the fender had been made for the Empress Josephine.

The scene in no way outshone the hostess; its colours, deep and glowing, were a background only to the radiant woman of bright complexion, dark eyebrows and brilliant eyes, with marble-white shoulders rising above her gown of sky-blue satin and her chestnut hair parted under a coronet of turquoises. She was indeed remarkably lovely, but her charm was stronger even than her beauty. The gaiety, warmth and sweetness she diffused made the people who talked to her feel at their best, delighted with themselves and her. The guests this evening were enjoying themselves amazingly, their talk and laughter was incessant, but fashionable and distinguished as they were, there was one curious thing about them: they were all men. Ladies did not attend evening parties given by the Countess of Blessington.

Her past, it is true, had been unconventional for a peeress. She was the child of a violent and disreputable Irishman named Power. The family lived at Clonmel, and when Margaret was fifteen her father married her off to a boon-companion of his own, a Captain

Farmer who was stationed in the neighbourhood. Farmer's treatment of her was so cruel and so abominable that three months after the wedding she ran away. Unfortunately she had nowhere to run except her father's house.

After some years of rough usage in a military neighbourhood as the beautiful daughter of a father who neither could protect her nor had any wish to, she was rescued by a Captain Jenkins, who, though a fellow-officer of her husband's, was a kind, generous and decent man. Farmer had disappeared to India and it was impossible for Jenkins to marry her, but he took her to his house in Hampshire and there, during her early twenties, Margaret Farmer enjoyed happiness and peace for the first time in her life. The qualities of mind 'she possessed enabled her to make the most of the advantages her situation offered. She was a clever girl who had had next to no education. The house in Hampshire had a large library and in it Margaret read, eagerly and continuously. While she lived with Captain Jenkins she acquired the knowledge of literature that was to last her a lifetime, for she never had such leisure to give to books again. At the same time, she received a very thorough, if somewhat one-sided social training. Jenkins entertained a good deal; his guests were, necessarily, those who could be asked where the lady of the house was not a wife, but their standards of breeding and conversation were more exacting than any she had known before. Margaret became a proficient in the art of talking and listening to cultivated men.

By nature she was brave, unselfish, gay and sympathetic. Her horrible experiences had not spoiled these qualities, but they had perhaps caused or intensified a certain trait in her. Michael Sadleir in his biography of Lady Blessington (*Blessington: D'Orsay, A Masquerade*) makes a convincing case for his theory that throughout her life she had no capacity for passion, that though she was married to two men and was reputed to be the mistress of two more, she never felt more for any man than affection; he suggests that it was the concentration of all her emotional energy into the one outlet that gave her affection its extraordinary tenderness and warmth. Extraordinary it was; the men who knew her as a hostess and a friend have left descriptions of the effect her kindness had on them: it had an emotional climate like that of some earthly paradise where warmth and sweetness were carried on gales of spring. Her sympathy was that of a mother while her beauty and

high spirits were still those of a girl. Even the relatives of Captain
Jenkins, who might naturally have been against her, were nothing
of the sort. Jenkins spent a great deal of money on clothes and
jewels for her, but his family considered that her society kept him
from the racecourse and the gaming-table, where he would have
spent more.

One of Jenkins's guests was an Irish viscount, Lord Mountjoy,
a man of great good nature but with over-bright, unsteady eyes
that suggested instability. Mountjoy had the distinguished
amateur's interest in the arts; in architecture, decoration, and the
collection of beautiful objects. He was very rich, rich enough to
buy anything he fancied. He fancied Margaret Farmer.

She was now well-read and had acquired a social training but
she was not fastidious. Vitality and cheerfulness such as hers perhaps incline to easiness and tolerance rather than discrimination,
and it was not surprising if the quality in a man she valued most
was good nature. Mountjoy was all good nature, and in due time
an amicable arrangement was come to by which Mountjoy gave
Jenkins £10,000 in consideration of what he had spent on Margaret,
and Margaret was established in London under Mountjoy's protection. The latter had been married to a woman whom he had
made his mistress some years before the death of her husband
allowed him to make her his wife. By this lady, he had a son and
daughter who were illegitimate and another son and daughter
born after the marriage. He did not seem much depressed at the
idea of having to wait an indefinite while before he could marry
his second wife, but this time the waiting was brief. Captain
Farmer returned from India in 1818, and by an unforeseen stroke
of good luck, fell out of a window dead drunk and killed himself.
Mountjoy had meanwhile succeeded to an earldom, and Margaret,
at the age of twenty-nine, became the Countess of Blessington.

No one could doubt Lord Blessington's good nature, but it required self-command to be able to live with him and preserve any
sort of composure. Lady Blessington was well-adapted to the trials
of her situation and they began at once. Lord Blessington took
his bride to Ireland and his manner of introducing her to his
friends was characteristic of a dramatic imagination unregulated
by tact or sense. In the drawing-room of his house in Dublin his
first wife's body had lain in state. The friends whom he invited
to meet him there, many of whom did not know of his second

marriage, had last been in that room when its walls were shrouded with black and wax lights were burning round a coffin covered with a black and silver pall. When the guests were assembled, the doors were thrown open and Blessington appeared with his new wife in her bridal finery on his arm.

The impression made by her blithe, tender-hearted charm on all who met her gratified her husband exceedingly. On her marriage he had her painted by Lawrence and the portrait was exhibited at the Academy of 1821. It shows a face not highly bred or distinguished, but of most winning beauty

> *. . . whose red and white*
> *Nature's own sweet and cunning hand laid on.*

The scanty, high-waisted satin dress is hardly whiter than her neck and arms, round one of which a pearl necklace is twisted as a bracelet. Except for an aquamarine on one finger and a minute posy of blue flowers between the breasts, the colour is all in the glowing face. The pose is characteristic: she leans forward in her chair, looking and listening with all her mind and heart. We are not left to wonder if she could really have been so charming, if the picture may not owe something at least to the painter's imagination. Thirty years later the journalist Patmore recalled seeing the portrait at its first showing, and Lady Blessington looking at it, leaning on her husband's arm. Patmore said: "As the original stood before it she fairly killed the copy."

She has been described by another eye-witness at this period of her life as "young and triumphant, gentle": ". . . these were," he said, "her halcyon days, every moment brought with it a fresh joy": and the delight she felt, showing itself in all the beauties of her face and form, was what made the impression on "her astonished and almost incredulous admirers". Even so, it would have been no simple matter to get such a woman accepted in the circles to which a Countess of Blessington should have belonged. Lord Blessington was not the man to make a success of such a delicate task, nor did he particularly care about it. Enough society came of its own accord to his house in St. James's Square to gratify his sociable instincts, and when the idea of European travel was put into his head, it stayed there. In 1822 he set off with his wife and a great retinue of retainers for a prolonged tour through France and Italy.

There had already been introduced to the Blessingtons in London a young Frenchman of great attractions, Alfred Grimod, Count D'Orsay. His ancestry was mixed. His grandfather had been a profiteer in the Revolutionary Wars and had bought the estates and with them the title of the Count D'Orsay. His father was one of Napoleon's officers, his mother the illegitimate daughter of a dancer by the Duke of Wurtemberg. Alfred D'Orsay moved in the first ranks of French society, such as they were, in the disturbed period between the First and Second Empires. His sister Ida had, in fact, married the Duc de Guiche. There was very little left of his grandfather's money and he was a young man with an almost unlimited capacity for spending money, but at the time the Blessingtons met him again, his commission in the Garde Royale was his chief means of support. Lord Blessington had taken a great liking to the handsome young man in London and was more than pleased to renew the acquaintance in Paris. D'Orsay's manners and appearance were charming and he had the unforced good spirits that elderly people find a great support. He at once became an intimate member of the Blessingtons' family party, and Lord Blessington could not endure the idea of parting with him when they went on to Italy. He approached D'Orsay's mother and promised her that if Alfred resigned his commission so that he could be free to act as Lord Blessington's *compagnon de voyage*, Lord Blessington would see him provided for, for the rest of his life.

D'Orsay was a typical product of the era which saw the breaking up of the aristocratic tradition and the sweeping influx of the wealthy middle class. Just as in the 1830s the last traces of the graceful and austere eighteenth-century taste were giving way to the ornate and florid in architecture, furniture and dress, so too the fashion in personality was undergoing a profound alteration. The ruling tone of the new era was that of the successful urban middle class; whether it were represented by the extraordinary genius of Dickens or the talent of Disraeli and Bulwer Lytton, the literary and social climate of the 1830s and 1840s was separated by a gulf from that of the first twenty years of the century, when art and society were still regulated after the pattern of the great age of taste. Twenty years earlier, D'Orsay would never have enjoyed his enormous social success. One need only compare D'Orsay with Brummel to see the chasm that lies between the ages of the dandy and the beau, although they seem to touch.

There was, however, one thing to be said in D'Orsay's favour. It is irretrievably damaging to a man's reputation, no matter what impression he makes on women, if he is despised by other men. D'Orsay was not. During his career in English society he was not only the fashion, the rage, "the thing", but he gained the liking, the respect even, of the men who knew him. Such good nature as can exist with complete selfishness, that physical magnetism that can be recognized but never explained, and physical courage shown in reckless horsemanship, perhaps account for D'Orsay's reputation among other men as a good fellow. He was undoubtedly popular with many of his own sex. The most important of these conquests, unhappily for Lord Blessington's wife, was Lord Blessington.

D'Orsay joined the Blessingtons' party on a footing between that of a protégé and an honoured guest. He soon appeared to occupy the position of an adopted son to Lord Blessington. In truth, his relation to Lady Blessington was not dissimilar, but as she was beautiful and little more than thirty, it was not to be wondered at that onlookers should give a different interpretation to this triangular ménage. Lord Blessington was careless and insensitive by nature and he had the aristocratic indifference to public opinion. His wife was neither aristocratic nor insensitive, and she was to find herself thrust into a situation for which neither nature nor heredity had given her any protection.

At first everything was delightful. The party went on to Genoa, where Lord Byron was living. He was in exile but the magic of his name was undiminished. The prospect of visiting him filled Lady Blessington with intense eagerness and awe. On their arrival she wrote in her journal: "And am I indeed in the same town with Byron? And tomorrow I may perhaps behold him!!!! I never felt before the same impatient longing to see anyone known to me only by his works." When she met him she was disappointed, but she wrote down every conversation with him, word for word as far as she could remember. Byron reported of her: "Very pretty, even of a morning," but the member of the party who seems really to have impressed him was D'Orsay. He found the Count charming. D'Orsay had written a journal of his experiences of London life, in which, like many foreigners who come and live on it, he was very severe upon English society, its pretensions and absurdities. As Byron had been driven from England at the height of his fame by the disapproval of this society, it was not surprising that he detected in the Count's work remarkable evidences of judgment; what is harder to understand is his describing D'Orsay as "an ideal Frenchman of the *ancien régime*".

Whatever the disappointment to her or to posterity, the meeting with Byron was the event of historical importance in Lady Blessington's life. A literary friendship of much more personal importance to her, however, was formed when the Blessingtons came to Florence. Here Walter Savage Landor, an old acquaintance of Lord Blessington's, was lying ill; Lord Blessington, in Landor's words, "brought his lady to see me and make me well again". Landor, sensitive and touchy but spiny as a hedgehog, quarrelled with so many people that he had an exaggerated friendship for the few who gained his heart. He was melted by the radiant kindness of Lady Blessington and at once conceived the hot-headed, partisan affection for her which he never lost. He very soon had occasion to show it.

In 1823, Lord Blessington had heard of the death of his heir, the ten-year-old Lord Mountjoy. His surviving son was the illegitimate Charles; his only legitimate child was now his daughter, the Lady Harriet Gardiner. The gossip among the English colony at Florence was that the Blessingtons were not living as man and wife; at all events it seemed clear that Lord Blessington was not expecting an heir from his second marriage, for he had fulfilled his promise of providing for Count D'Orsay by an extraordinary will. This said that when both his daughters had reached sixteen, D'Orsay should marry whichever he preferred and, in right of her, inherit the income from Lord Blessington's estates in Dublin. In 1827, the younger daughter, Lady Harriet, was fifteen and a half, and Lord Blessington considered that D'Orsay might now make his choice. Both girls were unknown to D'Orsay, who had never so much as seen either of them, but the Count did not need the guidance of personal considerations in this matter. He made his prudent choice of the legitimate Lady Harriet. To the great misgiving of her aunt, who had been taking care of her, Lady Harriet was sent for, to come to Florence and be married to the protégé of her father and stepmother.

Lady Blessington would have gained the confidence of most girls, but this situation defeated even her. Lady Harriet arrived, pale, shy and so reserved as to be almost mute. No one was surprised at this, but it gradually became clear to the family party that as she was at first, so she was going to remain. Lady Blessington's charm for most people was that she was gay, sympathetic and uncritical and that she created a domestic atmosphere of luxurious informality. Every one of these attributes combined to damn her in the eyes of the scared, affronted, censorious child. Harriet set her stepmother down as a bad woman. She would have done so on what she had heard of the past, without the horrible complication of the present, in which she was presented with a bridegroom who appeared to take no interest in herself and to be on terms of the closest intimacy with her father's wife.

Many years afterwards Harriet wrote a novel in French, of which the English translation was published under the title of *Clouded Happiness*. It contains a dreadful, unmistakable picture of Lady Blessington and D'Orsay as they appeared to her childish self. The villain is a bandit of savage ferocity, a blackmailer who does not stop at murder, but whose face has the calm beauty of an angel. His mistress and accomplice, Beatrice, "although lacking in true distinction both of feature and figure was remarkably beautiful with such beauty as Titian and Giorgione have immortalized; Beatrice's face lacked feminine charm but she had a certain frankness and her general manner was not at all repellent."

Lady Blessington can hardly be exonerated from all blame for this outrageous marriage. It is true that the *mariage de convenance* was still a normal thing in English society, that this one had been arranged by the girl's own parent and was no doing of hers, and that what appeared to be the overwhelming reason against it, the character of her own relations with D'Orsay, had no foundation in fact and that even the rumour of it was unknown to her. Nevertheless she was the lady of the house and, difficult as Harriet was, it should have been possible for the girl to go to her for help. She should have been able to sympathize with Harriet as being desperately unhappy; as it was, after her efforts had been rebuffed, she considered her merely as desperately disagreeable. On looking back to her own first marriage, she may well have asked herself what Harriet had to complain of: surrounded by care, affection, comfort and about to be married to so charming a man as D'Orsay. It was looking back, perhaps, which had caused her to do one thing for Harriet. She remembered no doubt that fifteen was the age at which she herself had been handed over to the unspeakable

Farmer, and she persuaded Lord Blessington to stipulate that the marriage should not be consummated till Harriet had reached nineteen.

The cheerful self-absorption, the almost idiotic irresponsibility of Lord Blessington had never been more obvious than in his thinking that he could bring about this marriage without public criticism. He was soon rudely disillusioned. It was necessary to get the consent of the British minister at Florence to the ceremony, and as D'Orsay was a Catholic, a Catholic service must be held as well as a Protestant one. Lord Burgersh had heard the gossip about the Blessington household and he now found himself asked to consent to what seemed, in view of the bride's youth, a peculiarly infamous arrangement. He did not challenge Lord Blessington on the matter, but he obstructed the proceedings in a roundabout way of his own. He insisted that the Protestant ceremony must be performed first. This gave such offence to the French minister that D'Orsay considered the affair at a standstill. Lady Blessington thereupon did a very ill-judged thing. Taking Lady Harriet with her, she called on Lord Burgersh. Whatever women might say of her, with men, at least, she had never encountered difficulty; but in the official presence of Lord Burgersh she found herself treated, with the minimum of words but unmistakably, as a woman not worthy of respect. Her discomfort was the worse because she had brought Lady Harriet there to witness it.

At home, her indignation was more than matched by that of her husband and D'Orsay, but Landor's outran them all. His letter to Lady Blessington on the affair was like a strong cordial. "I have said on other occasions," he wrote, "that nothing could surprise me of folly or indecorum in Lord Burgersh. I must now retract my words. . . . I am convinced that all the ministers of all the other courts of Europe have never been guilty of so many unbecoming and disgraceful actions as this man . . . and now his conscience will not permit him to sanction a father's disposal in marriage of his daughter with the very man who deserves her most."

The marriage was performed shortly afterwards at Rome, where the British minister was either less attentive to gossip than Lord Burgersh or had had less opportunity of hearing it.

The information about the young Countess D'Orsay is so scanty that it cannot be said whether the arrangement Lady Blessington

had made on her behalf was a relief to her or an affront. The only
fact about her at this time of which there is undeniable evidence,
is how she appeared to other people. Dr. Madden was a friend of
Lord Blessington and one of Lady Blessington's affectionate admirers; he would have been among the last of men to suggest
that Harriet was ill-treated by her father and stepmother or to
exaggerate the impression of what he saw; but his description of
Harriet, a few months after her marriage, when he saw her in her
family circle, was this: "There was no appearance of familiarity
with anyone round her, no air or look of womanhood, no semblance
of satisfaction in her new position. She seldom or never spoke . . .
strange and cold and apparently devoid of all vivacity and interest
in society."

The rest pursued their busy, distracting, pleasurable existence,
resigned or, by now, indifferent to the mute little image carried
in their train. They returned to Paris and Lord Blessington took
a lease of the Hotel Ney; he had always had a taste for interior
decorating and now he indulged it to the full. The whole house
was intended as a tribute to his wife, and on her rooms he lavished
particular pains, not allowing her to see them until they were
finished and then leading her through them like some benevolent
enchanter. Lady Blessington was in ecstasies over his affection and
his taste. Her bedroom was all pale blue and silver; her bed, borne
on silver swans, stood in an alcove lined with pleated white silk
trimmed with blue lace, and draped in blue. The carpet was pale
blue, the furniture silvered. Her bathroom had a sunk marble bath;
its windows and its sofa were draped in white muslin and lace; on
the painted ceiling Flora scattered flowers.

The great expense to which Lord Blessington had been put over
these arrangements did not deter him from moving shortly afterwards to another house and repeating his effects on a still more
magnificent scale. Here it was felt necessary to throw out an extra
room of nobler proportions than any the house already contained,
and this was accomplished by builders working at special rates in
consideration of their speed. At the same time a flower garden
was called into being by bringing in flower beds in deep tin-lined
containers. When all was finished the house in the rue Matignon
was a remarkable example of those impalpable effects, of distant
prospects seen through misted sunlight or the veil of waterfalls or
wreaths of cloud, so much admired in the romantic thirties; the

descriptions of the illusive, ethereal appearance of its rooms recall
the visions of the Opium Eater, of the early verses of Tennyson,
of the backcloths painted for the first romantic ballets. The salon
was divided from the library by a pair of glass doors. Mirrors at
opposite ends of each room reflected the terrace and the sky, the
glass doors and the opposing mirrors. Opening out of the library
was a glass aviary filled with brilliant birds. The gleam of the glass
doors, the vistas reflected in the silvery depths of the looking-
glasses created a mysterious aspect, luminous and unreal. Lady
Blessington said it was like fairyland.

The May of 1829 was hot; one afternoon Lord Blessington felt
ill but went out to ride; he was brought home in an apoplectic
stroke and died two days afterwards. The shock and distress to
his widow were great; she realized to the full the loss she had
suffered in the death of an affectionate husband. What she could
not realize was the calamitous future in store for her, deprived as
she was of the man who had protected her and committed to the
man who was going to ruin her.

Lord Blessington's will left his widow £2,000 a year, his plate
and movables and, for the remainder of its lease, the house in St.
James's Square. D'Orsay as the husband of Harriet was to have
£20,000, in addition to the £20,000 payable to him within a year
of his marriage, which he had not yet received. Besides these
capital sums he was to have an income of £10,000 a year from
Lord Blessington's Dublin estates. This income would descend to
any son of his by Harriet; in default of an heir, the estates would
revert to Charles Gardiner at his sister's death. It seemed clear
from the small provision left to Lady Blessington and the extremely
large bequests to D'Orsay that Lord Blessington had assumed that
his widow and his son-in-law would continue their joint establishment.

The arrangement was fatal to Lady Blessington in reputation,
prosperity and peace of mind, but even if there had been a friend
at hand with enough judgment to foresee and point this out to
her, it is more than doubtful if she would have listened. She
acknowledged no reason why they should part. Not only was it the
case that she had no passion for D'Orsay: it seems almost equally
certain that he had none for her, or for anybody. Like many men
who are extremely vain of their own beauty, his interest in women
was very slight. His affection, such as it was, was hers, and it was

returned by her with overflowing generosity. With her particular
deficiency, she probably would not have liked any man so well
who would have been capable of making sexual demands on her.
As it was, they were thoroughly congenial. Lord Blessington had
lifted them both into the sphere of wealth; he had given them both
his interests and his tastes. Unfortunately he had also encouraged
them in luxurious habits which it required a great deal of money
to maintain. If she had separated herself from D'Orsay, Lady
Blessington could have learned to retrench, however little she had
liked doing it. She was luxurious, but she was also inherently
honest, and when disaster had engulfed her, by dint of slaving
hard work and finally by selling up her home, she saw to it that
she died without owing a sixpence, but D'Orsay was afflicted with
what can only be described as pathological extravagance. He
would have run through any fortune, however large, and ruined
anyone whose finances were at his mercy.

On her widowhood Lady Blessington decided to return to England. She disposed of the lease of the house in St. James's Square,
and took one of a much smaller house in Seamore Place, off Park
Lane. Here she meant to set up as a society hostess, a salonnière.
Her position was very different from what it had been as a bride
twelve years before. She was now travelled and experienced in
the ways of European society in Paris, Genoa, Florence, Rome.
She had made distinguished acquaintances, she had brought back
from her travels a load of precious curios, beautiful furniture,
exquisite porcelain and a library of books. Everything she had
acquired, everything she had learned in the last dozen years, all
her accomplishments and all her natural gifts were to make her
brilliant in the sphere she had chosen.

But thunderclouds were piling up against her. The journalists
of the gutter Press had already been attracted to her like blue-
bottles to ripe fruit. Her past had been sensational, her present
gave grounds for rumour and she had married a peer. The combination made news-value of the most delicious kind. Before Lady
Blessington had returned to London, the *Age*, edited by West-
macott, had carried several paragraphs about her. One said: "The
Count makes the most loving of beaux-fils to his belle-mère . . .
they are scarcely ever asunder. Lady Blessington is really a most
charming woman." Shortly afterwards the *Satirist* published a
"Riddle by Lord Glengall".

My first the reverse of a curse is,
My second a very great weight is,
My whole neither better nor worse is
Than a dame from the land of potaties.
Of her daughter-in-law
She makes a cat's-paw.
(Ask the fair virgin bride
By Count D'Orsay's side.)

Lord Glengall was an early example of a peer's taking to dubious journalism.

More formidable than the journalists were the London hostesses; Lady Charleville, Lady Jersey, Lady Corke were all inimical to her. More hostile still was Lady Holland. The latter had been divorced and though she was now married to Lord Holland, even so distinguished a husband could not get her accepted in the first ranks of female society. Lady Holland was a hostess only to men, but she was no less inflexible than the ladies from whose society she herself was excluded; her situation exacerbated a naturally disagreeable temper; she felt she owed it to herself to be peculiarly vindictive against Lady Blessington. Most ominous of all, though it was not so realized at the time, was the fact that the unhappy Harriet's aunt, Miss Gardiner, was now living in London, with Harriet's elder sister Emily. Their house was a refuge if the Countess D'Orsay should need one.

The opening season of Lady Blessington's career as a hostess was, however, a great success. Her house had been arranged with all her own instinct for rich colour and with everything she had learned from Lord Blessington's taste. It was described as "a house of bijoux and a bijou of a house." The ruby and gold drawing-room, her own rooms of pale blue and silver, had been copied from their originals in the Hotel Ney. The dining-room was octagonal and lined with looking-glass. Lady Blessington was said to be one of the earliest hostesses to use flowers and dishes of fruit as a centrepiece to a dinner-table instead of the usual gold and silver plate. Her footmen waited in green and gold. The wine was as good as money could buy; the food had that excellence that cannot be bought and is attained only through the medium of a knowledgeable and exacting mistress and a first-rate cook. The library, a long-shaped room with an arched ceiling, overlooking Hyde Park,

LADY BLESSINGTON

Some women said she was immoral, coarse and unpresentable, but one who knew her well said "she never lost an opportunity of performing a gracious act".

THE DUCHESS OF LAUDERDALE

Lovely, clever and of strong character as she was, her influence on the man
she loved was wholly injurious.

was decorated in white and gold. Lady Blessington's were said to
be the first white bookcases seen in London. The shelves were
painted ivory, with strips of looking-glass between them, and their
tops displayed her collection of Sèvres porcelain in apple-green.
The carpet of this room was green, and under the hanging lamp
stood her armchair, covered in yellow satin. The table beside it
was piled with new books, reviews and magazines; she cut their
leaves with gold scissors that had belonged to Mary, Queen of
Scots. Lord Blessington had amused himself by having several
models made of his wife's beautiful hands; these now stood on
various tables. A pair of silver ones were clasped together, and
there were single hands in marble and alabaster.

The principal inmates of the house were worthy of their decora-
tive setting. At her first parties Lady Blessington was still wearing
weeds, but her white and red beauty could have asked nothing
kinder than the black dresses and the only ornaments allowed to
mourning, pearls, diamonds and jet. Her reputation as a beauty
was made instantly, but for obvious reasons she set no fashion.
D'Orsay, on the other hand, became the leader of men's fashions
without a rival. The impact made by him on London society was
terrific. Though a hyperbolical dandy, he was not effeminate in
physique. Carlyle described him as "a tall fellow of six foot three,
built like a tower with floods of dark auburn hair". His grip on
shaking hands was said to grind the victim's rings into the flesh.
His expression of emphatic bonhomie was rendered slightly alarming by the fact that his upper teeth were very widely spaced, giving
the appearance of fangs.

The first time he called on Mrs. Carlyle he wore a blue satin
cravat with yards of gold chain twisted round it, a blue velvet
waistcoat and a cream-coloured coat lined with cream-coloured
velvet. He arrived in "an equipage resplendent in sky blue and
silver." His beauty at first sight, Mrs. Carlyle said, was "of that
rather disgusting sort which seems to be—like genius—of no
sex," but she added that his conversation was "manly and unaffected," and that he was both witty and sensible. She likened
him in his finery to a diamond beetle, and an onlooker who saw
him in the park described him as "driving his tilbury like some
gorgeous dragon-fly skimming through the air". His bills with
tailors, shirt-makers, hatters, glovers, boot-makers and jewellers
were formidable, but even these were nothing to what he spent

F

on his riding horses, his hunters, on expeditions driving four-in-hand, on dinners to his friends, on betting at cards, races and prize fights.

His club was Crockfords', which had been founded for gamblers. He had not been long in London before he raised money on the £40,000 which was due to him from Lord Blessington's estate, and not long, again, before he had spent it. Forty years or more before the first of the Married Women's Property Acts, no husband was criticized for using his wife's money as his own, since it was, in fact, his own; but there was a point at which reckless extravagance in a penniless man who had married an heiress was looked on askance, and D'Orsay reached this point and passed it, going, as it is said on the turf, "well within himself".

In the daytime fashionable male society followed pastimes in which, with the exception of hunting, ladies did not join. The evenings were given to the amusements in which the sexes met. In D'Orsay's case, the evenings were spent as host at the parties where Lady Blessington was the hostess. His wife was almost unseen. Unlike most human couples, the D'Orsays followed the manner of birds, the female wearing sad colours, the male resplendent in brilliant plumage. Countess D'Orsay is described at one party as having "glided in, pale and silent" for a few moments and then retired "to nurse her influenza". There is otherwise almost no record of her presence on these occasions. Beside Lady Blessington, there were no women at all; the latter often had a sister or a niece in her ménage, and certain visitors of the female sex came to the house during the day, but the guests of the evening parties were men. A throng of them, now forgotten, filled the rooms, and some who are not forgotten: Bulwer Lytton, whose novels, *Eugene Aram, The Last Days of Pompeii, Rienzi*, made a huge contemporary success; the young Dickens, the young Disraeli, Thackeray and Leigh Hunt, as well as editors, reviewers and publishers. For each Lady Blessington had a manner that made him feel specially welcomed and at home.

This atmosphere was in striking contrast with that at Lady Holland's parties, where the hostess was perpetually ordering her husband or her guests to shut doors, open windows, poke fires, ring bells and run errands, and had once interrupted Macaulay's conversation by saying: "Enough of that, Macaulay, now tell us about something else." Lord Melbourne had one evening abruptly left her dinner-table, exclaiming: "I'll be damned if I dine with you again!" A visitor who saw Bulwer Lytton at one of Lady Blessington's parties said, "he ran up to her like a boy just let out of school."

The parties did not take place every night; sometimes Lady Blessington was at home to a few callers. On such an evening the American journalist Parker Willis made his acquaintance with her. He was shown into the library. "The picture to my eye as the door opened was a very lovely one," he said. "A woman of remarkable beauty half-buried in a fauteuil of yellow satin . . . a delicate white hand relieved on the back of a book, to which the eye was attracted by the blaze of its diamond rings." The scene was presently embellished by "the splendid person of Count D'Orsay in a careless attitude on the ottoman".

While D'Orsay lived after his fashion, his wife had found a life of her own. Her aunt Miss Gardiner was a friend of Lady Charleville, and through this connexion Harriet became acquainted with Lady Charleville's son, Lord Tullamoore, a young man who did not get on very well with his wife. Lord Tullamoore's relations with the Countess D'Orsay gave some disquiet to his mother and sister, but it was generally believed that though he was very much attracted by her, his attitude was that of a true friend, sympathizing and giving good advice. The friendship had, however, become very intimate and various witnesses said that the pair had been seen kissing each other.

The enmity between Lady Blessington and D'Orsay on the one hand and the Countess on the other, after no-one knows how much irritation and violent dislike, at last came to a head in a quarrel about a cook. The woman was found to be pregnant, and Lady Blessington, instead of acting in the recognized manner of the time and putting her and her boxes into the street, said that she should remain at Seamore Place. The Countess said that the cook ought to be dismissed. Lady Blessington was both indignant and angry at this harshness. She did what she very seldom did: she lost her temper and the stored-up feeling of five years burst out. She told Harriet that it did not lie in her mouth to dictate such a step; Harriet's own parents had lived together before they were married, and what of Harriet's present goings-on with Lord Tullamoore? D'Orsay joined the argument, calling Harriet "catin", in plain English, a whore. Harriet made the most effective answer that could have been devised: she left the house and threw herself on her aunt's protection.

It was a blow from which Lady Blessington's reputation never recovered. Up till now, the scandal about her position and D'Orsay's had been based, admittedly, on rumour, but the flight of the Countess D'Orsay gave the rumour such authority it could never afterwards be lived down. This event seemed to have breached a dam, and from now onwards misfortunes flooded in. The position of affairs between D'Orsay and his wife is obscure, but the provisions of Lord Blessington's will were such that they would give credibility to a sinister interpretation of D'Orsay's conduct. Since the Dublin estates would revert to the Gardiner family in default of Harriet's having a son by D'Orsay it was to the Gardiners' interest that the marriage should remain childless; if Harriet were to have a child by another man, two courses would be open to D'Orsay. He could father the child and thus secure the inheritance in his family, or he could disown it and divorce Harriet. If he did that, the law would allow him to keep her fortune. Lady Charleville told her daughter, and the information may have come through Lord Tullamoore from Harriet herself, that instead of waiting the prescribed four years, D'Orsay had consummated the marriage after three. As nothing that is known of his conduct suggests that he did this from any attachment to his wife, it seems possible that he may have been guided by two other considerations: the step would be necessary if he had any scheme of fathering a child that was not his own, and if Harriet were to leave him before the marriage had been consummated, she would be able to claim her fortune on the grounds of nullity.

That D'Orsay had conceived some discreditable plan, and that he had revealed it to Lady Blessington after Harriet's flight, either inadvertently or in obtuse and complacent egotism, seems to be suggested by letters which she wrote to her friend Mrs. Mathews, in which she implies that she had received an incurable wound at the hands of someone intimately connected with her. "Caesar defended himself against his foes, but when he saw his friend Brutus strike at him he gave up the struggle." It was necessary that D'Orsay should no longer inhabit her house now that his wife had left it, and he removed himself to an establishment in Curzon Street. Meanwhile the Gardiners brought an action attempting to set aside Lord Blessington's will. The trustees, finding themselves in difficulties, held back a part of Lady Blessington's jointure; though D'Orsay soon resumed his footing as master of ceremonies for the evening parties, he no longer made any contribution to the expenses of the household; Lady Blessington was in serious straits and she turned to authorship as a means of livelihood.

Writing came naturally to her; she had great fluency and she used it as a means of self-expression. Four years after her marriage she had published a book of sketches of London life, *The Magic Lantern,* and she had kept copious journals on her travels in France and Italy. She had besides what she called a Night Book, in which ideas and comments that had occurred to her during the day were written down before she went to bed. Encouraged by Bulwer Lytton, who was now the editor of the *New Monthly Magazine,* she took out what she had written of Byron in Genoa, and in July, 1832, there appeared in the *New Monthly* the first instalment of "Conversations of Lord Byron with the Countess of Blessington". The series ran for the next eighteen months. It created a sensation, and many of Byron's remarks on well-known figures such as Lady Holland were so severe, it was felt necessary to circulate the rumour that Lady Blessington had invented them. She published at intervals during the next twelve years, books of essays and autobiographical fragments: *The Idler in France, The Idler in Italy, Desultory Thoughts and Reflections,* and a round dozen of novels, of which the titles of three: *The Victims of Society, The Governess* and *Memoirs of a Femme-de-Chambre* give an idea of the rest. The work which occupied her most, however, was done in connexion with the Annuals.

These books were immensely in fashion for twenty years. The first of them, *The Forget-me-not,* had appeared in 1823, and as its success showed how large a public there was for this kind of work, it was quickly followed by *The Emerald, The Gem, The Amaranth, The Winter's Wreath, The Keepsake,* and many more. One of the most famous was *The Book of Beauty,* published by Charles Heath. This was meant to appeal to the snobbish instincts of the middle class, and its distinguishing feature was that of engraved portraits of beautiful society women, with appropriate verses on the opposite page. When poor Mrs. Nickleby fondly imagines that Kate is about to be married to Sir Mulberry Hawk, she envisages her daughter's portrait appearing in *The Book of Beauty,* with "Lines on contemplating the portrait of Lady Mulberry Hawk, by Sir Dingleby Dabber". "Perhaps some annual of more comprehensive design than its fellows might have a portrait of the mother of Lady Mulberry Hawk, with lines by the father of Sir Dingleby Dabber." Heath saw that it would be a *coup* if he could get the work produced under the name of a peeress. The 1833 edition of *The Book of Beauty*, bound in sapphire blue morocco, announced that it was edited by the Countess of Blessington.

The Annuals reflected a popular form of the Romantic Movement; their stories, poems and illustrations are frequently reminiscent of the early romantic ballet. *La Sylphide*, created for the great Taglioni and first danced by her in London in 1832, originated that series of ballets on similar themes: *Giselle*, *La Peri*, *Ondine*, in which the love story is that of a man possessed by a wraith. The scenery of these ballets, a castle crowning a tree-plumed crag against the sunset, the shores of a lake by moonlight, or twilight in a wood, was repeated over and over again in the engravings in the Annuals. Lady Blessington's own contribution to the first volume she edited, a piece taken from her Journal describing the Bay of Naples, is exactly to the taste of the time: "a golden barge advances; the oars keep time to the music and each stroke of them sends forth a silvery light; numerous lamps attached to the boat give it, at a little distance, the appearance of a vast shell of topaz, floating on a sea of sapphire."

The greater part of the items in the Annuals are to modern eyes lifeless and absurd; no-one now could give a moment's interest to the pictures of effeminate heroes with fierce moustaches and ladies with eyes of ineffable vacancy and waists about to break in half, or receive the faintest tremor from such anecdotes as The False Grave, The Skeleton Hand or The Ghost of the Private Theatricals. There are, however, a sprinkling of items of a realistic kind: Mrs. S. C. Hall's tale, "The Daily Teacher", is of no great merit, but the engraving by Parris which illustrates it, showing the dejected, exhausted girl snatching a few minutes' quiet in the empty schoolroom, has survived as a piece of social history. There is considerable effectiveness, too, in such a picture as that of a woman kneeling on the hearth burning love-letters, with Lady Blessington's own verses on the opposite page:

Hide their keen mockery, circling fire!

In 1840, Heath gave her the editorship of *The Keepsake*. This, bound in crimson watered silk stamped with a gold trophy of books, lyre and pallet and with pages thickly gilt, was the most famous of the Annuals and the exertions of Lady Blessington secured a number of contributions for it of unusually high standard. To find verses by Shelley, Keats, Coleridge and Tennyson scattered here and there among the Annuals is so incongruous, their presence is accepted as one of the curiosities of literature, but Lady Blessington secured for *The Keepsake* one contribution which is completely in the idiom of the popular taste and yet bears the touch of a master. Disraeli was a devoted admirer of Lady Blessington and of D'Orsay. In 1837 he had published his novel *Henrietta Temple*, which was dedicated to D'Orsay and which, in the character of Count Mirabel, contained a flattering portrait of him. He wrote something for *The Keepsake* because Lady Blessington asked him to, and trifling though it is, the buoyancy and brilliance of his contribution lift us into a different world.

"It is a scene of perpetual moonlight—never ceasing serenades, groups of gliding revellers, gardens, fountains, palaces!

"There are four green vistas and from each vista comes forth a damsel, each damsel in white raiment, each with a mask fashioned and glittering like a star. They meet and curtsey to the moon.

" 'O Lady Artemis!' the thrilling voices cry, 'O Lady Artemis! Endymion slumbers in thy bower but why are we alone?'

"There are four bright statues, bright heroic statues, mounted on emerald pedestals around the plot where the star-faced ladies sing.

"Lo! each statue from its pedestal leaps upon the earth, bends before a maiden, extends to her his hand and leads her with stately grace. Nymphs and heroes dance together. Yes, it is a scene of perpetual moonlight, never ceasing serenades, groups of gliding revellers, gardens, fountains, palaces!"

One of the heroes takes his nymph to a deserted grove by the side of a fountain. "The maiden slowly removed her starry mask and exhibited the crested head of a splendid serpent. Its eyes glittered with pristine fire and its tongue of blue and arrowy flame played between its delicate and ebon jaws.

" 'You are alarmed?' said the serpent.

" 'Only fascinated,' said the hero." They rejoin the throng, in time to see a procession sweeping by, of youths blowing silver horns, strange riders on white horses, a wild yet subdued chorus, a clash of cymbals, a chariot drawn by an ecstatic troop of nymphs and swains, in it a form whose melancholy beauty is like that of the setting moon. "The rout passes and in the fair and undisturbed light groups of dancers with twinkling yet soundless feet seem to sail over the ground. All is mystery, and so is life. Whither do they go and where do we?

"Yet it was a scene of perpetual moonlight, never ceasing serenades, groups of gliding revellers, gardens, fountains, palaces." The words seem to give one the spectacle of a ballet seen in a vision or a dream.

The work of editing was well paid but it was very hard. Lady Blessington had of course to write everything by hand and she had no secretary except that, from time to time, a niece helped her with the copying. It was not only hours and hours of writing that the task entailed; her social intercourse, her parties themselves were now turned into the means of securing contributions from desirable people. The charming character of her entertaining was not entirely spoiled; nothing could take away the attraction of a gathering at which Lady Blessington was the hostess; but the spontaneous desire of giving pleasure had been superseded by a commercial purpose and this began to be felt. It was said of her now: "Whenever a man of note was to be found, the enterprising Irish lady was sure to press him into her service . . . she urged him for contributions . . . and the higher the rank or greater the celebrity the better—all were made to furnish literary capital to their charming friend."

One of the drawbacks to this situation was that it deprived her of what had been her chief recreation. Now that entertaining was a matter of business, the pleasure and stimulus of it was largely removed and the never-ending sense of being at work added its depressing influence to the wretchedness that was growing on her. D'Orsay appeared to feel nothing of this; he at least enjoyed himself as much as ever, and gave no sign that he detected any failure of spirits in her. But Bulwer Lytton, one of her kindest friends, understood her very well, as his letters show. "That is a grand and true saying of yours: 'There are so few before whom one would condescend to appear otherwise than happy.'" Bulwer Lytton, after hideous domestic disturbance, had separated from his wife, a step which then involved severe public criticism, and Lady Blessington wrote to soothe and encourage him, as one who knew what it was to endure scandal and ostracism. She said: "A sort of silent respect for myself and contempt for the world has induced me to set its laws at defiance whenever I found them based on hypocrisy."

The lease of the house in Seamore Place expired in 1835 and rather than renew it Lady Blessington felt that she would prefer to take a house in peace and quiet outside the distracting clamour of London. At that date, Kensington answered this description and she settled herself in Gore House on what is now the site of the Albert Hall. This house had the solid, spacious qualities that make a comfortable homeliness. It was oblong with a mansard roof, three tiers of sash windows and one projecting french window opening on to a balcony. In front, a row of trees stood between it and the road. Inside there was room for everything and everybody, and the wages of domestic servants being then extremely low, the number required by a house of this size did not present the problem it would today. Lady Blessington arranged the rooms very much as she had had them in Seamore Place, except that she decorated the library entirely in green and had her yellow chair covered with apple-green silk.

Hans Andersen was one of her visitors and he described the garden at the back of Gore House. On the garden front there was "a great balcony richly overgrown with ivy and vines. Under the balcony grew many roses. There was a beautiful green sward and two pretty drooping willows". Beyond this was "a little green meadow with a cow grazing; all looked so country-like". Walter Savage Landor, gruffer and crosser than ever, came, to be charmed and mellowed as before by Lady Blessington. One day at dinner he was inveighing against the Psalms. She leaned towards him and said with her irresistible air: "Do write something better, Mr. Landor!" Whatever surroundings she made her own became dear to her friends, and when she was dead, Landor, a weary old man, wrote in a poem about his last visit to London, some lines about the lilacs on the terrace of Gore House:

> *White and dim purple breathed my favourite pair,*
> *Under thy terrace, hospitable heart.*

She might have been thoroughly happy in such a house but for the eating cares of making money, and the weary task, that needed

stronger and stronger efforts, of forcing a tired brain to produce
something of interest and amusement to other people. She was
now growing stout, a thing which, today, a woman with so much
remains of beauty would scarcely allow herself to do. Her sedentary
life was in part to blame. She had invented a head-dress for herself
which she always wore, a cap of gauze or lace with lappets which
tied under the chin, concealing the too full outline of her face.
People who described her appearance now, if they liked her, said
how well she managed her embonpoint; if they disliked her they
said she was old and coarse. She had never attempted to disguise
her age, and more than one visitor has recorded his surprise at
hearing her say what it was, her appearance was so much younger;
and now, among the many cares on her shoulders, the preservation
of her beauty was not one.

She was still a salonnière of celebrity and importance but first
and foremost she was a professional writer. The irksomeness, the
miserable fatigues of such work were not relieved by any moments
of creative pleasure in what she was doing. To *The Book of
Beauty* and *The Keepsake* succeeded *Gems of Beauty* and *Flowers
of Loveliness*, albums of pictures and letterpress of indescribable
fatuity. She said: "Light works may prove as heavy to the writer
as they too frequently do to the reader." Nor were her novels such
as would give the writer the relief of imagination. Their depressing
lack of achievement makes them now almost unreadable, though
they hit a certain range of taste in her own day. Charles Greville,
who disliked her and described her as "ignorant, vulgar and com-
monplace", was astonished that she was able to write anything
which sold. He said: "While it is very difficult to write good
books, it is not easy to compose even bad ones, and volumes have
come forth under her name for which hundreds of pounds have
been paid."

Though she was incapable of any sustained effort of imagination, she had, as one would expect, a very keen visual sense and
occasionally she uses this with startling effect. In *The Governess*,
one of the heroine's employers is a vile old woman called Mrs.
Vincent Robinson, who is obsessed by a mania for appearing
young, lovely and interesting. Her boudoir is draped with rose-
coloured silk covered with lace-edged muslin, the window-panes
are of gold-tinted glass to cast a "Claude Lorraine light"; in the
midst of these elegant surroundings sits the old woman in her

juvenile clothes, beneath which are visible "a pair of feet re-
sembling the tongues of reindeer, attached to legs like walking
sticks in tight silk cases".

The modern reader can find interest in some isolated detail of
domestic conditions of the 1830s. The hapless governess during her
first day at her post with a family in a London house pines for a
drink of water. A kindly kitchen-maid brings her a glass, but full
of "a discoloured liquid more opaque than any Clara had ever
tasted, and whose tepid state was not to be wondered at as it had
been in the confined atmosphere of the bedroom since early
morning". Her usual theme was one on which she could use every
scrap of domestic experience she had ever acquired, and this may
have accounted, with women readers, for some of her success.
She turned everything to use, now. Her Night Book, which she
once posted up before going to bed so that she could retain something in permanent form of the day's impressions of interest and
delight, was now used to store memoranda that could be expanded
into verses and articles.

D'Orsay had at first inhabited a little stucco house next door
to Gore House, but he used a semi-basement room in the latter as a
studio; he took likenesses with a certain skill and gracefulness,
though the subject was always in profile and always facing the
same way. His réclame brought him a great number of sitters,
to whom he charged fees. It was even said that he made enough
to keep himself in gloves, though this was probably an exaggeration.

After a time the stucco house was given up and he moved into
Gore House altogether, and Lady Blessington, besides giving
financial help to a sister and supporting nieces and a grand-niece,
had now the additional incentive to labour of having to keep the
roof over D'Orsay's exquisitely barbered head. He not only continued to play the host, as he had done at Seamore Place, delight-
ing all by his gaiety and good humour, he sometimes conducted
Lady Blessington's business interviews for her, in a manner peculiar
to himself. Saunders and Otley were publishing *Victims of Society*,
and when one of the firm called to see her, D'Orsay told him the
contract would not do. The publisher was offended by his manner
and said rather than put up with any more of it, he would prefer
to break off negotiations. D'Orsay exclaimed: "My dear sir!
Nothing personal is meant, I assure you. If you are Saunders, then

damn Otley. If by chance you are Otley, then damn Saunders."

Bulwer Lytton told a mutual friend: "It seems to me as if D'Orsay's blague were too much for her. People who live with those too high-spirited always get the life sucked out of them." If it had not been too hopeless a thing to wish for, any true friend of Lady Blessington's would have wanted her to get rid of D'Orsay. Many kind women have been in the same situation. Their friends scold them; they sigh, and say nobody understands!

In 1838 a judicial separation had been finally effected between D'Orsay and his wife. The terms gave D'Orsay a large sum, payable over several years, but he was so deeply in debt that he would not be able to touch any of it and Lady Blessington could expect no relief from him.

The Annuals which had enjoyed a burst of remarkable prosperity for twenty years lost the favour of the public as suddenly as they had gained it. In 1847, Heath went bankrupt owing Lady Blessington £700, and in the same year the trustees told her that, as a result of famine in Ireland, her jointure could not be paid.

D'Orsay considered that he had great claims upon the gratitude of Louis Napoleon, and when the latter was proclaimed President of the French Republic in 1848, D'Orsay first expected and then demanded in vigorous terms, through the British Minister in Paris, the offer of some handsome appointment. He would refuse it, he said, but for Napoleon's own sake the thing must be offered. The Minister must make it clear to Napoleon that D'Orsay must be given the chance of refusing something very considerable. If it should get about in England that Napoleon was treating D'Orsay with ingratitude, the English nation would be very angry. The Minister either did not feel able to make these representations to Louis Napoleon or he made them in vain. Nothing was offered and in the meantime D'Orsay's creditors, at long last, began to advance upon him. He could not go out on weekdays until after sundown for fear of having a writ served on him, but even in these straits his greatness of soul showed itself. An admirer brought him from Paris an umbrella with a richly jewelled handle. D'Orsay declared: "As long as I live, it will be a religion with me that whatever I have, whether a carriage or an umbrella, shall be of the best."

It was said that the writ was served on him at last one Saturday evening by a man who disguised himself as a pastrycook and got into Gore House carrying a tray of tarts. Lady Blessington's creditors, whose claims were small compared with those of D'Orsay, decided not to risk anything, and as D'Orsay was now exploded, they closed in on her to make sure of their money while they could get it. D'Orsay's method of handling the crisis was simple: he left for France under cover of darkness, not neglecting to carry with him his jewelled umbrella. He suggested that Lady Blessington should come, too, but she gently resisted him. This was not the way in which she preferred to settle her affairs.

Several of her friends offered to lend her money, but she refused it. She arranged for Gore House and its contents to be put up for sale, keeping nothing back except her personal necessities. She spent some of her last hours in England in discussing their own prospects with her servants and giving them recommendations to other employers. Then she and her niece left Gore House and went over to Paris, where they rejoined D'Orsay.

The sale took place during twelve days. Lady Jersey and Lady Hertford had never entered Lady Blessington's house before, but this was an occasion they could not miss. Amid all the horrid desolation of muddied floors, raucous voices, hostile curiosity and sharp appraisement, the servants who remained noticed that Thackeray was the visitor who showed real grief. What made the most impression on him was the sight of a dealer of unpleasant aspect sitting in Lady Blessington's green chair, examining a marble model of her hand resting on a book. The sale raised money to pay Lady Blessington's debts in full, some debts of D'Orsay's for which he had left her the responsibility and all the legacies she had devised to her servants. Fifteen hundred pounds remained over, but before the lawyers had received instructions from her as to what to do with this money, she died, early in the morning of 5 June, of heart failure following a bronchial attack. It was the most fortunate thing that had ever happened to her.

Two episodes of the sale at Gore House are pleasant to think of. Bulwer Lytton bought her edition of Byron's works that had been specially bound for her, and sent it to her in Paris, and Lord Hertford bought the portrait of her by Lawrence; thus we can see it today in the Wallace Collection.

The ladies who were too good to know Lady Blessington were unanimous that she was immoral, coarse and unpresentable, but of the few women who knew her well, one said: "She never lost an opportunity of performing a gracious act or of saying a gracious word." Another said: "That she was happy nowhere appears either in her letters or her diaries, yet hers was a life diffusing happiness. Her kindness was instinct, yet ardent as if it had been a passion."

As one looks at Lawrence's portrait of her in the perfection of her fresh smiling beauty, Shakespeare's question comes to mind:

Is she kind as she is fair?
For beauty dwells with kindness.

One would say that kindness is not always found with beauty, but that Shakespeare thought of a woman like this when he made the answer "yes".

CHAPTER 9

The Duchess of Lauderdale

The portrait by Lely hangs in the place of honour in the Round Gallery. It is the likeness of a slight young woman in the charming clothes of the time of Charles II. The dress with its low bosom, long bodice and voluminous sleeves is all of glistening blue satin. The wild and beautiful background, where a river rushes below autumnal trees and a stormy sky, throws up by its darkness a white complexion, eyes of darkest, densest blue and curling hair of a soft, pale reddish brown. And the face itself? It is very good-looking, undoubtedly; it has the unmistakable air of intellect and a strangely magnetic glance. It is also extremely disturbing.

Well it may be, for this is the portrait of the notorious Elizabeth Murray, Countess of Dysart in her own right and heiress of Ham House at Richmond, where the portrait hangs still. It shows her in her early twenties and one striking feature of it is that though it obviously represents an intellectual woman and a fashionable beauty, it has an odd look of a little girl. The face wears none of the self-conscious airs of beauty, it does not languish or sparkle or show a romantic pensiveness. It is calm with a child's self-possession and watchful with a child's determination not to be put upon. It is tranquil, remote, imperious, with a suggestion of passions as violent and single-minded as those of children.

The father of this arresting young person was William Murray, an unenobled Scot who, in the childhood of Charles I, had been his page and whipping-boy. Murray had gained a certain influence over his master, but by no means a despotic one. He was forced to use some persuasion to get the King to grant him a peerage, and when in 1643 he was at last created Earl of Dysart, he seems to have formed the opinion that loyalty would pay no further dividend. He acted a treacherous part in the Civil War and was said to have sold the King's secrets to the rebels for 40,000 marks. He was an unamiable and disconcerting character and his contemporaries did not like him the more for reversing the usual

behaviour of men when drunk and sober. When Murray was his
own man he spoke freely, with at least an appearance of candour;
when he was drunk, "which", said Bishop Burnet, "was very often",
he shut up like an oyster.

He had four daughters, and when Elizabeth, the eldest, was a
few years old, he acquired Ham House, a beautiful brick-built
Jacobean house standing among trees, in sight of a wooded reach
of the Thames. Murray improved the interior of the house a good
deal; in particular he built the splendid wooden staircase. Rising
from the marble floor of the hall, it is of dark wood; the balus-
trade is made of wooden panels, each one carved with a trophy of
weapons. The pillars at each turn of the stairs are crowned with
baskets of flowers and fruit. When Murray had the staircase made,
the trophies and the loaded baskets were picked out in gold.

Elizabeth Murray grew up in this house; when she was seventeen and her father was made an earl, she knew she would inherit
it as the future Countess of Dysart. It is unlikely, however, that she
had waited till this moment to show her domineering temper. Her
mother was a large, good-natured-looking woman; as for her three
sisters, it was the general opinion that beside Elizabeth they were
nothing at all. If there were one person in the household who was
thoroughly up to Elizabeth it was her father, the ruthless, unscrupulous, rapacious Scot whose caution was such that even his
drunkenness could not defeat it; but, unlikely as it might seem
at first sight, the fair, pretty, well-mannered little girl had a great
deal in common with this parent; two such birds of a feather were
not likely to fall out.

When the earldom was conferred on Murray, the Civil War was
already two years old, and possibly because of the disturbed condition of society there seems to have been some uncertainty as to
whether the creation would be considered valid. Sir Thomas
Knyvet visited Ham House several times in 1644, and he wrote to
his wife of the new Lady Dysart: "She is a very fine and discreet
lady, for at that rate she goes here, Madam at every word." Sir
Thomas added that she should be so, for all of him, he would scant
no courtesy, for he was revolving in his mind whether her eldest
daughter would not be a good match for his son. The eighteen-
year-old Elizabeth had charmed him. "Her sisters," he said, were
"pitiful, crooked things", but she was "indeed a pretty one, but
for her deep-coloured hair". However, said Sir Thomas, "such a

pretty, witty lass, with such a brave house and state as she is like to have, m'thinks might make a young fellow think her hair very beautiful". The intelligent, entertaining young lady with her calm and lively air had made a delightful impression on the good gentleman. "I am very much in her favour," he concluded. "She seems to be a very good, harmless, virtuous, witty little babble."

Elizabeth, it is plain, was not one of those women who lay out to entrap every man they see. To a man on whom she had no designs, she appeared bright, cool, gay and innocent. At eighteen she had had no incentive to show herself in another light. Nor was any such incentive provided by Sir Lionel Tollemache, the young Suffolk baronet whom she married at twenty-one. Sir Lionel was a mild youth and in spite of the enormous powers the law then gave a husband, he was able to exert little if any influence over this small creature.

Shortly after the marriage a very interesting picture was painted of Elizabeth, her husband and her sister Margaret. Sir Thomas Knyvet's saying that her hair was deep-coloured gives rise to the idea, in connexion with her portraits, that her hair was red and that she bleached it, first some, then many shades lighter; in Lely's portrait the hair is a peculiarly soft shade of reddish brown verging on apricot, while in the marriage picture she is painted with hair of silver blonde. In the latter, her sister Margaret, already thickening, sits beaming, complacent and disregarded, at one side of the picture. At the other, well in the background, stands Sir Lionel Tollemache, also disregarded. In the centre stands Elizabeth in a coral-coloured satin gown decorated with pearls, her hair falling behind her neck in a shower of moonlight fairness. Her head is held a little on one side, her expression is completely abstracted. Of whatever she is thinking it is not present company. She has a strange, self-contained soulless beauty like that of a fairy changeling. This beauty ripened and became voluptuous, but it remained unimpaired until late middle life, in spite of the usual prolonged period of child-bearing. She bore Sir Lionel eleven children, but the only ones to survive infancy were three sons and two daughters.

The Civil War had begun when Elizabeth was sixteen and had endured five years when she married Sir Lionel Tollemache. The length of the long-drawn struggle and the manifold issues involved made any clear-cut policy of loyalty a difficult matter for many families even when they were on the King's side. Elizabeth came

of a house where there was no tradition of any such thing. Her
father, who owed his fortune to the King, had not hesitated to sell
the King's interest, and she herself now discovered a strong turn
for Parliamentary generals. She became an intimate of no less a
one than Oliver Cromwell. He was dazzled by her, but when he
realized that the association was giving rise to talk, he dropped it
and even Elizabeth was powerless to make Cromwell waver in a
decision. Major-General Fleetwood, however, either felt that he did
not need to be so careful, or, as is probable, lacked Cromwell's
powers of will. His liaison with Lady Tollemache was public
property; people everywhere said she was his mistress. What Sir
Lionel Tollemache said is not recorded.

In 1650 her father died, and as Countess of Dysart Elizabeth
entered on the grand passion of her existence. John Maitland Earl
of Lauderdale was of Scots blood like herself. Ten years her elder,
he was a man of powerful physique, big and burly with a florid
complexion. The hair that was later concealed by a great peruke
was red. He was boisterous and rough, with a clownish sense of
humour, but he had other, unexpected qualities. Just as, in his
broad face with its pendulous, wet lower lip, the small eyes were
remarkably keen, so too the loud-mouthed bully and buffoon had
a highly trained intellect and a sarcastic wit, and the cumbrous
frame and somewhat slurred speech gave no warning of the acute
perception of character and the immense grasp of affairs that made
Lauderdale outstanding. He combined great coolness and a readiness to strike with the utmost force. He was also a man of formidable cruelty. It is all too easy to see why he attracted the wife of
Sir Lionel Tollemache.

Lauderdale was imprisoned by the Roundheads and Elizabeth
assured him that after the Battle of Worcester it was only her
personal intercession with Cromwell that saved his life. A man
of Lauderdale's acumen was not likely to believe that had Cromwell decided on his execution, the Countess of Dysart would have
been able to avert it. On the other hand, he was not the man to
condemn a fib told by a pretty woman who made it plain that she
wanted his attention, and he allowed himself to be invaded and
laid waste to with great good humour. But at the Restoration the
affair had to give place to more serious matters. Charles II created
him Secretary of State for Scotland and then High Commissioner
with almost kingly powers. Lauderdale's motto was: "Scottish

affairs in Scottish hands," but this meant in sum that the government of the country was to be carried on by himself and his friends; his task was to enforce obedience to the English Crown on the recalcitrant Scots and to compel the Scottish nonconformists who called themselves the Covenanters to accept the tenets of the English church. The fierce, haughty Scots pitted themselves against the implacable rule of a fellow Scotsman. The High Commissioner had his hands full. He allowed intrigue to languish.

Elizabeth was angry at his neglect, but she was not discouraged. She employed the whole strength of her mind and will to reclaiming his admiration and kindling his desire. Lauderdale frequently came down from Scotland—it was said of him that "he was never far from the King's ear", and the Countess of Dysart presented herself at court and took the place to which her rank and her personal gifts entitled her. She was well on in her thirties but her beauty made a triumphant appearance even among beautiful girls in their first youth. It was only a matter of time before Lauderdale was hooked, played with and brought floundering to the bank. Elizabeth was triumphant. Since Lauderdale had a wife and she had a husband her moral conduct could not be defended, but her judgment at least was vindicated. She had fixed her choice on a man who not only became utterly infatuated with her but remained completely contented by her.

Their mutual passion was soon a public scandal. One timorous gentleman whom Lauderdale offered to introduce to the Countess thanked him uneasily but wondered if it were discreet to call on a lady who was said to be his mistress? Lauderdale, who once said that he hated "damned insipid lies", and that when lies were needed, it was better to lie roundly, assured his friend that there was "nothing" between Lady Dysart and himself "save a vast fondness". Whether or not the gentleman was satisfied with this, it did not do for the Countess of Lauderdale, a disagreeable but much-tried woman, and she retired to Paris. People were apt to retire from the path of the Countess of Dysart.

And, sure enough, in 1668, Sir Lionel Tollemache died. With Lauderdale's wife abroad and her own husband dead, there was no holding Elizabeth. Lauderdale gave up any show of decorum or discretion; he "professed for her an open gallantry". Bishop Burnet said that her ascendancy over him was so absolute that people began to look down on him for being so enslaved: "He delivered himself up to all her humours and caprices." The bishop added: "She took upon herself to determine everything." No one who looks at the pose and the face of Lely's portrait will find any difficulty in believing it.

Burnet disliked her intensely, but he said: "She had a wonderful quickness of apprehension and an amazing vivacity in conversation." He said that her beauty was great but her intelligence even greater. She read continually; the subjects in which she was most interested were divinity, history, mathematics and philosophy.

It was strange that a woman of such intellect should have read so much to so very little purpose. Lovely, clever and of strong character as she was, her influence on the man she loved was wholly injurious. Lauderdale was bad to begin with and she made him worse. The full effects of her influence were not immediately seen, but the beginnings were ominous. She was the means of separating him from some of his best friends. Sir Robert Murray expressed some distrust of Lady Dysart and warned Lauderdale against surrendering his judgment to hers. From that time Lauderdale, once his close friend, became his mortal enemy. "So much," said an onlooker, "is friendship a weaker passion than amours and so foolish a thing is it for friends to interpose betwixt a man and his mistress."

When men or women have an uncontrollable determination to get their own way, it seems as if fate stands aside to let them have it. In 1671, the Countess of Lauderdale died in Paris, and then it was a question eagerly canvassed in society as to whether Lauderdale would marry the Countess of Dysart "to satisfy his fancy", or choose some young lady from whom he could expect an heir. The contemporary historian Mackenzie, another of the men whom Lady Dysart impressed but did not conciliate, said: "It was alleged by her friends that she was but forty-five and so might have her children." This implies that Mackenzie thought her older, but as she would appear to have been born in 1626 the estimate was a true one. None the less, Mackenzie admits that not only was her wit as charming as other women's beauty, but that "that extraordinary beauty she possessed when she was young, had not ceded to the age at which she was then arrived". Lauderdale's passion was such that "neither her age nor his affairs", nor the disapproval of his friends, had any weight with him. He married Elizabeth within six weeks of his wife's death.

The new Countess of Lauderdale was a Scotswoman and it was her ambition to make a great figure in Scotland. On the wedding day, 17 February, a great feast was given in Edinburgh Castle and as many guns were fired as on His Majesty's birthday. This caused some surprise, but the Scots did not fully understand what was in store for them until the following year. In 1672, Lauderdale was given a dukedom and "came down to Scotland in a vast magnificence with his new lady". The Duchess of Lauderdale's name has been handed down as "famous for diamonds and temper", but indeed the charges against her were much blacker than such a phrase implies. Lauderdale's régime had always been severe, but after 1672 it became abominable. In the seventeenth century corruption had to be flagrant before it was considered blameworthy, but Lauderdale's government now became execrated for the shameless rapacity with which it was carried on; there was, it was said, "such a spirit of violence and injustice and such a ravenous sale of all things among them". Opinion at the time had no hesitation in saying that this was owing to the influence of the new Duchess. Even before her policy had discovered itself, her manners had riled the nation. Burnet said: "She carried all things with a haughtiness that would have been shocking even in a queen."

The climax of this behaviour was reached when the Duke opened a new session of the Scottish parliament and the Duchess caused chairs to be placed for herself and her attendant ladies and sat "in great state" to hear her husband's speech. This was something that no woman—no queen, even, except Mary, Queen of Scots, the reigning sovereign—had ever done. At such unexampled presumption, a bellow of fury went up from the outraged Scots. Who was this Duchess of Lauderdale, was demanded on every side. It did not take them long to find the answer; she was nobody. Her father, before he had badgered an earldom out of Charles I, had been plain William Murray; her mother, Catherine Bruce of Clackmannan. As for her own doings, they were matter for halfpenny broadsides to be hawked at street corners rather than for discussion in polite society. Yet there she sat, in her velvet and ermine, her diamonds and her coronet, looking as if the ancient nobility of Scotland were barely good enough for her to wipe her shoes on. The writers of lampoons addressed themselves to their task with alacrity. They proved that they had got up the Duchess's past, and for the present, they added the Earl of Atholl to her lovers. "A Satire on the Duchess of Lauderdale" is vigorous and coarse and yet it recalls irresistibly in its picture of her mannerisms, the exquisite portrait of her youth:

> *She is Bess of my heart, she was Bess of Old Noll.*
> *She was once Fleetwood's Bess, she is now of Atholl ...*
> *With a head on one side and a hand lifted high*
> *She kills us with frowning and makes us to die ...*
> *And now she usurps both the sceptre and crown.*
> *And thinks to destroy with a flap of her gown.*

Mackenzie's complaint shows that the Duchess had not altered her tactics since the days of Lauderdale's early infatuation when she had taken it on herself to decide everything. He said that there was "too much meddling", and the cry was that "we had two commissioners". Her chief and overriding concern was to use her husband's position to extract money. She not only encouraged and supported him in his rapacity but she took an active part herself in the business. She acted as the agent in selling appointments in her husband's power and took immense bribes from Scottish officials for ensuring that they should be allowed to levy illegal taxes. Burnet appealed to her to consider the state of injustice and oppression that the country was groaning under, but, he said, "I saw she got too much by it to be in any way concerned at it." He described her "ravening covetousness", and declared, at last, that he believed she would stick at nothing to gain what she wanted. He tried an appeal to Lauderdale himself, but with no more success. "He was so drunk with his prosperity that he despised everything that was said to him."

A very interesting pamphlet with the title: *An Impeachment of the Duke and Duchess of Lauderdale by the City of Edinburgh* which addresses itself to the King, shows that the Duchess was credited with a part as active as her husband's in the system of extortion:

"The Duchess of Lauderdale did also endeavour to get more money from them and did with great wrath threaten the Magistrates in plain terms for not giving her a present, notwithstanding all the good she said she had done for them: reckoning the favours your Majesty hath at any time been pleased to bestow on them as done by herself."

The greater part of the money wrung from the Scottish nation the Duchess spent on enriching Ham House. This house in which she had lived since she was a little girl, which had been her own possession since she was twenty-four, is a monument to her and her passion and her strength of will such as few people leave behind them. She and her husband threw themselves into the project of enlarging the house and redecorating and furnishing the rooms with mutual energy and enthusiasm, though, it was said, "her Duke was much governed by her". The servants' and children's quarters were in the upper story; the Duke and Duchess lived and entertained in the range of apartments on the ground floor and the floor above. These consisted of a series of large rooms leading into each other, and at each end of the range very small rooms giving on to small staircases immediately outside, so that, unlike the great chambers, they could be entered privately. The lavish extravagance of the Duchess ended abruptly with her; her descendants at once began a policy of vigorous retrenchment; they bought nothing new and put away a good deal of what was already there; as this has been brought out again with a saving of two centuries' wear and tear, it is possible to gain some idea of how the Duchess chose to arrange and decorate.

The wood in which all the rooms is panelled is a dark brown with mouldings picked out in gilt and beautiful gilded locks and handles to the tall and narrow doors. The dining-room had a marble floor and its walls were covered with white leather stamped with gold; those of the Blue Drawing-Room were covered with panels of violet-blue silk bordered with velvet of darker blue. Some of the rooms were hung with tapestry whose pearly, ashen grounds set off their mild but strong tones of blue, green and cornelian. Some were hung with crimson damask, some with green. The White Closet had panelling painted and veined to look like white marble. The furniture which an inventory made for her shows to have been the Duchess's own, was designed to show a gem-like brilliance against sombre walls. She had yellow satin chairs embroidered in scrolls of crimson cord, rose-red brocaded chairs supported on gold dolphins, a wonderful cabinet made of sticks of ivory, an ebony table ornamented with chased silver, bearing in the middle of its top her monogram in silver surmounted by a countess's coronet. She had cane-seated wooden chairs lacquered with brilliant designs and ebony cabinets inlaid with lustrous mother-of-pearl, rosy, green and blue. The chimney furniture, tongs, shovels, pokers, bellows, the grates themselves and the pans for burning charcoal were richly decorated with solid silver.

Although the whole scheme of decoration is in the same strongly marked taste, it is not the great rooms, the alternations of drawing-room and stately bedchamber, that give the strongest sense of personal occupation, but those small closets, a few yards square, with one lofty, narrow sash window and a little chimney-piece. In one of these, known as "the Duchess's closet", she kept an equipage in oriental lacquer for brewing tea, that fashionable drink newly imported from the East, and with it a lacquered box "for sweetmeats". Over the chimney-piece of the small White Closet is a painting of Ham House from the garden front; the house, the Lauderdales' alterations and enlargements of it newly complete, stands in the background, rectangular and symmetrical as a house on a sampler. The foreground is a lawn between two lines of slight young trees and statues on marble plinths. Ladies and gentlemen pass over the grass, hounds playing between them. Advancing from the house to join the group come the Duke and Duchess, arm in arm. The Duke wears a great feathered hat over his periwig, and the Garter Star on his breast. The Duchess wears no hat on her light shining hair; her head barely tops her husband's shoulder; but her figure is not the less impressive of the two.

The picture shows the era of the house when it was visited by John Evelyn, who wrote in his diary for 1678: "After dinner I walked to Ham to see the house and garden of the Duke of Lauderdale which is indeed inferior to few of the best villas in Italy itself; the house furnished like a great prince's; the parterres, flower-gardens, orangeries, groves, avenues, courts, statues, perspectives, fountains, aviaries, and all this at the banks of the sweetest river in the world, must needs be admirable."

Lely had painted Elizabeth Dysart in his youth and her own, and now that they were both elderly, he was summoned to paint her again, sitting by Lauderdale's side. The portrait of Lauderdale is disagreeable, gross, debauched and cruel, but no one would expect to see him anything else. Of the Duchess it is shocking, because in the sensual, dissipated, greedy face of the elderly woman, one can see traces of the sprite-like girl. To be soulless is charming at twenty but it is a characteristic that becomes less and less attractive with advancing age.

Lauderdale's tyrannous policy, which had long been abhorred in Scotland, was finally condemned in England also. He never lost the King's friendship, but he was blamed with increasing vehemence in the House of Commons, and as his health was failing, he was driven to resign his offices in 1680. He went to Tunbridge Wells to take the waters, but for the remaining two years of his life he was much of an invalid. It was said that during this period the Duchess showed him no tenderness and very little patience. Was it to be wondered at? The man she had chosen, with whom she had identified herself, allowing neither his marriage nor her own to prevent her, was not this corpulent creature, prone to apoplexy, moving goutily with the aid of a stick. The Duke had known her thoroughly for over twenty years; he should not have been surprised by her conduct and very likely he was not. A man of such knowledge of the world had probably accepted the truth of the Spanish proverb: "Life says: Take what you want: and pay for it."

When he died in 1682, the Duchess, who had already had some experience of litigation when she called in the law to harass her Scottish victims, now applied her very considerable abilities to getting everything she could from the Lauderdale family. She possessed in a high degree both the knowledge and the temperament necessary for such work. When Lauderdale's first wife died, she left by will a collection of her personal jewellery to her friend Lady Boghall. On her death the jewels had been sent back to Lauderdale and therefore had fallen into the hands of his second Countess. When an application for them was made on Lady Boghall's behalf, the Countess merely laughed. She kept the jewels by the simple expedient of saying she would not give them up, and Lady Boghall, who had no wish to make her dead friend's gift the subject of an odious law-suit, abandoned the matter. The Lauderdale family were not so accommodating, but they fared no better. The Duchess arranged a most magnificent and costly funeral for her husband which included a procession from Tunbridge Wells, where he died, to Haddington, outside Edinburgh, where he was buried. The family regarded this pious act of the widow with some respect until they discovered that the Duchess had so arranged matters that the entire cost was to be borne by themselves. This, however, was nothing to what was to come.

The lawyers, whose female clients were as a rule desolate widows

or helpless orphaned girls, were accustomed to having to soothe
and support them as well as to tell them what to do. They found
themselves cast for an entirely different rôle when called on to
act for the Duchess of Lauderdale. To take the Duchess's instructions was a legal education in itself. A brilliant picture of her as the
litigious Widow Blackacre in Wycherley's *Plain Dealer* shows her
instructing the counsel engaged for her numerous cases in Westminster Hall. The Duke had raised a large sum on the property at
Ham and had bought with it the estate of Duddingstone in the
neighbourhood of Edinburgh. The rents of the estate had been
paid to the Duchess in recognition of the fact that her property
had been used to make the purchase, but in spite of this, she now
demanded that the Lauderdale family should repay her the purchase money for Duddingstone, while leaving the estate in her own
hands. A bare statement of the facts as afterwards disinterred does
not, of course, give any idea of the form in which the Duchess
presented them. The matter was made the subject of a law-suit,
which was heard in Scotland before Lord Fountainehall; at a
crucial point in the case, the evidence rested on the Duchess's un-
supported word. She gave it readily in her own favour and the
victims could find no means of disproving it. Lord Fountainehall
sympathized with them, but it was idle to suppose that anyone
could do more. As his Lordship said: "Shall an estate gained
without conscience be lost by it?" The Lauderdale family never
recovered from this reverse.

For fifteen years longer the Duchess lived at Ham, becoming
something of a legend to the new generation. There would seem
to have been some coming and going of her married sons and
daughters and their children, for the inventory shows that after
the Duke's death, "two chairs for children, one black and the
other japanned", had been added to the furniture of the Marble
Dining-Room. But her marriage to Sir Lionel Tollemache had
meant very little to her and there is no evidence that the children
of it had meant more. The whole force of her existence had been
concentrated upon Lauderdale, and there is one room in Ham
House where her achievement has been enshrined. The small closet
at the end of the first floor was known as the Queen's Closet because it opened out of a bedchamber once prepared for a visit
from the Queen of Charles II; but it is in fact something much
more interesting. It became the private sitting-room of the Duke

and Duchess and it conveys still a startling sense of ownership. In a shallow recess, backed by a tapestry worked with the Duke of Lauderdale's arms, stand two "sleeping chairs" with adjustable backs for letting down. They are covered with rose-red brocade and rest on gilded feet. The small hearth is made of black scagliola inlaid with coloured flowers, and in the middle of it, and in the middle of the parquet floor and on the sill of the tall sash window, are inlaid the interlaced letters: J. E. L. for John and Elizabeth Lauderdale, surmounted by a ducal coronet.

Elizabeth did what very few women have been able to do. She loved the beautiful house of her childhood; she married the man she loved and she brought him to live in it with her; but no one who looks at the picture of her sitting by his side can envy her in her triumph or repress a sensation of horror. Till the last century there was a saying that in the hours of early morning, her ghost was sometimes seen descending the great stair. If the past has an imperishable quality, certain states of existence in one life must have an importance of their own although they are at variance with the tenor of the life as a whole. The little closet with the interlaced initials has its meaning, although she was unkind to her husband when he was diseased and helpless. If her ghost does walk, one may hope that it is not in the guise of the hard-faced, elderly voluptuary of the later picture, but that it is the girl who loved the house and was filled with pride and pleasure to have it for her own who is seen on its stair, where the light of early morning awakes the sheaves of gilded weapons and the baskets of gold fruit.

CHAPTER 10

Mary Fitton

A whitely wanton with a velvet brow
And two pitch balls stuck in her face for eyes!

So the heroine is described in a play acted at Court in 1597, the last decade of Elizabeth's reign. Four young men are in love with four ladies, and the leading man is laughed at for his choice because she is "black", that is: black-haired and black-eyed. She is none the less the most fascinating of the quartette. Her name is Rosaline; the play, Shakespeare's comedy, *Love's Labour's Lost*.

The ideal beauty of Western countries has always been fair. In the long reign of Elizabeth, the prejudice in favour of fairness was so strong that a woman of dazzling attractions who was yet dark seemed to be a paradox, a sport of nature. There were no doubt fewer dark beauties on view to combat the prejudice, the Celtic element of the race being then largely confined within their native Cornwall and Wales. In a population of barely four million, the Court was the sole centre of taste and fashion, and the Queen herself inspired the fashion of the Court. Elizabeth's own hair was light. In youth it had been a red-blonde; in age it was replaced by a red wig.

Queen Elizabeth in her last years was so extraordinary a creature that the convention of treating her as a goddess was something more than mere ridiculous flattery of a vain old woman. When she appeared to the public, pale, high-nosed, in stiff dresses, scintillating all over with points of many-coloured fire, people felt that they were in the presence of a supernatural being. Her favour meant the height of success to an ambitious man, but a success which had to be maintained by constant effort and which a rival might at any time take away. From 1590 till his dreadful end in 1601, the place of chief favourite was held by the Earl of Essex; but no likely young man needed to despair of the Queen's favour, and in 1599 his family and friends pushed forward a candidate who for once was thoroughly unwilling. William Herbert, soon to succeed his father as third Earl of Pembroke, was intellectual and of a sombre attractiveness. He was, however, languid, careless and self-absorbed, the last person to succeed as a courtier, as well-wishers were constantly pointing out to his anxious relations. The Earl was devoted to poetry; he wrote it himself, and he was so much interested in the work of the rising playwright Shakespeare that when, after Shakespeare's death, his friends published the first collected edition of his plays, they dedicated it to the Earl of Pembroke because he had been the author's chief patron.

Besides poetry, Pembroke had another, even more absorbing preoccupation. He was devoted to women. He was not indifferent to beauty but what enchanted him most was vivacity: women who had an "extraordinary wit and spirit and knowledge", such as "gave great pleasure to their conversation". Among his own poems are some verses showing the restless, passionate agitation which was his idea of love.

> *Into what poison do they dip*
> *Their arrows and their darts,*
> *That touching but an eye or lip*
> *The pain goes to our hearts?*

What consuming passion did he feel in this year 1600? With whom was he in love so much that his moody absence of mind, his extravagant melancholy, made him the despair of his worldly advisers?

The Earl's close companion was another young man who wrote verses, Sir Benjamin Rudyerd, and among Rudyerd's poems is one addressed to a young lady about whom two things are made clear: she was not his—was that because she was already the property of his dearest friend?—and her eyes and hair were black. *On black hair and eyes* is the title, and Rudyerd not only praises them, he defends them as if against hostile criticism, as Rosaline's lover defended hers.

> *Why should you think (rare Creature) that you lack*
> *Perfection, 'cause your eyes and hair are black? ...*
> *Rich diamonds shine brightest, being set*
> *And compassèd within a foil of jet.*

Nor was it fit that Nature should have made
So bright a sun to shine without some shade . . .
Nor hath Dame Nature her black art revealed
To outward parts alone, some lie concealed.
For as by heads of springs men often know
The nature of the streams that glide below
So your black hair and eyes do give direction
To make me think the rest of that complexion
*   . . . Pardon I pray*
If my rude Muse presumeth to display
Secrets unknown or hath her bounds o'er past
In praising sweetness that I ne'er did taste.
Starved men may know there's meat, and blind men may,
Though hid from light, presume there is a day.

A dark, sparkling girl had been complimented in a Court play by a poet in whom Pembroke was interested. A girl with black hair and eyes like diamonds and jet had been celebrated in a poem by the Earl's closest friend. The Earl himself was in the throes of a passion; we know the lady had black hair from the coloured effigy of her kneeling upon her family tomb; she was twenty-two years old and since her appointment as a Maid of Honour, five years before, she had been one of the most striking figures in that band of girls who, dressed on state occasions in white and silver, attended the unpredictable and terrifying Queen. Her name was Mary Fitton.

The first mention of her and the Earl together on a public occasion is in June, 1600, at the wedding of Pembroke's cousin, Lord Herbert, with another of the Maids of Honour, Lady Ann Russell. The atmosphere of the Court was one of uncertainty, gloom and terror, for the long quarrel between the Queen and the Earl of Essex was approaching its climax. Essex was already under arrest at his house in the Strand; the Queen was at Greenwich Palace, where, said a letter-writer, "she uses to walk much in the park, and takes great walks out of the park and round about the park and thus while the poor Earl of Essex was a prisoner in his own house and she was debating his fate in her breast, but she seemed to think of nothing but Ann Russell's wedding with Lord Herbert."

The wedding feast took place in Lord Cobham's house at Black-friars, and after supper eight Maids of Honour came in to perform "a strange dance, newly invented". This band of lovely creatures, their hair loose upon their shoulders, in cloth of silver with mantles of carnation taffeta cast under one arm, was led by Mary Fitton. The carnation and silver might have been chosen for her; Pembroke could hardly have seen her make a more brilliant appearance. At the close of the dance, the girls approached ladies in the audience, asking them to dance. Mary Fitton, as leader of the troupe, invited the Queen. Elizabeth, always pleased by a spectacle, had perhaps for a brief space forgotten her agony of mind. She asked graciously what character Mary Fitton represented. The girl answered: "Affection." The word awoke the barely sleeping torments of Elizabeth's anger and her suffering. The distractions of music, dancing, homage, lost their power.

"'Affection!' said the Queen. 'Affection's false!' Nevertheless Her Majesty arose and danced."

Had Mary only known it, the Queen's words had a dreadful meaning for herself, but she could not apply it. The passion of the two lovers was something in a less exalted sphere than that of the Queen's struggle with Essex, but its intensity blotted out worldly wisdom, caution or even sense. When the Queen appointed a Maid of Honour she made herself responsible to the girl's parents. A man who compromised a girl under the Queen's protection found himself in a situation of grave danger. Like all English sovereigns to the time of Charles I, Elizabeth had the power of arbitrary arrest. She could imprison at her pleasure, not only without trial but without showing cause other than that it was her pleasure. A man who offended her might find himself in prison for a wholly indefinite period. As for a girl who brought scandal upon such a select circle, banishment from Court was the least she could expect; she might share her lover's imprisonment, though not in the same habitation. Drastic as these penalties appear, it was necessary that the Queen should have some method of safeguarding the young ladies for whose good name their fathers held her liable. The position was made harsher for amorous girls and their lovers because of the personal jealousy with which the Queen was supposed to resent lovemaking addressed to anyone but herself.

A man as self-absorbed as Pembroke and a girl as spirited as Mary Fitton were a pair, if any were, to override and ignore these obstacles. "One Mrs. Martin who dwelt at the Chopping Knife in

Ludgate" is known to have said of Mary Fitton that "during the time the Earl of Pembroke favoured her, she would put off her head-tire and tuck up her clothes and take a large white cloak and march as though she had been a man, to meet the said Earl out of the court." A girl of whom nothing could be seen but close-lying hair, a cloak and stockinged legs might pass for a youth in Elizabethan dress, if, like Portia, she "turned two mincing steps into a manly stride"; and Mary Fitton "marched" like a man. Who was this high-spirited creature, who disguised herself like a girl in one of Shakespeare's plays?

The Fittons were a Cheshire family who lived at Gawsworth. Sir Edward Fitton and his lady had two sons and two daughters, Ann and Mary. The latter, born in 1577, was twenty-two in the fateful year 1600. Ann, three years her elder, had married at sixteen and was settled, the wife of Mr. Newdigate, at Arbury in Warwickshire. The elder sister had that sort of extraordinary sweetness that drew affection from everyone round her, as may be seen in the letters written to her and preserved in the Newdigate family. Tenderness, fondness, romantic affection in all varieties and degrees were poured out upon her. There were her father and mother, who felt Cheshire a long way from Warwickshire when Ann's first baby was born. Sir Edward wrote: "Good Nan, God in heaven bless thee; God bless your little one." Her mother wrote the postscript: "I pray God bless thee and my little (grand) daughter. I long exceedingly to hear how you both do. An we can do you any good, let us know it and it shall be done." There was Ann's great-uncle, old Mr. Francis Fitton, who wrote to "Mine own especial good niece, Mrs. Newdigate", saying, "wanting to know if you would be at home this winter was only that I meant to come and see you if possibly I might."

Young Sir Henry Carey wrote to say that now Ann had left the Fittons' town house for Warwickshire, London was so dull, there was nothing to write about except that: "I love you and ever will and so, betake you to your rest, being about to take my own. Strand, this present Monday 1596." The elderly Sir Fulke Greville, statesman and man of letters, who was M.P. for Warwickshire and took himself very seriously, maintained a tender, intimate, though an entirely proper correspondence with his young neighbour.

The person who might have been expected to write to her

oftenest and at most length was, however, no letter-writer. Her sister Mary, appointed at Court in 1595, was immediately so much taken up with her duties and the distractions of a brilliant social success that she not only wrote but seldom : when she did write she used those false excuses for not writing more that are almost worse than total neglect. One of her letters begins, it is true, "To my dearest sister, Mrs. Ann Newdigate", and says that nothing can be more welcome than a letter from her; but as to any sort of reply, Mary will not undertake to write one, "lest my lines too tedious were"; and, continues this sparkling and affairée young person, "time that limits all things, bars me of words, which else could never cease to tell how dear you are".

Time barred Mary from writing to her mother, either. Lady Fitton was obliged to ask if Ann had any news of her. "If you hear anything of your sister, I pray you, let me know, for I never heard from her since."

Indeed, though Ann Newdigate might hear next to nothing from her sister, she heard a good deal about her. Ann, a honey-pot herself, had for one enamoured elderly gentleman the additional charm of being Mary's sister. Sir William Knollys, forty-eight when Mary Fitton was seventeen, was one of the Comp-trollers of the Queen's Household and a privy counsellor. When Mary was appointed to her post, her father wrote to Sir William, asking him to keep an eye on her. Sir William accepted the trust with eagerness, it might almost be said with avidity. He replied to Sir Edward Fitton's letter: "I will in no wise fail to fulfil your desire in playing the good shepherd and will, to my power, defend the innocent lamb from the wolfish cruelty and fox-like subtlety of the tame beasts of this place." It was not long before the innocent lamb had utterly bewitched him.

Sir William's wife was a great many years older than he, but as it was to prove, she had nine more years of life in her. Before many weeks had passed the good shepherd was writing to Ann New-digate, candidly expressing his impatience for his wife's death. His situation was harassing in the extreme. He was devoured by love and longing, he saw no immediate prospect of release, and meantime he was continually tormented by the sight of the beasts in full cry after the fascinating quarry. His plight was caused by the fact that though he was more than twice Mary Fitton's age, and held no personal attraction for her whatever, she was too astute to discourage such an influential lover. Sir William was not eminent from his office only; his sister was the second wife of the Earl of Leicester and the mother of the Earl of Essex. He was, there-fore, as brother-in-law of the old favourite and uncle of the young one, in that small, inner circle immediately next the Queen. The penalty for this was that he was regarded as too useful to let go. Mary had nothing to fear from him; besotted though he was, he was elderly and responsible. If Lady Knollys were to die suddenly, Mary would find herself awkwardly placed, but Lady Knollys showed no sign of dying: none at all, as her husband lamented time and again in his letters to Ann Newdigate.

Ann was a young wife and mother, devoted to the cares of her family and household, but it is clear that she had that form of sexual magnetism that not only attracts men but gives them a sense of complete ease and freedom in conversation. Sir William wrote and wrote; his letters, cumbrous with allegory and metaphor in the worst manner of the time, were none the less startlingly clear in meaning. "By continual frosts my looking for any fruit of my garden is vain, unless the old tree be cut down and a new graft of a good kind planted." His miseries kept him on the rack. "My hopes are mixed with despair and my desires starved with expectation, but were my enjoying assured, I could willingly endure purgatory for a season to purchase my heaven at the last." But oddly enough, it was only his wife whom he saw as the obstacle to his desires. "My ground is covered with the bramble and the briar, which, until it be grubbed and cut up, there is no hope of good." It had not so far occurred to him that if the bramble were grubbed up, there might remain even thornier barriers in his path. Nor does Mary's sister seem to have enlightened him. In that pro-found silence about herself and her affairs which she had no time to break, Mary may have left Ann without confidential informa-tion. Sir William on his side left almost nothing of his feelings untold, though occasionally he made a gesture of prudence to his young confidante. "But I must cry silence lest I speak too loud, committing this secret only to yourself."

His woes gave him and his correspondent no respite. To make matters worse he developed toothache. Worst of all, Mary went to bed without saying good night to him. She had, no doubt, other things to think about, but to Sir William it was the last straw. That and the toothache even checked his ardour for letter-writing

and explained the reason for "these few lines scribbled in haste".
Ann was expecting another baby and Sir William added: "Wishing you a good delivery of your burden and your sister in the same
case justifiable." He thought only of that happy contingency in
which he himself would be justified in putting Mary in her sister's
case. Soon, however, a faint note of uneasiness sounds in his letters.
"I leave you to God's protection, myself to your dearest sister's
true love and her to a constant resolution to love only him who
loves her best. Your most assured friend, I would fain say brother."
The poor gentleman had begun to have some misgivings as to
Mary's being able to stick to such a resolution if she made it. Such
uneasiness added fuel to his flames. Ann's daughter was born in
1598, and Sir William was asked to stand godfather. He waived his
right of naming the infant. "Give it what name shall please you."
Then he was fain to go back a little on his word. "Imagine what
name I love best, and that do I nominate." The baby was accordingly christened Mary.

The next year, in 1599, Mary herself had a sort of illness. "The
mother" was a name given to hysterical fits of crying and distress.
They may have been of many origins, sleeplessness, anxiety, agitation from overwrought nerves. Mary's attack was severe enough
for her to be released from her duties and sent to her family's town
house to recover. The secretary to the Sidney family informed
them: "Mistress Fitton is sick and gone to her father's." She was
soon recovered, but on her return she found Sir William in a
lamentable way. To the private miseries of a disappointed lover
he now added acute anxiety as to the behaviour of his nephew
Essex. He was in such a state of dismay that it made him absolutely
tiresome. Mary reprimanded him. His only consolation was to
write to Ann about his dire apprehensions for Essex's safety and
their unfortunate effect on his manners. "I leave you to imagine
the discomforts I take hereof, when your sister is fain to blame
me for my melancholy and small respect to her, who, when I am
myself is the only comfort of my heart. She is well now and hath
not been troubled with the mother for a long time. I would God,"
exclaimed the unfortunate lover, "I might as lawfully make her
a mother as you are."

The parents who lived in Cheshire naturally knew nothing of
Mary Fitton's goings-on, nor was it surprising that a sister in
Warwickshire should know little or nothing if Mary chose to keep

her in the dark. The strange thing is that Sir William Knollys, living under the same roof as Mary, should have known as little of her doings as anybody. Clearly she was a young woman who could keep her own counsel, however ill-starred her secret path might be. What were her private concerns? She may, at some time between 1595 and 1600, have been involved in an intrigue that is now, with all its ambiguities and uncertainties, and in spite of the fact that of the three people concerned in it we do not know the names of two, reckoned among the famous love affairs of the world. The mere possibility (and scholars will not allow that it is more) that Mary Fitton was the woman concerned, has lent her name a magic, for of the two men's names, the one we know is Shakespeare's.

Shakespeare the actor and playwright, the poet who had gained court patronage, was already in the first dawn of his tremendous fame. He had written a series of sonnets which, though they were not printed till 1609, were already circulated in manuscript in 1599. The sonnets appear to tell a coherent story; they describe the poet's romantic friendship with a young nobleman whom he urges to marry and beget children so that posterity may see a copy of his beauty; succeeding sonnets describe the poet's passion for a woman with black eyes and hair. Like the lines put into the mouth of Rosaline's lover, like Sir Benjamin Rudyerd's poem *Black Hair and Eyes*, these sonnets admit the strange sombre colouring but assert that it is no blemish. His mistress's brows, he says, are raven-black, her eyes of the same colour, as if they were in mourning:

> *Yet so they mourn, becoming of their woe*
> *That every tongue says, Beauty should look so.*

A single sonnet unfolds the crisis of the story. The dark mistress who enslaves him still has now seduced his friend:

> *Of him, myself and thee I am forsaken,*
> *A torment thrice threefold to be thus crossed.*

And the next one completes the tale:

> *So, now I have confessed that he is thine.*

"He" and "thee" are words of no identity, but the impact of the poet's emotion is so powerful that there are moments in reading when we feel we know everything about this man and woman except their names. And those? The publisher dedicated the printed version "To the only begetter of these ensuing sonnets, Mr. W. H.", thereby leaving behind him one of the riddles of all time. There is no warrant to say more than that the initials are those of Pembroke's name, William Herbert.

But in one of her affairs concealment was abruptly snatched from Mary Fitton. In one at least there was no secrecy and no uncertainty. In January, 1601, the truth exploded with dire effect, laying the edifice of her career, her Court favour, her reputation, in ruins. Sir Robert Cecil wrote to a friend: "There is a misfortune befallen Mistress Fitton, for she is proved with child, and the Earl of Pembroke, being examined, confesseth the fact but utterly renounceth all marriage. I fear they will both dwell in the Tower for the Queen hath vowed to send them thither."

The Queen's intention was carried out on Pembroke but Mary Fitton was less harshly treated. She was "committed" to the house of Lady Hawkins, and here, in February, she was delivered of a dead boy. The other Maids of Honour were found by the courtiers to be much sobered by this example. "Fitton's afflictions," said Sir John Stanhope, acted as "a discouragement of the rest."

There were others whom the afflictions discouraged even more than the Maids of Honour. Sir William Knollys was struck to the earth. He wrote to Ann: "accounting myself the most unfortunate man alive to find that which I had laid up in my heart to be my comfort is to be my greatest discomfort."

The parents' dismay was dreadful. Sir Edward Fitton brought his wife to London and meantime tried to get his daughter released from Lady Hawkins's custody and given to him, but this could not be done merely for the asking. Ann, in Warwickshire, was ill; he wrote to the daughter who was his one comfort: "Sweet Nan, I am very sorry that you are not well. I am in some hope of your sister's enlargement shortly, but what will be the end with the Earl I cannot tell." Lady Fitton added a postscript. "My own good Nan, Beware how you take physic. Let me know how you do. When we hear any good news you shall hear from me."

The only news the Fittons could consider good would be that Pembroke consented to marry their daughter. Mary herself was

filled with vehement conviction that he would; she was possessed
of the idea that if she remained near him he must shortly give the
consent which it was impossible that in the end he should not give,
but the conviction was based on her memory of his passion, and
memory belongs to the past. Sir Edward Fitton did not share her
confidence. He was an unremarkable father of a brilliant daughter,
but of the two he had the sounder knowledge of men. He decided
that as soon as Mary was fit to travel she must go home rather than
linger in London, not able to show her face. Three months after
the confinement, when nothing had been gained, the long,
laborious journey to Cheshire was begun. It was too much for her
as it was. They were obliged to make a long halt at Stanner, and
while they waited, Sir Edward wrote to Sir Robert Cecil, saying
that his daughter was "still confident of her chance", but he said,
"for myself, I expect no good from him that in all this time hath
not showed any kindness." His distrust of the Earl was shared
by the rest of the family. Old Francis Fitton wrote to his darling
Ann his gloomy prognostications of her sister's fate: "Mine own
sweet niece . . . God grant all be for the best but for aught I know
or can see, I see nothing better nor cause of better hope than
before."

They would have seen none at all if they had read the Earl of
Pembroke's poems. Mary Fitton's case was outwardly no different
from that of Elizabeth Throckmorton, whom Sir Walter Ralegh
had got with child and who had been imprisoned with him in
1592. On their release, Sir Walter Ralegh had married her and
taken her and his infant son to Sherborne, where they lived in great
happiness. But Ralegh's temperament was not that of Pembroke.
The latter epitomized all those views of sexual morality which
teach that a man despises a woman who gives way to his demands.
His poem *To a Lady residing at Court* is ominous indeed in the
light of his own conduct.

> *Then this advice, fair Creature, take from me.*
> *Let none pluck fruit unless he take the tree.*
> *For if with one, with thousands thou'lt turn whore.*
> *Break ice in one place and it cracks the more.*

Mary Fitton's career at Court was irrevocably closed. One opening remained to her which would have kept her in some sort of

connexion with the society of the great world, but she rejected it impatiently. She had borne with Sir William Knollys when there was something to be got by it, but now, after so much hope and ecstasy, disappointment and suffering, the idea of submitting once again to his tediousness was unendurable. Sir William withdrew with a certain dignity. He wrote to Ann of her "unkind sister", from whom he had deserved something better than "so long silence. But," he added, "I am pleased since she will have it so."

Mary had failed in her great enterprise, but she was not long forlorn, for she was one of those women at whose approach men start up out of the ground. The Fittons had a charming cousin eight years older than herself, Sir Richard Leveson, a sea-captain with red-gold hair. His wife was out of her mind, and it was natural he should make the most of a friendship with his attractive cousins. Ann had been his first object, but though he wrote to her under the nick-name of "Sweet Wife", sending messages to her small daughter as "Little Mistress Waspsnest", with Ann there had been no question of anything but affection.

Mary, now staying often with her sister in Warwickshire, occupied a different position with regard to him. His domestic misfortune, their family relationship, her compromising past, above all her astonishing attractions, the raven darkness of her hair and eyes and the brilliance of her charm, seemed to mark them out for an unceremonious, intimate footing with each other. Mary could no longer buy her clothes in London and Sir Richard sent her down a strange new ruff to her sister's house. When he died four years later, his cousin Mary had borne two daughters, said to be his, and the saying is given weight by a mysterious clause in his will which directs the executors to employ one hundred pounds yearly (the equivalent of some thousands of our money) "to such uses and purposes, and such person and persons as I shall appoint unto them by some private instructions from myself."

When Sir Richard had commanded the *Repulse*, one of his fellow-captains, commanding the *Lyon's Whelp*, had been Captain William Polewhele. Sir Richard had perhaps commended his cousin Mary and her infant daughters to his friend before he died. At all events, within two years of his death, Captain Polewhele, though no match for a Fitton, married Mary. Sir Edward Fitton had died the year before and old Lady Fitton, left alone to uphold the family dignity, was extremely angry. Besides the mésalliance, a further exasperation that put her almost beside herself was that Captain Polewhele had seen his own advantage in the fact that the neighbours spoke very freely of Mary. Lady Fitton poured out her mortification and grief in letters to Ann: "My Lady Frances Egerton said she was the vilest woman under the sun. But Polewhele is a very knave and taketh the disgrace of his wife to make the world think him worthy of her and that she deserved no better." Even when the marriage was accomplished and Mary, well within the year, had borne a son, Lady Fitton was not appeased. "I take no joy to hear of your sister nor of that boy. If it had pleased God when I did bear her that she and I had been buried it had saved me from a great deal of sorrow and grief. Write no more to me of her."

The rest of the family did not share this implacable resentment. They may have thought that to have Mary married at all was something. Old Francis Fitton in his will left Captain Polewhele his "best horse", "a token of my love to him and to my said cousin his now wife". Polewhele himself died in 1610 before the birth of his daughter, and Mary married another sailor, Captain Lougher, whom she outlived, dying herself in 1647 at the age of 70. Many years before that her kneeling effigy, in painted stone, had been placed with her sister's and those of two brothers, on her parents' tomb in Gawsworth church. On the carved hair under the head-dress remains of pigment show that it was painted black.

Time doth transfix the flourish set on youth.

When the sonnets were published in 1609, did the book come into her hands? If it did, she may have read it merely as fashionable poetry, or she may have seen in it a vivid evocation of that span of her existence which had been extinguished with the abruptness of a falling star. She could not have known that the mere suggestion of her being connected with the poet would touch her with immortality.

Bibliography

The sources for these sketches are in almost every case numerous and fragmentary. I have listed below one or two of the chief ones for each.

i. MARTHA RAY

Love and Madness, Sir Herbert Croft, London, 1780.
The Case and Memoirs of Miss Reay, London, 1779.
The Case and Memoirs of the late Rev. Mr. James Hackman and of his dealings with the late Miss Martha Reay, London, 1779.

ii. ELIZABETH TUDOR

Imprisonment of the Princess Elizabeth, John Foxe, Acts and Monuments, London, 1563.
The Girlhood of Queen Elizabeth in Contemporary Letters, Frank A. Mumby, London, 1909.

iii. THE DUCHESS OF MARLBOROUGH

The Queen's Comrade: Life and Times of the Duchess of Marlborough, Joseph F. Molloy, 1901.
An Account of the Conduct of the Dowager Duchess of Marlborough, from her first coming to the Court, to the year 1710, ed. Nathaniel Hooke, London, 1742.

iv. FAIR ROSAMOND

The French Chronicle of London, Camden Society, 1844.
Itinerary of John Leland, vol. ii, ed. Thomas Hearne, Oxford, 1710.
"Eleanor of Aquitaine", Agnes Strickland, *Lives of the Queens of England*, London, 1869.

v. ELIZABETH INCHBALD

Memoirs of Mrs. Inchbald, ed. James Boaden, London, 1833.

vi. BECKY WELLS

Memoirs of the Life of Mrs. Sumbel, late Wells, Written by herself, including her correspondence with Major Topham, Mr. Reynolds etc., 3 vols., London, 1811.

vii. HARRIETTE WILSON

Memoirs of Harriette Wilson written by herself, 35th edition, with an appendix containing an account of the action for libel brought by Robert Blore against the publisher of the book, 4 vols., London, 1825.

viii. LADY BLESSINGTON

Blessington: D'Orsay, a Masquerade, Michael Sadleir, London, 1933.
Literary Life and Correspondence of the Countess of Blessington, R. R. Madden, London, 1855.

ix. THE DUCHESS OF LAUDERDALE

History of his own Times, Bishop Burnet, London, 1734.
Memoirs of the Affairs of Scotland from the Restoration of Charles II, Sir George Mackenzie, Edinburgh, 1821.
The Hamilton Papers, ed. S. R. Gardiner, Camden Society, 1880.

x. MARY FITTON

Shakespeare's Sonnets, Thomas Tyler, London, 1886.
East Cheshire, vol. ii., J. P. Earwaker.
Gossip from a Muniment Room: Passages in the lives of Anne and Mary Fitton, 1574–1618, transcribed and edited by Lady Newdigate-Newdegate, London, 1897.

INDEX